This book makes available for the first time an empirical study of the transformations in religious beliefs that have occurred amongst English Catholics since the Second Vatican Council of 1962–5. It complements Dr Hornsby-Smith's well received *Roman Catholics in England* (1987) which provides the social and historical context for this present study.

In *Roman Catholic beliefs in England*, Michael Hornsby-Smith explores Catholic beliefs over a range of concerns from doctrinal matters to questions of personal and social morality and assesses how religious beliefs are differentiated between different types of Catholics. He also examines the legitimacy accorded by English Catholics to both papal authority and religious authority in general.

This study is based on extensive interviews with lay members of the bishops' advisory commissions, Catholic electors, people who attended the public events during the Pope's visit in 1982 and grassroots parishioners. From this evidence, Michael Hornsby-Smith convincingly demonstrates the prevalence of 'customary religion', that is the continuation of beliefs and practices derived from official religion but no longer subject to the control of the Church. He argues that English Catholics have gradually withdrawn legitimacy from the clerical leadership and increasingly 'make up their own minds', particularly in the area of personal morality. The author concludes by reflecting on the implications of his findings for the secularisation thesis.

Roman Catholic beliefs in England

Roman Catholic beliefs in England

Customary Catholicism and transformations of religious authority

Michael P. Hornsby-Smith

Senior Lecturer in Sociology, University of Surrey

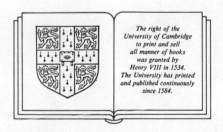

The right of the
University of Cambridge
to print and sell
all manner of books
was granted by
Henry VIII in 1534.
The University has printed
and published continuously
since 1584.

CAMBRIDGE UNIVERSITY PRESS

Cambridge

New York   Port Chester

Melbourne   Sydney

Published by the Press Syndicate of the University of Cambridge
The Pitt Building, Trumpington Street, Cambridge CB2 1RP
40 West 20th Street, New York, NY 10011, USA
10 Stamford Road, Oakleigh, Melbourne 3166, Australia

First published in 1991

Printed in Great Britain at the University Press, Cambridge

British Library cataloguing in publication data
Hornsby-Smith, Michael P.
 Roman Catholic beliefs in England
 1. England. Catholic Church. Attitudes of Catholics
 I. Title
 282.42

Library of Congress cataloguing in publication data
Hornsby-Smith, Michael P.
 Roman Catholic beliefs in England: Customary Catholicism and
 transformations of religious authority / Michael P. Hornsby-Smith.
  p. cm.
 Includes bibliographical references.
 ISBN 0–521–36327–6
  1. Catholics – England – Religious life.
 2. England – Social life and customs
 3. Catholic Church – England – History – 20th century.
 4. Catholic Church – England – Teaching office.
 5. England – Church history – 20th century.
 6. Religion and sociology – England – History – 20th century.
 I. Title
 BX1493.2.H668 1991
 282'.42'09045–dc20   90–34003 CIP

ISBN 0 521 36327 6 hardback

CE

To
LENNIE
with all my love and thanks for our thirty years together
and to
PENNY, PETER AND RAY
generous collaborators and good friends

CONTENTS

PART II: THE RELIGIOUS BELIEFS OF ENGLISH CATHOLICS

Contents

TABLES

PREFACE

'Are you really a Roman Catholic?' I asked my aunt with interest. She replied promptly and seriously, 'Yes, my dear, only I just don't believe in all the things they believe in.' (Graham Greene, *Travels with my Aunt*, 1972: 151)

This book has been conceived as a complement to *Roman Catholics in England* (Cambridge University Press, 1987), which reported a number of studies of the social structural aspects of English Catholicism and how these had changed as a result of post-war social and post-Vatican religious change. Thus evidence of the heterogeneity of English Catholics, their social mobility experiences, changing marriage patterns and competing elite groups, and the assimilation of Irish Catholics, were the primary concern in arguing that the defensive walls, which up to the 1950s, had separated the 'fortress' Church from contamination with the outside world, had steadily been dissolved.

In this second book, the focus is on the consequences of these structural changes, in terms of patterns of belief and morality and views of religious authority, for the whole range of Catholics, from those institutionally involved with the Church at the national level to ordinary self-identifying Catholics at the parish level, such as Henry Pulling's 'aunt' in Graham Greene's novel, whether they attend Mass regularly or not. It has been a long time in the writing. The data which have been reported in it were collected in four separate research projects in the decade from the mid-1970s to the mid-1980s.

It is unlikely that the researches which are reviewed would have been commenced without two grants from the British Social Science Research Council (as it was then called in happier times) for the interviewing programmes with members of the bishops' commissions, and random samples of Catholics in two London and two Preston parishes. The Nuffield Foundation made available the small grant, at very short notice, which facilitated the interviews with people attending the six public events at Wembley, Coventry, Liverpool, Manchester, York and Cardiff, during the historic visit of Pope John-Paul II in 1982.

A cursory examination of the bibliography will demonstrate that much of the work which is reported here was undertaken collaboratively. I am indebted to a generation of generous colleagues who have worked with me over the past fifteen years or so. In particular, I wish to dedicate this book with gratitude to Penny Mansfield, Peter Reilly and Ray Lee who were successively the research officers on the two S.S.R.C.-funded projects. I count myself fortunate to have had such conscientious, sociologically alert and insightful colleagues, and hope that this book, in spite of its somewhat slow gestation, will be an acceptable testimony to the many hard and often uncomfortable interviews we carried out, as well as to their numerous reflections and draft reports. It is gratifying to record that our friendship has outlasted our research collaboration.

During the pope's visit, Ray Lee and several other colleagues, especially Jennifer Brown, Betsy Cordingley, Constance Elliott, Joan O'Bryne and Ann Scurfield, kindly collaborated by interviewing people at various locations. Without their help this project would have been stillborn and I gratefully acknowledge the generous way they gave up a very hot Bank Holiday weekend.

Over the course of nearly fifteen years research on English Catholics I have incurred too many debts to record in detail. In this book the results of several hundred interviews have been reported. Perhaps only other researchers, whose analyses depend on the collection of focused and tape-recorded interview data, will appreciate fully the significant work of the interviewers, who conscientiously probed and prompted various samples of respondents, almost all of them strangers, to tell us something about their understanding of their Catholicism and the meaning it had for them. But their efforts would have been of no avail had it not been for the courtesy and generosity of those people who agreed to tell us their stories and give us their accounts of what it meant to be a Catholic. To all those who have contributed in any way to this research I wish to express a very sincere thanks.

This preface was drafted at Charles de Gaulle airport in Paris as I waited for the flight home after a Council meeting of the Société Internationale de Sociologie des Religions. It was a happy reminder of the friendship, stimulation and sociological insights which have been generously given by the wider community of sociologists of religion. They have kindly provided thoughtful and constructive comments on various drafts over the years. The intellectual climate in Britain has become crudely instrumental in recent years and their collaboration and encouragement is a happy reminder of more lasting values. I am pleased to express my gratitude to those who commented critically but constructively on early drafts, especially Eileen Barker, Joan Brothers, Jennifer Brown, Grace Davie, Christie Davies,

Graham Howes, Ray Lee and Joan O'Bryne. Any failure to respond to their suggestions is, of course, entirely mine. My thanks are also due to Melanie Cottrell who generously gave me a copy of her perceptive and important thesis.

I am pleased to acknowledge permissions to use materials which first appeared elsewhere. Much of chapter 2 was first published in *Accounts and Action* edited by Nigel Gilbert and Peter Abell. An earlier version of chapter 3 first appeared as a University of Surrey Occasional Paper. Chapter 5 is a substantially expanded version of a paper written with Ray Lee and Peter Reilly which first appeared in the *Review of Religious Research*. Some sections of chapter 6 first appeared in *The Month* and the main argument of chapter 7 was presented with Penny Mansfield in an article in *New Blackfriars*. Chapter 9 is a substantially revised version of a paper first given at an Implicit Religion conference organised by Edward Bailey at Ilkley. I am also grateful to Michael Holdsworth for encouraging me to write two books on English Catholics, and to his colleagues at Cambridge University Press for their painstaking work in seeing them through to publication.

Finally, to my wife Lennie. Thank you for your love and our first thirty years together. I wish I had the words to express adequately my gratitude for your tolerance, support and encouragement when the writing has not been going well, to have faith and keep going in the sociologist's vocation of demystification, for 'the truth will set you free' (Jn. 8: 32).

PART I
INTRODUCTION

I
FROM IDENTITY TO COMMITMENT

1.1 Beliefs and belonging

This book aims to explore the ways in which Roman Catholics in England in the last quarter of the twentieth century make religious sense of their everyday lives. At one level it is concerned to explore the nature of their religious beliefs over the whole range of concerns, from doctrinal matters to questions of personal and social morality. These include such controversial issues as contraception, abortion and divorce, and concerns such as the celibacy of priests, fasting regulations, Mass attendance requirements, and rules governing religiously 'mixed' marriages, which might better be regarded as matters of Church rules and discipline. On another level it aims to explore underlying questions of religious meaning, belonging and commitment, the nature of the Catholic identity, and its salience. Behind all these concerns there is the matter of religious authority, the ways in which it is interpreted, legitimated, delimited, ignored or transformed by different types of Catholics.

For the purposes of this book the term English Catholics will be used to describe all those self-identifying or baptised Roman Catholics who are living in England, regardless of the origins of their religious affiliation. Thus nearly one in nine are converts to Roman Catholicism, while one quarter are first generation immigrants and an additional one-fifth are second generation immigrants (Hornsby-Smith and Lee, 1979: 43–5, 179–87; Hornsby-Smith, 1986; 1987: 23–6).

This study has been conceived as complementary to my earlier book *Roman Catholics in England* (1987) which was based largely on quantitative findings from survey research with representative samples of Catholics. It described structural aspects of English Catholicism such as the extent of social and geographical mobility, the assimilation of Irish Catholics, patterns of Catholic marriage and family life, the characteristics of Catholic elites committed to reform in the Church, and the broad framework of Catholic attitudes on major social, moral, political and religious issues. Such a structural analysis provides the social and historical context within which the present study is located. In contrast to the earlier study, the present book will be substantially grounded in more qualitative data derived from taped interviews with Catholics who report a wide range of institutional involvement, from the members of national commissions set up to advise the bishops, to random samples of electors in a number of parishes. Questions of representativeness are not so important for our purposes, which are to present and interpret the variety of religious accounts given by English Catholics in response to focused interviewing. In reporting these variations we shall quote liberally from the interview transcripts. Apart from the exploration of doctrinal beliefs and sexual attitudes, our interviews also investigated responses to parish life, liturgical change, the role of the priest and his relationships with lay people, ecumenism, justice and peace issues, and the authority which our respondents accorded to the teachings of the religious leaders in the Church from the Pope to the local parish priest.

It is appropriate here to make brief reference to the status which will be accorded to the accounts given by lay Catholics, in focused interviews, of their religious beliefs, their sense of belonging and commitment, and the salience which their Catholicism held for them. Some of the methodological issues arising from the accounts given by different types of Catholics will be discussed in the following chapter. Here we are concerned simply to note that the analysis of actors' accounts is problematic and contested within sociology (Gilbert and Abell, 1983).

Peter Abell has distinguished four positions taken by contemporary sociologists from the 'ethnomethodological', that 'no inferences are possible from accounts of actions to actions themselves', to the 'behaviourist', that 'inferences from accounts of actions to actions themselves are impossible as the former are intrinsically unreliable and ephemeral' (1983: 173–4). In a similar manner, Wallis and Bruce (1983) distinguish between ethnomethodological approaches which insist that actors' accounts are all we can ever know from structuralist and functionalist, for example marxist, approaches which discount such accounts as merely epiphenomenal. The view taken here corresponds to Abell's second position:

that inferences are possible from accounts of actions to actions themselves but that *both* the inference *and* the analysis of account giving hold intrinsic interest for the sociologist. (1983: 174; emphasis in original)

In this book our concern will be with the first of these tasks and the regarding of interviewees' accounts as data which can be used, along with other data such as contextual factors to situate the interview material, in the making of inferences about action. Thus we will have particular regard for our respondents' interview accounts because:

since actors have privileged access to their intentions and beliefs, the presumption must be that their characterizations of their actions and their accounts of why they are performing them are the correct ones. (Wallis and Bruce, 1983: 99)

However, 'actors' accounts, like sociologists' accounts, are efforts to conceptualize and explain behaviour and beliefs, and both are equally hypothetical' and fallible. In spite of this, sociological explanations, which may be considered to be 'a more systematic form of commonsense', differ from those of actors not only in being more systematic but also more concerned with conceptualising and generalising (1983: 103–5). Wallis and Bruce conclude by observing that:

No-one will adequately explain social action who does not understand how individuals interpret their world. But no-one will understand how individuals interpret their world who is not aware of the social and historical context within which they do it. (1983: 109)

1.2 Social and religious context

Thus in order to understand the accounts which English Catholics give of their religious beliefs, it is first necessary to locate them historically in their social and religious context. Our data were collected over the decade from the mid-1970s to the mid-1980s. We commenced our research nearly three decades after the end of the

traumatic events of the Second World War. During this post-war
period the world had learned to live with the threat of nuclear
annihilation, the 'cold war', and 'peaceful coexistence' between the
two great ideologically opposed blocks of western capitalism and
soviet communism. These three decades also saw the end of the long
period of European colonialism and the emergence of dozens of new,
politically independent nations. For Britain this meant coming to
terms with a major loss of international status and power, as but one
among many medium-sized industrial nations competing fiercely for
world markets. It was perhaps peculiarly handicapped by
institutional obsolescence, the legacy of its earlier historical emergence as the first industrial nation. All the same, at home the period
saw the construction of the Welfare State and a long period of
continuous economic growth and rising affluence sufficient to prompt
the proclamation from Harold Macmillan that 'you've never had it so
good'. It was a period which saw the revolution of rising expectations, the emergence of mass leisure industries, the growth of car
ownership and the mobility it gave, and, in particular, the near
universality of television ownership. For the first time authority
figures, whether cabinet ministers or the Cardinal Archbishop of
Westminster, were subject to detailed cross-examination in one's
own front room, and in the process became vulnerable to critical
evaluation in a way that had never been possible before. Post-war
reconstruction and urban development projects resulted in more
comfortable homes, and a more privatised home-centredness focused
around the nuclear, rather than the extended, family was said to have
emerged.

Our research was also undertaken at a time of great religious
upheaval in the Roman Catholic Church. We commenced our
interviewing programme nearly a decade after the ending of the
Second Vatican Council in 1965. This general council of the Church
was only the second to be called since the Counter-Reformation
Council of Trent (1545–63) and the First Vatican Council (1869–70),
which was aborted by the taking of Rome by nationalist forces and
the ending of the temporal power of the papacy. The latter council
had defined the doctrine of papal infallibility, but in a way which had
resulted in its wide misinterpretation and exaggeration. The Second
Vatican Council was regarded as having completed the unfinished
business of the earlier council and, especially in its major Dogmatic
Constitution on the Church, *Lumen Gentium* (Abbott, 1966: 14–101),

placed the doctrine of papal infallibility in the context of an extended theology of the 'People of God'. Apart from that, the Council had been called by Pope John XXIII to 'let some fresh air into the Church' and promote within her an *aggiornamento* or 'bringing up to date' (Butler, 1981: 6). The participation of lay people in the Church and in its mission to transform the world in favour of the Kingdom values of justice, peace and love, was afforded much greater emphasis, and strong encouragement was given to the ecumenical movement. Given the major transformations taking place world-wide after the Second World War there was certainly a need for institutional renewal in the light of the changing social and historical context and the emergence of new needs requiring new responses to mission.

The combined effect of these social and religious transformations in the post-war world was 'the dissolution of the English Catholic subculture' (Hornsby-Smith, 1987: 208–14). Up to the 1950s English Catholicism had been characterised by a distinctive subculture with an all-embracing Catholic institutional life centered around the parish and school and with its own norms, values and beliefs (Coman, 1977: 4–5). This subculture had been forged in a fortress model of the Church, defended by policies favouring marital endogamy and segregated religious worship and schooling, which were buttressed not only by institutional rules and sanctions but also by community pressures to safeguard the preciously distinctive Catholic identity. The strong Irish background of most English Catholics reinforced this sense of belonging to a religio-ethnic minority with its own separate and proud identity.

The processes of change in the post-war years were gradual and took place over several decades. There was no dramatic collapsing of the fortress walls as a result of an explosive attack from without. Rather there was a steady dissolving of the walls in the solvent of rapid external social change after the Second World War and the internal processes of renewal encouraged by the Vatican Council's programme of reform. Peter Coman characterised the process in the following terms:

The gradual assimilation through education and mixed marriage, the dissent over traditional teaching in birth regulation, the questioning of the limits of papal authority, the gradual substitution of English for Latin in the liturgy, the tentative movements towards ecumenism, the softening of traditional disapproval of mixed marriages and the abolition of Friday abstinence. (1977: 105)

The 1978 survey of English Catholics had shown, for example, that whereas over two-thirds of married Catholics before 1960 had a Catholic partner, among those married in the 1970s, the proportion had fallen to only one-third (Hornsby-Smith, 1987: 94). These, and other changes, led to 'the weakening of the traditional Roman Catholic sense of boundary and demarcation in relation to the wider community ... [and] the weakening of a general Roman Catholic identity' (Coman, 1977: 106). Mary Douglas articulated the concern of many:

Friday no longer rings the great cosmic symbols of expiation and atonement: it is not symbolic at all, but a practical day for the organisation of charity. *Now the English Catholics are like everyone else.* (Douglas, 1973: 67; italics added)

Most Catholics experienced the effects of the changes primarily at the parish level (Hornsby-Smith, 1989). The Mass was said in English and the priest faced the congregation in order to symbolise the communal nature of the eucharistic celebration and the full participation of lay people in it. During the Mass lay people read selections from scripture in English, articulated in bidding prayers the petitions and everyday concerns of the members of the parish, and, more recently, served as special ministers at Communion which was increasingly given under both kinds, that is the consecrated wine as well as the host. The full participation of lay people at all levels in the life of the Church was reflected in their membership of bishops' advisory bodies at both diocesan and national levels and in the slowly increasing number of parish councils. In their response to the National Pastoral Congress in 1980, the bishops of England and Wales eulogised the concept of *The Sharing Church* (Anon, 1981: 307–28). While the practice very often fell far short of the new theological thinking in the Church, there is no doubting the magnitude of the shifts in self-understanding to which members of the Roman Catholic Church were asked to respond after the Second Vatican Council.

While most English Catholics adapted well to the changes as they were gradually, and sometimes reluctantly, introduced, there were some unanticipated consequences. Thus Anthony Archer has suggested that, whereas the Church up to the 1950s had been an important source of identity for working-class Catholics, the post-Vatican Church has increasingly become a vehicle for the achievement of the aspirations of articulate middle-class enthusiasts who are in open competition with older forms of clerical domination. But the liturgical changes so enthusiastically welcomed by middle-class reformers, in fact articulated new forms of elitism, 'cut off many of the ritual streams that had previously nourished Catholics and covered over many of the accumulated pools in which popular Catholicism had found its strength'. While 'the new Mass proved only too vulnerable to congregational as well as clerical sabotage', it was basically classist in origin: 'its very language was that of a particular class', familiar in the courtroom and the classroom. In this sense Archer interprets the changes as new forms of class oppression, and it is hardly surprising that, with the dissolution of a distinctive Catholic identity, 'working-class indifference coincided ... with the relinquishment of an Irish identity, and their subsequent failure to find anything of particular interest to them in the Catholic Church' (Archer, 1986: 141–5, 234–6).

Archer's claim has some validity, though it overlooks the extent to which lay people generally were excluded from full participation in the life of the Church in the pre-Vatican years. What seems to be beyond dispute is that, with the dissolution of the distinctive Catholic subculture, there was an associated shift in the nature of Catholic belonging to the Church. No longer was being a Catholic a part of one's intrinsic identity, an indication of ancestry and membership of an identifiably distinct religio-ethnic community, something normally ascribed. Now Catholics were increasingly required to make a positive choice and affirm the calling to participate fully in the work of the whole 'People of God'. From being a given aspect of their cultural identity which they accepted passively, Catholics were invited to see their Catholic faith as having meaning, and requiring from them a positive commitment to the task of mission in the world. Whereas previously 'cradle' Catholics regarded themselves as Catholics unless they positively 'opted out', there is a sense in which in the post-Vatican Church, Catholics were being asked to 'opt in', rather as converts had always had to. It seems, therefore, that the basis of meaningful belonging for the English Catholic has been transformed from one of religio-ethnic identity to one of voluntary religious commitment.

1.3 Research aims

This book is concerned to explore the religious transformations which have taken place in English Catholicism in the second half of the twentieth century. Here the study of religious change in a Liverpool suburban parish by Theodore Koopmanschap in the 1970s is of great value. In particular he explored transformations in the quest for community, liturgical worship, the belief system and morality, and these issues are similar to those we have addressed in our own studies. In his interpretation of his in-depth interviews with ninety-five adult Roman Catholics in his research parish in 1972, he utilises John Bowker's concept of 'route-finding activity' as the principal characteristic of religion (1973: 82) and finds value in Lévi-Strauss's notion of 'bricolage' (1966: 16–36; Koopmanschap, 1978: 39). He concludes that:

old symbols must make sense in *this* industrial society and encompass, differentiate and synthesise modern multi-faceted and fragmented social experience.

It is precisely at the crossroads between tradition and modernity, between old symbols of old authoritarian social structures and new social experience that the contemporary Roman Catholic is called to perform his bricolage. (1978: 49)

We shall be concerned, like Koopmanschap, to explore how English Catholics 'reshuffle the myths and values of their religious tradition in order to make them fit new experiences' (1978: 223) in a more affluent, highly mobile and more tolerant or religiously indifferent society.

We shall also take note of the challenging and insightful study of middle-class religion in England in the 1980s by Melanie Cottrell (1985). Her research was designed to test a number of hypotheses derived from Luckmann's 'invisible' religion thesis (1970). Her data came from the life stories of 34 middle-class people in the south of England in the early 1980s, in interviews which typically lasted three to five hours. For the 'religiously devoted', church religion did provide a transcendent meaning system. But, contrary to Luckmann's hypothesis, for the majority of her respondents, including many regular church-goers, religion was not a matter of intrinsic importance. Most people had meaning systems which contained no transcendent theme. The outlook of the majority was this-worldly and pragmatic. Church religion had been pushed to the margins of life and consciousness and there were no secular substitutes. Drawing on the work of Mary Douglas (1973; 1975; 1978), Cottrell found that the prevailing cosmology corresponded to a competitive individualism and was strongly influenced by rationality, empiricism, pluralism and relativism. It will be one aim of this present study to judge the extent to which Cottrell's analysis has relevance for English Catholics who differ widely in the degree to which they are institutionally involved.

In broad terms this book will endeavour to address four different but related sets of issues. Firstly, it will attempt to describe what meanings English Catholics attached to being a Roman Catholic at this time, how they saw the nature of their religious identity, and to what sort of institution they regarded themselves as belonging. Here the recent Presidential Address to the Society for the Scientific Study of Religion is helpful. Phillip Hammond, following Hans Mol (1978), distinguished two kinds of identity: one which is involuntarily held, such as is the case of an oppressed religio-ethnic immigrant minority, which is nourished in primary, face-to-face, groups and community interaction, and the second which is transient and dependent on the nature of social encounters and where a great deal of social interaction takes place outside primary groups. Thus Hammond distinguishes two views of the Church in contemporary society:

On the one hand, there is ... the 'collective-expressive' view, in which involvement is largely involuntary because it emerges out of overlapping primary group ties not easily avoided. On the other hand, there is the 'individual-expressive' view, in which involvement is largely voluntary and independent of other social ties ... the social conditions eroding the first view are the same conditions that permit, perhaps even encourage, the second view. (1988: 5)

Following Luckmann's contrast between church-related and invisible religion (1970), Hammond suggests that people can be located on a grid in terms of their involvement in overlapping primary groups and in secondary groups. This leads him to distinguish two main types of religious identity. Firstly, church-affiliated people who place a high stress on primary group involvement and on 'localism' (Roof, 1978) and a low stress on secondary group involvement are said to have a 'collective-expressive' involvement in the Church and the first type of 'involuntary, immutable' religious identity. Secondly, those with a low local involvement but high secondary group ties are said to have an 'individual-expressive' involvement in the Church and a 'transient, changeable' religious identity (1988: 6).

Hammond's theory seems likely to be of value in the case of English Catholics for whom the defensive walls of a fortress Church have largely been dissolved in the solvent of post-war social change and post-conciliar religious change. It is worth noting, however, that hypothetically two other types of identity might exist. Thus Hammond suggests that where people are highly involved in both primary and secondary groups, such as might be the case for the 'post-ethnic' Roman Catholic Church in the United States, there might be 'pressure on the Church to move out of a paternalistic mode' (1988: 6; fn. 3). In other words, one might predict that under these circumstances there are likely to be conflicts within the Church over the legitimacy accorded to the religious authority of the clerical leadership. It will be shown that these reflections of Hammond are helpful in the analysis of our interview data with English Catholics in the 1970s and 1980s.

The second issue which this book will consider is the range and nature of Catholic beliefs and, in particular, how religious beliefs are differentiated both among themselves and between different types of Catholics. Previous work based largely on the analysis of quantitative structured interview data (Hornsby-Smith, Lee and Turcan, 1982; Hornsby-Smith, 1987: 47–66) has indicated a considerable degree of heterodoxy of belief among English Catholics. This present study, based on the results of focused interviewing which generated more qualitative forms of data, will explore further the wide variations in the levels of knowledge and comprehension as well as the coherence and consistency of Catholic beliefs. In his study of cargo cults, Worsley warned against imputing 'a spurious unity ... on to other people's belief systems' (1970: 300–1). In this book we will explore the relevance of this warning of inconsistencies and incoherence in the beliefs and attitudes of contemporary English Catholics.

Thirdly, it will be concerned with variations in the salience of the religious beliefs or of the sense of belonging to the Roman Catholic Church. In a recent review of the literature, Hoge and de Zulueta defined salience narrowly as 'the self-perceived importance of religion as such to an individual' (1985: 23), leaving the question of the relevance of religion for various areas of life to be determined by empirical enquiry. On the basis of a national probability sample in the United States in 1981, they concluded that in general terms American Christianity had an impact on members' values and attitudes in only a limited realm, chiefly family life, sexuality and personal honesty, and always in a conservative direction. For Catholics only there was also a close relationship between self-perceived religious salience and the desire for greater respect for authority in the future. It was also reported that religious salience had a strong and linear relationship with orthodoxy. These matters will be explored further in the case of English Catholics in this present study. For our purposes the salience of an individual's religious beliefs or attitudes is here taken to refer to their prominence, significance and relevance in terms of their implications for action in the everyday lives of Catholics, notably for religious practices and for social behaviour, such as political participation and involvement, which may be religiously informed.

The final area of investigation relates to the question of religious authority. The evidence from our previous quantitative work is that Catholics differ widely in terms of their beliefs, attitudes and practices. In 1978 nearly one-third of a national, representative sample of English Catholics regarded the statement, 'under certain conditions, when he speaks on matters of faith and morals the Pope is infallible', as being false (Hornsby-Smith and Lee, 1979: 193). In this book we will explore in greater detail the understandings which English Catholics have of papal authority. More generally, we will be concerned with the legitimacy which is accorded to pope, bishops and priests over the whole range of concerns from creedal issues to other doctrines, teachings on personal and social morality, (including contraception, divorce and abortion), and matters of institutional discipline (such as the Sunday Mass obligation and rules relating to 'mixed' marriages and intercommunion).

Thus from these considerations five main aims of this present study can be identified:

(a) The reporting of systematic comparisons in the accounts they offer of a range of types of English Catholics who differ in the salience they attach to religious matters in their everyday lives, in their religious commitment and institutional involvement, the nature of their Catholic identity, and their sense of belonging to a distinctive Catholic community between one and two decades after the end of the Second Vatican Council.

(b) The interpretation of patterns of religious belonging and the salience of religious explanations of the everyday world, in terms of the social processes which have occurred in British society since the end of the Second World War, notably the dissolution of the distinctive, defensive Catholic subculture.

(c) The explanation of such changes as have taken place in doctrinal beliefs, sexual attitudes, responses to liturgical changes, atti-

tudes to justice and peace issues, ecumenism, the parochial
clergy and parish life, the meanings attributed to the problems,
dilemmas and emergent needs found in everyday lay lives, the
legitimacy accorded the religious leaders in the Church and the
transformations of religious authority, in terms of the concepts of
belonging and identity, coherence and consistency, salience and
commitment.

(d) The making of comparisons wherever possible with developments in Roman Catholicism in other societies, especially in
Western Europe, the United States and Australia, since the
Second Vatican Council, in order to contribute to the analysis of
global transformations of Roman Catholicism (Gannon, 1988).

(e) The utilisation of our data in addressing recent theories of
secularisation, regarded as a multi-dimensional concept and
distinguishing between laicization, religious involvement and
religious change (Dobbelaere, 1981), and advocating the less
value-loaded notion of religious transformations.

1.4 Data sources

The data presented in this study have been derived from four distinct
sources.

(a) *Bishops' advisors*: In a feasibility study of the Roman Catholic
Community in England, sponsored by the then British Social Science
Research Council (S.S.R.C.), Penny Mansfield and I interviewed
seventy-one of the eighty-three lay members of the Laity, Ecumenical, International Justice and Peace, Social Welfare and Racial
Justice Commissions of the Bishops' Conference of England and
Wales in 1974/5. The interviews, which were generally tape-recorded
and which on average lasted two hours, were focused on four main
areas: the manner of appointment of lay members to the various
commissions; their description and assessment of the work of their
commission; their religious attitudes, especially in the areas of the
teaching of the Church, images of God, and the nature of authority in
the Church; and the social, educational and religious backgrounds of
commission members. For our present purposes we will restrict
ourselves in the main to data relating to the third of these four areas.
The relevant questions from our interview guide have been given in
Appendix 1.

In this first part of our research, apart from studying the extent and nature of lay participation in the new decision-making machinery in the Church set up after the Second Vatican Council, we were concerned to investigate the religious orientations of those lay people who had been sponsored or coopted by the clerical leadership for these advisory roles. In particular we wished to explore their understanding of the nature of religious authority in the Church and their comments on the ways in which they considered the exercise of religious authority had changed in recent years. Penny Mansfield and I introduced the issue using the three questions which Kokosalakis had employed in his study in a Liverpool parish in the 1960s (Appendix 1, Questions 1–3; Kokosalakis, 1971: 27).

At this early stage in our research we were also much taken with the conceptualisation of conflicts of authority in the Church by François Houtart (1969), who distinguished three types of contestation in the Church: individual, joint and social movements. Houtart hypothesised that there were two groups of people in the Church with opposing concepts of God and the Church. These groups perceived authority differently. For one group it was seen as a value, while the second group saw it only as a means to be used to facilitate the achievement of the goals of the institutional Church. In our interview guide (Appendix 1, Questions 5–10) we attempted to operationalise Houtart's concepts. In the further exploration of tensions and conflicts in the Church we invited commission members to comment on Michael Winter's critical comparisons between parishes and small basic christian communities, and his challenge that the Church was in practice more concerned with the maintenance of its existing structures and privileges than with mission (1973; see also Appendix 1, Questions 12 and 25). In this initial work we also wished to test David Martin's hypothesis that social mobility, in creating a new Catholic middle class in closer contact with Protestants and Humanists of similar status, will inevitably lead to 'unspoken divergence' from Catholic norms and eventually to 'audible dissent'. Martin argued that:

Intellectuals begin by inventing verbal subterfuges and, when they can bear these no longer, erupt against authority; the working class either obeys or silently pursues its way in the usual manner of erring humanity. The Catholic system can cope with large-scale divergence, but it cannot brook overt disruption and challenge, and it is precisely this that occurs as more and more climb out of the overlapping ghettos of class and religious separatism. (1972: 187–8)

Such considerations were reflected in our first interview guide (Appendix 1, Questions 12 and 13).

(b) *Parish electors and activists*: In a second study sponsored by the S.S.R.C., Penny Mansfield, Peter Reilly, Ray Lee and I carried out surveys in each of four parishes: an inner-London parish and a commuter parish about twenty miles from the centre of London, and an inner-city parish and a suburban parish in Preston, Lancashire in 1975/77. In each parish random samples of electors were selected using sampling fractions adjusted to achieve around sixty Roman Catholic electors. In addition, in each parish, around 20 parishioners, identified by parish priests as being actively involved in the life of the parishes were interviewed. Two types of interview were carried out with the parish samples: Stage 1 structured interviews mainly to obtain the measures of social mobility used in the earlier study (Hornsby-Smith, 1987), and focused Stage II interviews. The latter were generally tape-recorded, and ranged from half an hour to two hours in length.

The Stage II interviews focused around four main areas. In the first place we wished to explore the nature of the religious socialisation of our respondents in order to contextualise their current religious orientations. Thus for 'cradle' Catholics we were interested to learn about the strength of the Catholic subculture and the way in which it both constrained and supported the religious beliefs and practices of their families of origin. For those who were in 'mixed' marriages we wished to explore the nature and extent of the pressures to which they had been subjected and the subsequent consequences for them in terms of their level of commitment or antagonism. We also asked our respondents to indicate to what extent, in their experience, the present situation in the Church had changed in recent years.

Secondly, we invited our respondents to discuss their religious beliefs and practices. Following Houtart (1969), as in the previous study, we hypothesised a relationship between the respondents' image of God and their views about the nature of the Church and religious authority. Hence we prefaced a discussion about the teaching of the Church with an invitation to articulate, as best they could, how they saw God. In this we anticipated the analysis of the religious imagination which Greeley developed in the United States (1981).

In the third part of our interviews we invited our respondents to comment on recent changes in the Church and in particular on those liturgical changes which regular Mass attenders would have experienced by the 1970s. We also explored their views about lay participation in the Church and how they saw the proper role of the priest. Finally, we focused on the local parish and asked our respondents to comment critically on the extent to which they regarded it as a 'community', the reality of lay participation in decision-making in their parish and the nature of priest–lay relations. Apart from identifying the range of both traditional Catholic organisations in the life of the parish and the extent of new developments, such as house Masses, prayer groups or study groups, we also asked respondents to describe and evaluate such changes as they had experienced in their parish in recent years.

In this book we will only be considering findings relating to the Stage II interviews with 183 Catholic electors. The interview guide used in the parish studies has been given in Appendix II.

(c) *Catholics attending papal events*: Several colleagues and I tape-recorded short interviews with people who attended one of the six public events at Wembley, Coventry, Liverpool, Manchester, York and Cardiff during the visit of Pope John-Paul II to Britain in May-June 1982. Each interviewer contacted people randomly, usually in or near their own corral or designated area, and aimed to achieve equal numbers of males and females in each of the over- and under-35 age categories. A total of 194 interviews, each averaging 10 minutes in length, were available for analysis. They were chiefly concerned to explore people's motives in coming to the event and their attitudes to papal authority and obedience to the teachings of the Church. The interview guide used has been given in Appendix III.

We had hypothesised that the people who were most likely to attend these set events, often after travelling considerable distances overnight and at some inconvenience and discomfort, would be traditional Catholics with an 'ultramontane' attitude towards the pope. We supposed that they would regard him very much as a 'man apart' with sacred qualities and a privileged religious authority which would be tinged with aspects of a 'creeping infallibility'. We also expected that this would be the case particularly for Irish Catholics though we anticipated that assertions of a Roman triumphalism might decline with length of stay in the more secularised British society.

Such considerations were reflected in our brief interview guide and in the sequence of our questions. We first tried to ascertain the main reasons for the informant's coming to the event and then asked what they thought about the pope and his teaching. In particular, we tried to probe, as far as we could within the very limited time constraints, whether there were any matters on which the respondents considered they were entitled to make up their own minds. We wished to explore whether they felt obliged to follow a religious authority and the extent to which this was related to the 'charisma of office' of the papacy (Weber, 1964: 366).

While in this book we will be concerned mainly with the analysis of the tape-recorded interviews, we also followed-up the Roman Catholic respondents by means of a postal questionnaire four months after the pope's visit. In this way we hoped to make allowance for any effects which were due to the special excitement associated with a unique historical event. Brief reference, therefore, will be made to the findings from the 120 returned questionnaires. These attempted to identify the different expectations people might have had for attending the event and also to probe further about our respondents' attitudes to Pope John-Paul's leadership style, his teaching and to papal authority in general.

(d) *Everyday lives of lay people*: An exploratory study, with an opportunistic sample of twelve relatively articulate and 'committed' lay Catholics, was carried out in 1986/7 in the run-up to the 1987 Synod of Bishops in Rome on the vocation of the laity. The sample included both men and women from both the north and south of England, came from a variety of occupations from Member of Parliament to three single parents and a redundant highway engineer, and covered a wide range of both personal and professional experiences of suffering and deprivation. Seven of the sample responded to an invitation to contribute to the project by drafting an account of their everyday lives, while interviews with the remaining five were tape-recorded. In order to ensure some measure of coherence in the project, informants were offered six key areas as guidelines for their contributions: the concept of the lay vocation, coping with everyday needs, moral dilemmas and priorities, sources of support, the lay experience of the Church, and the nature of lay spirituality (Hornsby-Smith, 1988: 2–3). It was stressed that these were intended to be suggestive rather than constraining, and contributors were invited to feel free to convey the flavour of what it was like to be a lay person in their particular work or field in whatever way they felt would be most appropriate. In the last analysis, no battery of questions can ever cater for every contingency, but it was hoped to convey something of the everyday quality and variability of the lives of ordinary lay people in a wide range of occupations and circumstances. Somewhat similar explorations of 'the spirituality of work' have recently been published for nurses and teachers by the National Center for the Laity in the United States (Droel, 1989a; 1989b).

In sum our four main data sources comprise around 500 hours or more of taped interviews with a very wide range of English Catholics in terms of their age, sex, institutional involvement, regional, social class and occupational distributions. It seems likely that these sources comprise the most comprehensive collection of interview material relating to English Catholics between one and two decades after the end of the Second Vatican Council.

1.5 Outline of book

This book, then, will present the analyses of our interviews with samples of English Catholics from both sexes and a wide range of age, social class, regional and ethnic backgrounds, and levels of institutional involvement. The interviews date from the mid-1970s to the mid-1980s, that is roughly three to four decades after the end of the traumatic global events of the Second World War, and one to two decades after the end of the Second Vatican Council, which aimed to reform the Roman Catholic Church the better to face the challenges of the modern age. There seems little doubt that, as a result of massive social and religious changes in recent decades, the nature of English Catholicism has been very substantially transformed from a defensive subculture which existed until the early post-war years. The fortress walls which once attempted, with some if limited success, to insulate this religio-ethnic community from the corrosive effects of outside influences, appeared largely to have dissolved away by the 1980s. In the process the nature of the English Catholic identity seems likely to have been transformed.

Hammond (1988) suggestively has distinguished between the 'collective-expressive' and 'individual-expressive' views of the Church. The former might be said to have characterised the easily mobilised Catholic community with its strong and all embracing institutional life, hierarchical structure, clerical leadership, and mechanical solidarity in the era of the fortress Church. On the other hand, the 'individual–expressive' view of the Church appears to prevail in the contemporary society, where 'English Catholics are like everyone else' and where continuing commitment is much more likely to be voluntarily chosen but changeable, and where the Church (or parish) is regarded as but one of several more-or-less salient institutions in the life of the individual Catholic. It is the task of this book to throw some light on such transformations in English Catholicism, which have clearly taken place over the past quarter of a century or more, by considering in detail the accounts which different types of Catholics give of their religion.

We commence this task in chapter 2 with an analysis of some of the methodological difficulties of interpreting the results of interviews with Catholics who differ widely in the degree of salience which they attribute to the Catholic Church, the degree of commitment they manifest, and the degree to which they are able to verbalise about these matters. The result is that accounts vary significantly in terms of their coherence and consistency, the relative emphasis they place on explanations, justifications and excuses, and the status which tends to be accorded them by the researcher. This bias is likely to be particularly problematic in the case of those Catholics who are weakly attached to the institutional Church.

The main body of the book is divided into two main parts: a consideration of accounts of their religious beliefs by lay Catholics with varying attachments to the institutional Church, and the corresponding transformations of religious authority which can be discerned. Chapter 3 reports some of the findings from a preliminary enquiry undertaken in anticipation of the Synod of Bishops in Rome in 1987. This suggested that relatively committed and articulate Catholics had a weakly defined sense of a lay vocation or 'calling' and were unable to articulate to any great extent how they coped with moral dilemmas at work or determined their priorities as between work, home and parish. While some social support was given to some individuals in some circumstances, a general finding was that for all the rhetoric of 'community', a great deal of parish life was impoverished. In spite of this there was evidence of the emergence of a richly varied lay spirituality in tune with the rhythms of everyday lay lives.

In chapter 4 some of the findings from interviews with core Catholics who were members of the bishops' commissions and advisory groups will be reported. The focus in this chapter will be aspects of personal religiosity, such as images of God, and observations about the teaching of the Church, especially in the areas of personal and social morality. Similar issues will be addressed in the following chapter for nominal Catholics at the parish level. The concept of 'customary' religion, which is derived from official religion without being under its control and subject to processes of trivialisation, conventionality, apathy, convenience and self-interest, will be discussed and illustrated from our interview material.

The first chapter in the second main section of the book will report on the responses of those Catholics sufficiently committed to attend one of the public events in England and Wales during the visit of Pope John-Paul II to Britain in 1982. The 'paradox' of the overwhelmingly favourable responses to the pope as a person and very wide variations in the responses to his teaching are indicative of the major transformations which have taken place in the matter of religious authority in recent decades.

Chapter 7 uses a theoretical framework proposed by Houtart (1969) to examine the responses of active Catholics on the national advisory commissions to questions of religious authority. A typology of the objects and means of contestation will be employed and it will be argued that what Martin (1972) had called 'verbal subterfuges' were in fact new interpretations of authority which enabled the contestants to co-exist with other members of the institutional Church.

Chapter 8 will explore the responses of ordinary parishioners to questions of religious authority. Consideration will be given to the responses of ordinary parishioners on the controversial issues of contraception, abortion and divorce. An attempt will be made to distinguish major differences in the interpretation of religious authority between older and younger Catholics.

In chapter 9, the final chapter of this part of the book, the relevance of the Weberian categories of legitimacy and authority for our understanding of the transformations in religious authority which have taken place in English Catholicism over the past few decades will be explored. It will be argued that the modifications suggested by Harrison (1971) in his study of the American Baptist Convention, also have value for the understanding of questions of religious authority among English Catholics.

The final chapter of the book will review the attempt to account sociologically for the transformations which have been identified among English Catholics, both in terms of the coherence of their religious beliefs, and in terms of the legitimacy which they accord to the clerical leadership in the Church from the pope to the local parish priest. In a concluding section the relevance of these findings for secularisation theory will be addressed. While strong reservations will be expressed about the viability of the concept and its ideological usage, it will be argued that, while there is clearly evidence of increasing laicization in the Church and of major religious changes especially since the Second Vatican Council, it would be misleading to interpret these simply as evidence of secularisation. Furthermore, while there have also been significant reductions in the levels of religious involvement, at least in terms of some of the traditional indicators, it is also necessary to take due notice of the evidence of new forms of religious belonging and commitment. What evidence there is suggests major transformations in the nature of religious belonging and identity in the Roman Catholic Church in England and Wales. Membership of the Church is no longer an ascribed characteristic of a large religio-ethnic minority, but more an indication of a chosen commitment, for a variety of religious and social reasons, to embryonic community-like groupings held together in a loose network under a more facilitative and enabling form of religious authority than was the case up to the 1950s.

In his recent book on *The Sources of Social Power*, Michael Mann has drawn attention to 'the complexity and obduracy of facts', that 'there are more social and historical data than we can digest', and that 'the real world ... is messy and imperfectly documented'. This is undoubtedly true of Roman Catholicism in England in the last quarter of the twentieth century. Mann has admirably captured the flavour of the sometimes desperate process by which the social researcher attempts to make sense of the almost limitless complexities of everyday life:

We select our data, see whether they confirm or reject our theoretical hunches, refine the latter, collect more data, and continue zigzagging across between theory and data until we have established a plausible account of how this society, in this time and place, 'works'. (1986: vii)

In this book we will be zigzagging between committed national advisors to the bishops and other institutionally involved activists or 'core' Catholics, on the one hand, and 'ordinary' Catholics-in-the-pews and dormant or alienated Catholics, on the other hand, of different backgrounds and in different parts of the country, in order to seek some sort of understanding of the transformations which have clearly taken place over the past three or four decades. It remains for the reader to judge the plausibility of the account which is offered.

VARIETIES OF CATHOLIC ACCOUNTS

2.1 Methodological Problems

Before we commence the task of analysing our interview data, it is appropriate to offer a cautionary note and address some of the methodological difficulties which arise in interpreting the results of interviews with Catholics, who differ widely in the degree to which they attribute salience to the institutional Church, the level of their commitment to it and to its normative belief system, and in their ability to verbalise about religious matters generally. It will be suggested that the accounts given by different Catholics vary significantly in terms of their coherence and consistency and in the relative emphasis which they place on explanations, justifications and excuses. One result is a tendency for the researcher to accord differential status to the accounts of different categories of Catholics. It is important to recognise, however, that any tendency to discount the accounts of marginalised or non-verbal Catholics constitutes a bias in the analysis. In this chapter, therefore, we will identify some of the methodological issues of coping with interviewee variability, and construct a typology of accounts in terms of their attachment to the normative belief system, their knowledge of competing models of the Church and their legitimating theologies, and the salience of their religious beliefs for both religious practice and social action in their everyday lives. We will also examine the key concepts of salience and commitment and the issues of the consistency and inconsistency, coherence and incoherence of religious beliefs.

In the course of our interviewing programme it became very obvious that the respondents in our various samples, from the members of the bishops' advisory commissions and parish activists to ordinary Mass attending Catholics and those who had long ceased to have any regular contact with institutional Catholicism, differed widely in their levels of religious knowledge, comprehension, salience and commitment. Yet it was an important aim of our research to explore the range of religious meanings, variations in the sense of religious belonging, and attitudes towards religious (and especially papal) authority, for the whole spectrum of those who were either self-identifying Roman Catholics or who had at one stage in their lives been baptised in a Catholic ceremony, so that canonically they would have been regarded as such by the clerical leadership in the Church.

In this section we will describe aspects of the research process, and our attempt as researchers to interpret our responses to the growing realisation that the accounts given by English Catholics of their religious beliefs and practices in the mid-1970s varied systematically according to the degree to which the respondent was involved in the institutional life of Roman Catholicism. Not only did the evaluation of recent changes in the Roman Catholic Church following the Second Vatican Council, particularly in liturgical matters, differ widely, but so also did both the knowledge of these changes and their salience for our respondents. For some, these changes were a matter of tremendous importance and conflict in a Church in ferment, while others either had not been aware of them or regarded them as of no importance whatsoever.

In our endeavours to interpret the responses of Catholics to the recent changes in the Church, it became increasingly apparent that not only were we concerned with differential patterns of acceptance and rejection of the changes, but also with differential degrees to which these changes, and religious matters generally, were salient for different groups of respondents. It became clear that not only was there considerable variation in the patterns of beliefs of Catholics, but also the assumption that an individual's beliefs constituted a coherent system was shown to be highly problematic. Furthermore, the salience of religious beliefs, if there were any, varied widely. In an early attempt to reflect this growing awareness we referred to the general absence of a religious ideology on the part of many Catholics. Thus:

we found that the more active or involved Catholics very largely seemed to
have understood, accepted and adapted to these various changes. Amongst
ordinary Catholics, on the other hand, there was less understanding of the
changes, though in most cases a fairly similar acceptance and adaptation to
them. At the parish level we did not find a widespread sense of any new
ideological orientation or commitment to the post-Vatican theology ...
theological innovation meant little at the grass-roots level ... It seems clear
... that even for some of the more articulate informants, there was little sense
that the transition to new liturgical forms symbolised a fundamental shift in
the self-awareness of the Roman Catholic community. The changes were
simply liked or disliked. (Hornsby-Smith, Lee and Reilly, 1977: 407)

In the early stages of our research an analytical framework which
assumed a coherent and consistent belief and value system, varying
along an ideological dimension from 'religiously traditional' to
'religiously progressive', was not seriously disturbed by our first
batch of interviews with lay 'activists' who had high levels of
institutional involvement, especially in the new participatory structures set up at the national level after the Second Vatican Council.
Accordingly, at this stage we tended to treat the respondents'
accounts as unproblematic, that is, as accurate statements and
explanations of their beliefs and not seriously distorted in any way,
for example by self-interest or status-striving. In retrospect this could
be interpreted as a tendency to allocate privileged status to key
informants and possibly as an instance of confusing the construction
of an ideal-type of religious belief system with a value-judgement
about the religious content (Weber, 1949: 98).

It was only later, in subsequent interviews with randomly selected
samples of Catholic electors in four parishes, one inner-city and one
suburban parish in each of the London and Preston areas, that it
became apparent that our implicit assumptions regarding the coherence and consistency of the religious world-view of Catholics were not
valid. Not only were there variations in the attitudes to the recent
changes in the Church, particularly in its forms of liturgical worship,
between respondents differentially located along a traditionalism–
progressivism dimension, but there was also evidence both of a
considerable degree of heterogeneity of belief and practice, and of a
wide variation in the salience of institutional religion among self-
identifying Catholics. The analysis and interpretation of the accounts
given by Catholics of their beliefs and practices were clearly shown to
be more problematic than had originally been assumed.

For the researchers this meant a shift of emphasis from the mapping of differential responses to the reforms emanating from the Second Vatican Council to the tentative exploration of the various dimensions of the world-views of Catholics, in the growing realisation that many of our respondents did not have a coherent or consistent knowledge, belief or value-system, and indeed, that the researchers were asking questions about matters on which, in many cases, the respondents had no knowledge and had never previously had occasion to consider. Similar problems had been faced by Abercrombie and his colleagues in their study of the relationships between religion and superstition (1970: 128).

It became clear that we were no longer involved in the study of variations within 'official' religion, but in the exploration of what Towler called 'common' religion (Towler and Chamberlain, 1973; Towler, 1974) and we later came to regard as 'customary' religion (Hornsby-Smith, Lee and Reilly, 1985). To some extent, therefore, the categorisation of these findings in terms of variations in the salience of a religious ideology was itself an over-simplification. In the course of these shifts of direction in our research into contemporary English Catholicism there was a corresponding shift of research style from focused interviews (Merton and Kendall, 1956) using relatively structured interview guides, which assumed some shared knowledge and concern for the salience of the dimension of religious ideology, to a far more exploratory and tentative search for 'religious' meanings where there was apparently no shared set of concepts or language. We will discuss our findings and the relevance of the analyses of Cottrell (1985) and others later in chapter 5.

Our research findings led us to reconsider the nature of the Catholic belief and value 'systems' and to reject a supposedly unproblematic model of Catholic orthodoxy, with heterodoxy simply conceived of as deviation from the norm. It also led to the realisation that the researcher's account of the respondent's religious beliefs, meanings and actions was the product of an implicit process of negotiation in which the respondent accounts were mediated by, and selectively filtered through, the researcher's own preconceptions and frames of meaning. This realisation was facilitated within the research team by the fact that the four researchers then involved did not share a single view about the state of Roman Catholicism in England or the same valuation of the implications of the Second Vatican Council. On the other hand we could reasonably claim the advantages of multiple triangulation of researcher, value-orientation, and to some extent of theoretical perspective and methodological approach (Denzin, 1970; Blaikie, 1988)

2.2   Comparative approaches

Throughout this book the points discussed in the previous section will be illustrated by selections from interview transcripts with three of four broad categories of Catholics:

(a) Core members, in particular lay members of the national commissions set up following the Second Vatican Council to advise the bishops. In general, while these respondents might differ in their religious ideologies (for example on the traditionalism–progressivism dimension), they not only shared, to a large extent, a knowledge of and acceptance of the official belief and value system of the Church, but also the salience of a religious world-view. In Cottrell's terms, these were the 'religiously devoted' (1985: 149). They can be regarded as a 'cognitive minority' whose religious world-view 'differs significantly from the one generally taken for granted in (our) society' (Berger, 1971: 18; 1973: 156).

(b) Parish 'activists', so designated by their parish priests. These corresponded roughly to Fichter's 'nuclear' and 'leading' parishioners (1954: 21–39) and reported high levels of both associational and communal involvement (Lenski, 1963: 22–4). Like the previous group, they largely accepted the official belief and value system of the Church, though their knowledge of the conciliar teaching tended to be less and they were less prepared to relate it to everyday living. We have not drawn on our interviews with parish activists in this book since they are, in many respects, an intermediate category between 'core' and 'ordinary' practising Catholics.

(c) The 'practising' Catholics with a minimum level of institutional involvement, such as attendance at Mass more than once a year. These Catholics manifested considerable variations in terms of orthodoxy and heterodoxy of religious beliefs, attitudes and practices, so that it could not be said that they shared a common belief and value system. They did, however, appear largely to share the view that 'religious' matters were of some consequence to them in the way they lived their lives. These Catholics approximate to Fichter's two categories of 'modal' and 'marginal' parishioners (1954: 40–67) but there are good grounds for describing the regular attenders as 'passive' rather than using the statistically incorrect term 'modal' (Hornsby-Smith, 1989: 180).

(d) The 'dormant' Catholics (Fichter, 1954; 17, 68–79) who identified themselves as Roman Catholics but who had only negligible attachment to the institutional Church either in terms of beliefs or in terms of religious practice. For these Catholics not only was there very little or no evidence of any coherent or consistent religious world-view, but there was also evidence that religious matters had negligible salience for them and were of no consequence in the way they lived their lives. It seems they differ little from those Cottrell calls the 'nominally and non-religious' (1985: 165–78).In this book we have described the 'practising' and 'dormant' Catholics as 'ordinary' Catholics.

As the researchers moved from interviewing core activists to Catholics who were on the periphery of the institutional Church and who barely retained a Catholic identity, it seemed that the research problem with which they had commenced the study was becoming increasingly incomprehensible to the respondents and thus to require some reformulation. As we noted previously, a further cycle of zigzagging 'between theory and data until we have established a plausible account' (Mann, 1986: vii) was undertaken.

We noted, for example, that those Catholics who were actively involved in the institutional Church, and especially those lay members of the national commissions set up to advise the Bishops' Conference, were generally aware of the significance of the Second Vatican Council and were able to give accounts of their religious beliefs, attitudes and practices in broadly theological terms and with a reasonably coherent and consistent world-view. Since this accorded with the expectations of the researchers, the respondent accounts were regarded as unproblematic for analysis purposes.

Yet with hindsight it is clear that these initial analyses were undertaken uncritically and there remained for the researcher the problem of identifying the relevant criteria to justify such differential allocation of status between respondents. It is suggested that there really is no way of avoiding this methodological issue, and that some selection of what is to count is inevitable where there is a mass of data to be analysed, as is typically the case with observational studies or in-depth interviewing. In the last analysis, the researcher selects those data which are relevant for his theoretical purposes, as Mann pointed out (1986). At the same time it is incumbent on the researcher to give appropriate attention to the questions of representativeness, reliability and validity.

In this present study, it is suggested that the implicit criteria employed were the contributions made by the respondent accounts to the coherence and consistency of the analyst's account of his findings. These were generally greater in the case of knowledgeable and articulate activists whose accounts tended, therefore, to be given disproportionate weight. In this connection it is interesting to note Weber's acknowledgement that:

in the great majority of cases actual action goes on in a state of inarticulate half-consciousness or actual consciousness of its subjective meaning. The actor is more likely to 'be aware' of it in a vague sense that he is to 'know' what he is doing or be explicitly self-conscious about it. In most cases his action is governed by impulse or habit. Only occasionally and, in the uniform action of large numbers, often only in the case of a few individuals, is the subjective meaning of the action, whether rational or irrational, brought clearly into consciousness. The ideal type of meaningful action where the meaning is fully conscious and explicit is a marginal case. (Weber, 1968: 21–2)

This became more apparent in our later interviews with grass-roots Catholics, where we gradually became aware that questions of religious ideology, conformity to a traditional pre-Vatican model of a closed and static Church, or adherence to a progressive post-Vatican model of a more open and dynamic Church, were simply of no consequence. These respondents were largely unconcerned about theological debates and evaluated the consequences of these debates, for example about the liturgical innovations or modifications in fasting or abstinence disciplines, simply in terms of their relative convenience or inconvenience. Hence the early assumption of the researchers, that what they considered to be salient would also be salient to their respondents, was clearly shown to be erroneous, and with hindsight naive.

In the case of the dormant Catholics who had, in practice, largely severed their connection with institutional Catholicism, there was not even any knowledge that the Roman Catholic Church had changed in recent decades, whether in terms of its theology, with which they, like most practising Catholics, were completely unconcerned, or in terms of its styles of worship and leadership. Under these circumstances the interviews became more exploratory and appeared to be probing areas which various authors have referred to as 'common' religion (Towler and Chamberlain, 1973; Towler, 1974), 'invisible' religion (Luckmann, 1970), 'customary' religion (Hornsby-Smith, Lee and Reilly, 1985) or 'folk', 'popular', or 'implicit' religion (Bailey, 1986). It seemed that for dormant Catholics, religion provided a 'God of the gaps', that is a fall-back set of beliefs when all else failed (Abercrombie et al, 1970: 123). The heterodoxy of beliefs and practices of grass-roots Catholics, which was fully documented in *Roman Catholics in England* (Hornsby-Smith, 1987), raised methodological problems of considerable significance during the analysis of the taped, focused interviews which is the concern of this present book.

How does the researcher investigate the hidden world of the 'taken-for-granted' (Schutz, 1972: 74), especially when it concerns religious world-views or what David Martin calls 'subterranean theologies', that is a 'series of interlocking attitudes about fairness, about the sources of contemporary social difficulties, the choice of superhuman cultural heros, the selection of significant metaphor, and notions about how and why people act' in the way they do (1969: 109)?

Peter Berger has pointed out that in the modern world probably a majority of people seem to get on quite well without a sense of the supernatural (1971: 18; see also Cottrell, 1985). What people find plausible or credible requires appropriate structures of support, 'social networks or conversational fabrics', therapeutic practices and legitimations. A taken-for-granted, implicit Catholicism (1971: 50–3), might have been appropriate in the stage of the 'fortress', pre-Vatican Church or for those who wished to opt for a sect-like intransigent stance in the modern world. But where the accommodation option of *aggiornamento* has been selected in a situation of pluralism, there is a 'crisis of credibility'. In these circumstances, 'what certainty there is must be dredged up from within the subjective consciousness of the individual, since it can no longer be derived from the external, socially shared and taken-for-granted world' (1973: 156). In pursuing this task, the role of the sociologist is

to report people's 'knowledge' and its consequences (1971: 19).
Empirical inquiries must be pursued by patient induction and with
an openness to the fullness of human experience in a:

spirit of relentless honesty, which is not so much disrespectful of established
religious authority as ruthless with one's own religious hopes . . . animated by
patient openness and humility before all available intimations of religious
truth. (1971: 106–7)

It is hoped that this present study has been pursued in such a
spirit. Our experience suggested that the research process of seeking
accounts by interviewing procedures must be flexible if it is to cope
with the absence of knowledge, beliefs and salience. This flexibility
had to embrace changes not only in the formulation of the research
aims and methods, but also changes in the criteria employed to
determine significance.

This brings us to the question of 'triangulation' as a means of
reducing bias and improving validity. Webb and his colleagues
(1966) advocated 'multiple operationism', the use of a 'triangulation
of measurement processes', including 'unobtrusive measures' as an
appropriate response to the problems of bias and validity. Denzin
suggested that the use of multiple methods raised the investigator
'above the personalistic biases that stem from single methodologies',
but went further and urged a policy of multiple triangulation 'when
researchers combine in one investigation multiple observers, theoretical perspectives, sources of data, and methodologies' as the
'soundest strategy of theory construction' (1970: 310; 300).

Nevertheless it is important to pay attention to recent criticisms of
the concept of triangulation. Thus Blaikie (1988) has called for a
moratorium on its use, and is critical of Denzin's eclecticism and
'inappropriate combinations of methods and data sources' where
these are based on incommensurable ontological and epistemological
assumptions of different methodological perspectives, in particular
positivism and interpretivism.

Nigel and Jane Fielding have also stressed that 'triangulation, or
the multiple-strategy approach, is no guarantee of internal and
external validity', though they recognise that the use of different
methods to look at a particular situation 'stimulates an awareness
that there is no one "truth", even in relation to quite specific,
discrete, and limited incidents' (1986: 24–5). In their critique of
Denzin's treatment of multiple triangulation, they argue that:

theoretical triangulation does not necessarily increase validity. Theories are generally the product of quite different traditions, so that when they are combined one may get a fuller picture, but not a more 'objective' one. Similarly, different methods have emerged as a product of different theoretical traditions, and therefore combining them can add range and depth, but not accuracy ... there is a case for triangulation ... We should combine theories and methods carefully and purposefully with the intention of adding breadth or depth to our analysis, but not for the purpose of pursuing 'objective' truth'. (1986: 33)

It is the fact that the selected theories and methods 'fit together which adds to the plausibility of the researcher's interpretation'. Thus they advocate a 'dualist' view, complementing a perspective which explores structural aspects of the research problem with one that investigates key aspects of its meaning for the participants (1986: 34).

In the research reported in this book, an approach to multiple triangulation was made in that there were, in the various studies with different groups of Catholics and in different locations, several different researchers with different theoretical orientations. A variety of qualitative and quantitative research methods, including both structured and focused interviews, participant and non-participant observation, were employed. While it was originally envisaged that this would reduce the chances of systematic bias and improve the validity of our interpretations, it seems more correct to regard the more qualitative findings reported in this book as being complementary to those reported in *Roman Catholics in England* (Hornsby-Smith, 1987). Thus in the 'dualist' view suggested by the Fieldings, the former book was concerned with the structural aspects of English Catholicism while this present book is concerned more with the question of the meaning which their religion has for different groups of Catholics.

2.3   A typology of Catholic accounts

On the basis of these reflections about the methodological and theoretical difficulties of investigating the religious beliefs, attitudes and values of English Catholics, it is suggested that the four categories of respondent in the present research could usefully be differentiated in terms of the following three dimensions as summarised in Table 2.1:

Introduction

Table 2.1. *Classification of respondent category and type of account*

	Respondent Category			
	Priests, National advisers	Parish activists	Weekly attenders	Dormant Catholics
Religious Characteristics				
Attachment to beliefs	+	+	+	−
Knowledge and ideological legitimations	+	+	−	−
Salience for religious and social action	+	−	−	−
Type of account				
Coherence and consistency	high	medium	low	lowest
Researcher allocation of status	high	medium	low	low
Most prominent features	explanation	justifications	justifications and excuses	excuses

(*Source*: Hornsby-Smith, 1983: 148)

(a) belief: attachment to the core elements of the official belief system;
(b) ideology: knowledge and relevance of the different models of the Church and of their legitimation; and
(c) salience: prominence of religious beliefs for both religious and social action.

Respondent accounts varied in terms of their coherence and consistency and correspondingly, as we have indicated, in terms of the status which tended to be allocated to them by researchers. It is suggested that the accounts also differed in terms of their most prominent features. In the case of the national advisers, their interview responses were generally accorded privileged status and treated as unproblematic, that is as more-or-less accurate statements of the respondents' beliefs. They typically consisted of 'explanations' of their beliefs and behaviour and the researchers tended to regard them as relatively undistorted by self-interest.

In the case of the other three categories of respondent, progressively lower status was accorded to their accounts which progressively declined in terms of their coherence and consistency, at least in terms of the original research questions. Following the useful review offered by Scott and Lyman, these accounts were more likely to have the characteristic of statements 'made by a social actor to explain unanticipated or untoward behaviour' (Scott and Lyman, 1968: 46). Two types of accounts are distinguished:

(a) *justifications* which are 'accounts in which one accepts responsibility for the act in question, but denies the perjorative quality associated with it', and

(b) *excuses* which are 'accounts in which one admits that the act in question is bad, wrong, or inappropriate but denies full responsibility'. (1968: 47)

In terms of this distinction, it appeared that in the present research the activists were more likely to offer justifications (for example, for intercommunicating in non-Catholic churches) while the dormant Catholics were more likely to offer excuses (for example, for lack of religious practice).

In all areas of social life greater credence and weight is given to some accounts rather than others. Similarly, as Mann pointed out, the researcher invariably has to face the matter of what data to select from a huge mass of potentially relevant findings. The problematic nature of all interview accounts remains, and in particular the differential allocation to status to accounts offered by different respondents. In studies of the 'taken-for-granted' aspects of social life, such as is the case of religious beliefs of people for whom religion appears to have no salience, or more generally in cases 'where the dependent variable "evaporates" to vanishing point', the researcher is perhaps best advised to supplement interview methods with observational studies in natural settings such as parishes. This was done to a limited extent in the studies reported in this book. Even so, the problem of 'siding' with some versions rather than others, and of the selection of data accorded significance, still has to be faced. In general it seems that the researcher typically uses the criterion of the contribution of data to the coherence and consistency of his own account of his findings and his tentative theoretical interpretations.

2.4   Consistency, coherence and complexity

Somewhat enigmatically, the Fieldings assert that 'consistency and complexity are crucial to an adequate analysis of social action' (1986: 69). In this connection, we have indicated that at the beginning of our research we tended to pay more attention to, and attribute a privileged status to, those interviews which appeared to have a consistency of religious orientation and a coherence of religious beliefs and attitudes. This was because they appeared to contribute to our early analyses, which were conceived of largely in unidimensional terms as indicating a conflict within the Church between the 'progressives', who supported and promoted the shifts of religious ideology and pastoral emphases promulgated by the Second Vatican Council, on the one hand, and the 'traditionalists', on the other hand, who rejected and resisted them. We increasingly came to realise, however, that the concepts of consistency and coherence are extremely problematic and that the social reality is that the religion of English Catholics is extremely inconsistent, incoherent and complex.

Reference was made in the previous chapter to Worsley's warning against imputing 'a spurious unity ... on to other people's belief systems' and attempting the 'over-systematisation of belief' (1970: 300–1). The relevance of this warning emerged clearly in our study of structural aspects of contemporary Roman Catholicism in England. Evidence was reviewed which indicated that the commonly held view that the Catholic Church was unusually monolithic in its religious beliefs and practices, and that lay people were especially conformist in a 'priest-ridden' Church, was erroneous. Rather, the empirical evidence from surveys carried out in the 1970s showed that there were considerable variations in the religious identity, beliefs and practices, institutional involvement and sexual morality among English Catholics. This led to the identification of ten different types of Catholics. Only 9 per cent were found to be orthodox in terms of both an unqualified belief in the doctrine of the consecration of the bread and wine in the Eucharist and in a traditional opposition to 'artificial methods of birth control' (Types A and C). The largest single group (Type J), comprising over one-fifth of all Catholics, was that of the heterodox non-attenders (Hornsby-Smith, 1987: 47–66).

The *consistency* of a religious world-view refers to the extent to which the different elements are compatible rather than contradictory.

Thus, not only would the different elements of the belief system reflect the same underlying principles, but the association between the belief system and other dimensions of the world-view, such as religious practice, knowledge and experience (Stark and Glock, 1968), would also be high. Thus it would be consistent for a person who espoused a post-Vatican theology to favour liturgical reform, more lay participation at every level in the Church, and an enabling style of priestly authority. Broadly speaking, such a person would be regarded as a 'progressive'. It would be inconsistent for such a person to claim to welcome the reforms of the Second Vatican Council but resist the setting up of parish councils or the authorisation of lay special ministers of communion. Similarly, it would be consistent for a person of a Lefebvre-like persuasion to reject the conciliar reforms, seek to retain the Latin Mass and relate deferentially to the priest, regarding him as a sacred 'man apart'. Broadly speaking, such a person would be viewed as a 'traditionalist'. It would, however, be inconsistent for such a person to advocate the retention of the Latin Mass while at the same time encouraging the use of lay readers or special ministers of communion.

The *coherence* of a belief system refers to the extent to which the different constituent elements are complementary to each other and have some overriding theological principle. Thus a coherent belief system might stress the transcendent nature of the creator God, the hierarchical nature of the Church, papal authority, the priest as a sacred 'man apart', and the role of the lay person as subordinate to, and supportive of, that of the clergy. Conversely, a belief system which placed a greater emphasis on the immanent nature of God, the Church as the pilgrim 'people of God', the collegiality of the bishops, the full participation of lay people in all aspects of the mission of the Church, and an enabling style of priestly leadership, would also be coherent. To the extent to which various mixed combinations of beliefs coexist, it could be said that there was evidence of incoherence in the belief system.

For English Catholics in general, if one were simply to consider the two dimensions of belief and practice as being crucial, and with belief dichotomised as either orthodox or heterodox and practice as either conformity to the weekly Mass attendance norm or not, then there are four possibilities: the orthodox attenders (Types A-D, 31 per cent), the heterodox attenders (Type E, 5 per cent), the orthodox non-attenders (Types F and H, 21 per cent) and the heterodox non-attenders (Types G, J and non-identifying Catholics, 35 per cent). Of these four collapsed categories, the first and fourth (66 per cent of English Catholics) are consistent at least in terms of the two indicators selected. The remaining two categories (26 per cent) are inconsistent. However, when one probes further, additional elements of inconsistency emerge. For example, two-thirds of the 'orthodox attenders' reject the official teaching of the Church on birth control and only one-third are sufficiently involved to be members of a parish organisation (Hornsby-Smith, 1987: 51).

In the analysis of the delegates to the National Pastoral Congress in 1980, seven distinct types were distinguished in terms of six criteria: progressive morality, progressive theology, progressive liturgy, community emphasis, socio-political religious involvement and an anti-nuclear defence stance. In terms of these criteria, only 15 per cent of the delegates were 'progressive' on all dimensions and only 4 per cent 'traditionalist' on all dimensions (Hornsby-Smith et al, 1987: 244). Thus, even in terms of relatively crude quantitative measures, there is considerable evidence of inconsistency. This becomes even more apparent when analysing the more qualitative focused interview data. An indication that this might long have been the case is the observation of Madeline Kerr in her classic study of a Liverpool slum in the 1950s:

The hold which the Catholic Church acquires over the children seems to persist ... only in the form of prohibitions of conduct, and this *not always very logically*. For example, Ship Street regards birth control as a sin but abortion before the age of three months a perfectly legitimate measure.' (1958: 137; italics added).

In the United States, Andrew Greeley has indicated something of the flavour of inconsistency in his identification of the communal Catholics who are:

loyal to the Catholic collectivity and at least sympathetic towards its heritage ... [but who] refuse to take seriously the teaching authority of the leadership of the institutional Church ... [and manifest] a new and self-consciously selective style of affiliating with the Catholic tradition. (Greeley, 1977: 272)

This would seem to appeal very much to Catholic 'yuppies', assertively self-confident with their educational qualifications, achieved professional status and social and geographical experiences. Some Catholics may have an ability to articulate the complexities of their religious faith, but many (and by no means only the minimally educated) have an extremely limited knowledge of Catholic beliefs and values and/or capacity to articulate them in an interview situation. Thus not only does one find strong elements of contradiction and ambiguity of meanings given in verbalised accounts, but there are additional problems for the researcher in attempting to understand the significance and meaning of poorly articulated responses to interviewer probes on matters which the respondent may never consciously have addressed before.

The sociologist must, therefore, be sensitive to any propensity on his part to assume ordered relationships between elements of belief and action, or to expect rational explanations of these, or to give undue weight to the accounts of those who conform most closely to his expectations of consistency and coherence. In our field research it became evident that such expectations were quite unrealistic for many people and that the everyday reality was complex and often contradictory and ambiguous. This was not simply because of the 'multidimensionality' of religion (Stark and Glock, 1968; Mueller, 1980). Nor could it be interpreted easily in terms of Weber's distinctions between instrumental and value-rationality, affectivity and habituation (1968: 24–6).

Our interview data did seem to be consistent with Cottrell's findings that, apart from those for whom Church religion was a central life-value, individuals did not exhibit a search for general meaning, but pragmatically, instrumentally and individually ordered their lives within a network of structural links, mutual dependencies and obligations. For many people 'religion is not a matter of intrinsic importance. Ignorance about religion is widespread, beliefs are extremely vague and people are uncertain of their feelings' (1985: 158). Our data pointed towards an uncertain world of a Catholic form of diffused religion, 'a sort of "lay religion" which "betrays" orthodox religious values but which adapts and reinserts itself into [everyday] contingent realities' (Cipriani, 1984: 38). There is, in other words, a need for a 'sociological construction of inconsistency' (1984: 30).

Put into a wider context, it is the concern of cultural studies generally to address these issues, and to show how the coordination of diverse beliefs and values reflects conflicts and power struggles in the wider society, and in this case the Church, and the attempts by different groups to assert and impose particular definitions of what is to count as consistent, coherent and commonsensical. Such issues were at the core of Gramsci's analysis of religion, especially at the 'common sense' level where the 'popular religion' of different groups of people manifests itself:

> Every religion, even Catholicism (indeed Catholicism more than any, precisely because of its efforts to retain a 'surface' unity and avoid splintering into national Churches and social stratifications), is in reality a multiplicity of distinct and often contradictory religions: there is one Catholicism for the peasants, one for the *petits-bourgeois* and town workers, one for women, and one for intellectuals which is itself variegated and disconnected. (Gramsci, 1971: 420; Fulton, 1987: 203)

This leads us to the consideration of the *salience* of religion for respondents and its relationship to measures of religious commitment.

2.5   Salience and commitment

Finally we will consider briefly variations in the salience of religion in people's everyday lives and in their levels of religious commitment. In general terms salience is concerned with the 'consequential' dimension of religiosity, that is 'the effects of religious belief, practice, experience, and knowledge in persons' day-to-day lives' (Stark and Glock, 1968: 16). Roof and Perkins regarded religious salience as 'the importance an individual attaches to being 'religious' and defined it as 'an orientation toward religious commitment, similar to that implied in Allport's intrinsic religiosity, in which belief is regarded as bearing significance and meaning in everyday life situations' (Allport, 1950, 1966; quoted in Roof and Perkins, 1975: 111, 116). That some ambiguities exist in the relationship between salience and commitment is indicated by the fact that two of the thirteen scales developed by King and Hunt (1975) for the exploration of the multidimensionality of religious commitment refer to salience (Roof, 1979: 24-9). Clearly there is a danger of some circularity if the concepts are not operationalised independently. In this book the salience of the religious beliefs or attitudes for an individual is taken to refer to their prominence, significance and relevance for the individual in terms of their implications for action, notably for religious practices and for religiously informed social behaviour such as political participation and involvement.

In Table 2.1 we suggested that among English Catholics high levels of salience of their religious beliefs for both religious and social action were to be found only among the national advisers. Unlike the three other categories of respondent, these were able to offer consistent and coherent explanations of their actions in terms of these beliefs. In the case of the parish activists and weekly Mass attenders, as well as the dormant Catholics, the salience of their religious beliefs, especially for action in their everyday lives, for example in politics or at work, was not high. Yet levels of religious practice, often regarded as a key measure of commitment, were high for the activists and regular attenders.

This is consistent with the findings reported by Melanie Cottrell who distinguished four categories of respondent. For the 'religious' in her sample, church religion provided an overarching frame of general meaning and significance in all aspects of their lives. However, this was not the case with any of her other categories including the 'non-religious church-goers' for whom religion was not intrinsically important. The 'nominally religious' tended to cease religious practice because they could not be bothered. Cottrell's data supported Luckmann's (1970) analysis that religion has no significant place in the lives of most people and for many regular attenders, churchgoing is largely a habitual social action unconnected with religious purposes (1985: 146–82). Religious practice, therefore, is not by itself an adequate measure of the salience of religion for the individual over a range of different substantive areas.

In a recent review of the literature, Hoge and de Zulueta defined salience narrowly as 'the importance of religion to the individual' (1985: 23), leaving the question of the relevance of religion in various areas of social life, such as personal and sexual morality and issues such as contraception, divorce and abortion, on the one hand, and social and political morality in such areas as racial discrimination, economic policies and social justice, acceptable defence strategies and international relations, on the other hand, to be determined by empirical enquiry. On the basis of a national probability sample in 1981, they concluded that in general terms American Christianity had an impact on members' values and attitudes in only a limited realm, chiefly family life, sexuality and personal honesty, and always in a conservative direction. For Catholics only, there was also a close relationship between self-perceived religious salience and the desire for greater respect for authority in the future. It was also reported that religious salience had a strong and linear relationship with orthodoxy.

There are also difficulties in the way in which the concept of commitment has been defined, interpreted and used in empirical research. In a major review of the literature, Roof has defined religious commitment as 'an individual's beliefs and behaviour in relation to the supernatural and/or high intensity values' (1979: 18) leaving open the question of whether the meaning system is church-oriented or not. Much of his review relates to attempts to measure quantitatively various dimensions of religiosity. There seems to be a general ambiguity in the literature as to whether religious commitment is an independent variable causally related to various measures of religious belief, practice and involvement, as dependent variables, or whether these measures are in fact different indicators of commitment. Is commitment a cause or a consequence of religiosity?

Secondly, most of the empirical studies of commitment have confined themselves to the analysis of the relationships with religious beliefs and attitudes and both associational and communal forms of involvement. There seem to have been few studies which have explicitly investigated the relationship between religious commitment and behavioural measures of social activism, as opposed to the attitudes of Church members towards political issues and involvement. Distinctions between different objects of commitment: God, the local congregation or religious community, the wider societal or global community, humankind across generations, or to social transformations in search of 'Kingdom' values, are often not clearly made. The result is that one is frequently left with rather trivial and tautological findings that people committed to their local religious communities have high levels of interaction with fellow-members with whom they share many beliefs.

Becker (1960) suggested that a commitment arises when an individual makes a 'side bet', linking extraneous interests (such as self-esteem or the promise of salvation) with a consistent line of activity (such as regular religious practice). The 'side bets' are often a consequence of participation in a social institution, for example a parish. He further argued that to understand commitment fully, an analysis of the individual's system of values, what things are desired and what losses feared, was necessary to explain a consistent line of action. In Becker's treatment it is important to avoid the tautological proposition that 'commitment produces consistent lines of activity' by specifying the characteristics of commitment independently of the behaviour it is intended to explain, for example, action in the economic or political spheres.

A recurring theme is that there are basically two main clusters indicative of religious commitment: those aspects concerned with meaning, belief, feelings and experiences, on the one hand, and those pertaining to belonging, including religious participation, communal interaction and social involvement, on the other hand (Greeley, 1972: 69–70; Kanter, 1972: 64–70: Himmelfarb, 1975). Thus McGaw (1979) showed that a charismatic Presbyterian congregation was more effective at providing meaning and belonging to its members through stronger closure, strictness, consensus on authority, and cohesion than was an otherwise comparable mainline congregation.

Such findings have led to the investigation of the social bases of commitment and a theory of religious plausibility in terms of Merton's distinction between local and cosmopolitan influentials (1957: 387–420). In particular, Roof (1978) has demonstrated, for liberal Protestants, the importance of local community attachments in sustaining traditional religious beliefs and behaviour. Similarly, Cornwall (1987) showed that personal community relationships had the strongest direct influence on belief and commitment and that early religious socialisation is important mainly because it channels individuals into supportive communities of believers.

From one point of view, the findings from these various studies present the Roman Catholic Church with major problems in the selection of both pastoral goals and the choice of means for their attainment. On the basis of the research evidence, mainly from American Protestant Churches, it seems likely that the promotion of parishioner interaction and the cultivation of a sense of belonging would contribute to increased religiosity in terms of beliefs, practices and parish involvement. Strategies of closure, strictness, consensus on authority relations and cohesion, as in a 'fortress' Church, would contribute to a greater sense of religious meaning and belonging to adherents (McGaw, 1979). Such strategies, however, appear to conflict with the traditional inclusive membership policies of the Catholic Church and other mainline Churches. At the same time, what evidence there is suggests that it is likely that an emphasis on localism would also be associated with conservative religious consequences (Roof, 1978). In the case of the Catholic community this might manifest itself as a reassertion of a traditional differentiation between religion and politics and a rejection of the active pursuit of social justice. It seems possible, therefore, that strategies of parish renewal which stress the building-up of strong local attachments, might be conducive to the development of a commitment to traditional beliefs and practices. On the other hand, if one measures religious commitment in terms of altruism (Neal, 1982) or some form of social activism, then a greater emphasis on cosmopolitan influences would seem to be necessary.

Conclusions

We have reviewed a number of the methodological problems which must be borne in mind in interpreting the interview data from different types of English Catholics in the rest of this book. Many of these problems are intrinsic to the research enterprise and bear on the recognition that the findings reported do not, and cannot, purport to be 'the whole truth'. Rather they are data which have been collected by the researcher using probes and prompts related to *his* original purposes. In a finite interview situation these are subject to further exploration or closure generally depending on the judgement of the interviewer in the light of his understanding of the research goals and his calculus of the rewards and costs of alternative lines of enquiry. Furthermore, in the analysis process itself, it is the researcher who judges what is to be counted as relevant or interesting. The purpose of this present chapter has been to provide a basis from which the reader might in turn be able to evaluate the researcher's account of Roman Catholic beliefs and attitudes towards religious authority which have been given. Thus attention has been drawn to the problems of interpreting variations in the levels of coherence, consistency and articulation on the part of respondents differentially located in the institutional Church. Reference has also been made to the debates, still largely unresolved, over the use of such key concepts as salience and commitment.

With these points in mind, we turn now to consider our empirical data relating to the everyday lives of English Catholics between the mid-1970s and the mid-1980s (chapters 3 to 5) and the evidence for transformations in religious authority in the Church (chapters 6 to 9).

PART II

THE RELIGIOUS BELIEFS OF THE ENGLISH CATHOLICS

3

THE EVERYDAY LIVES OF LAY CATHOLICS

3.1 An exploratory study

There is very little research evidence which relates directly to the ways in which ordinary Catholics make religious sense of their everyday lives, with all their 'hopes and joys', but also their unremitting demands and dilemmas and the perennial problems of survival and security and coping with personal disasters and unanticipated contingencies. How do ordinary Catholics cope with their secular lives in their daily domestic and work routines? What difference does their religion make to the way they handle everyday reality and their determination of priorities and resolution of dilemmas? These were some of the questions which we attempted to address in an exploratory study of English Catholic lay people in 1986/7.

A second concern was to question a variety of 'taken-for-granted' assumptions on the part of both laity and clergy, about the nature of the Church, appropriate priest–lay relations, styles of priestly authority and lay subordination and compliance (Etzioni, 1961), religious rituals and the everyweek routines of the liturgical cycle, and forms of lay participation in the Church more than two decades after the Second Vatican Council reforms. Evidence will be presented which indicates that at least for some lay people, many of these issues are both problematic and contested (Houtart, 1969). There are similar indications from Catholic laity in the United States (Droel and Pierce, 1987; Droel, 1989a and 1989b) and Ireland (MacRéamoinn, 1986).

The study originated in the context of the substantial exclusion of lay people from the deliberations of the 1987 Synod of Bishops in Rome on 'The Vocation and Mission of the Laity in the Church and in the World', though in his post-synodal Apostolic Exhortation, Pope John-Paul II acknowledged 'a valuable contribution' from 'a qualified representation of the lay faithful' (*Christifideles Laici*, s.2 in John Paul II, 1989: 6). It was also suspected that clerically defined or inferred and 'taken-for-granted' assumptions about lay people were erroneous or inadequate, firstly in their understanding of the realities of everyday domestic and work lives, and secondly in their assumptions about the non-problematic nature of everyday or everyweek clergy–lay relations, especially at the parish level, and about lay expectations of appropriate styles of clergy authority in the contemporary Church.

In our analysis, as we indicated in the previous chapter, the accounts of lay Catholics, and their meanings and interpretations, will be regarded as their privileged 'definitions of the situation' (Gilbert and Abell, 1983). Adapting W. I. Thomas's well-known observation, if lay people define situations as real, they are likely to be real in their social structural consequences for the Church they are in the process of constructing, for the forms of clergy–lay relationships which are in the process of emerging, and for the styles of religious authority on which they are prepared to bestow legitimacy. The approach taken, therefore, was broadly Weberian (1949), in that it aimed to take seriously lay accounts of the religious meanings of their everyday lives and regarded this as essential, if explanations of the prevailing social and community relationships within the Church were to be causally adequate at the level of meaning. Any lack of fit between the taken-for-granted assumptions of religious leaders about the laity, and those of the laity themselves, or any evidence that these assumptions are not so taken-for-granted by the laity, would be likely to have important implications for the social structures of contemporary Catholicism, for example for the compliance of the lower participants, the laity.

Given the suspicion that there was likely to have been a lack-of-fit between the bishops' interpretations of the everyday lives, vocation and mission of lay people, and those of lay people themselves, it was considered to be important to follow Blumer's injunction to 'get in touch with the empirical social world' (1954: 4). Hence the purpose was to explore the realities of the everyday domestic and work lives of a sample of lay Catholics and the religious meanings which they attributed to them, and not to accept uncritically accounts of these realities by religious leaders or authority figures or compliant or submissive laity in terms of what they would like them to be. It was regarded as important to explore the extent to which the social realities were in fact 'not-so-obvious'.

In this exploratory study, the opportunistic sample consisted of twelve relatively articulate and 'committed' lay Catholics, with both men and women, from both the more deprived north of England and the more prosperous south, and ranging from those who could be regarded as having some sort of decision-making powers, such as a Member of Parliament, a retired senior executive and professional social workers, to the relatively powerless, such as three single parents and a man recently made redundant from his job. Thus although the sample was in no sense statistically 'representative' of English Catholics, it covered a wide range of both personal and professional experiences of suffering and deprivation. In the following sections of this chapter we will review those responses, particularly in the areas of the lay vocation, coping with everyday problems and dilemmas, the extent to which experiences of support were derived from local parishes, and constructions of spiritualities in tune with the normal rhythms of everyday lay lives.

3.2 The lay vocation

The first area we wished to explore was the sense which lay people had of their everyday domestic or work roles as a 'vocation'. The sociological treatment of vocation derives ultimately from Max Weber's analysis of Luther's conception of the 'calling' (1930: 62–3, 80–1) and his two lectures on the vocations of politics and science (1948: 77–156). For Weber the concept refers to a specific inner-call to a specialised task with its own unique combination of ethical demands which differentiate it from other vocations. In the Catholic treatment of vocation, the specific calling comes from God and must be interpreted prudentially and with discernment. Thus Yves Congar in terms reminiscent of Weber, writes that the lay person's 'particular Christian calling is to bring glory to God and the reign of Christ *in and through that work* (of the world)' (1965: 390–1; emphasis in original).

Among Catholics generally, the term 'vocation' is commonly taken to refer to the calling to the priesthood or membership of a religious order (Congar, 1965: 427) and indeed, the bulk of references to vocation in the documents of the Second Vatican Council have this restricted meaning (Abbott, 1966). Nevertheless, in the recent official teaching of the Church, a clear picture of the vocation of the lay person does emerge. The task of the laity is to 'work for the sanctification of the world from within, in the manner of leaven' (*Lumen Gentium*, s.31, in Abbott, 1966: 58) or 'salt of the earth' (*Lumen Gentium*, s.33, in Abbott, 1966: 59), and to 'take on the renewal of the temporal order as their own special obligation' (*Apostolicam Actuositatem*, s.7, in Abbott, 1966: 498). For Pope Paul VI, writing ten years after the Second Vatican Council, the particular field of evangelising activity of lay people is:

the vast and complicated world of politics, society and economics, but also the world of culture, of the sciences and the arts, of international life, of the mass media. It also includes other realities which are open to evangelisation, such as human love, the family, the education of children and adolescents, professional work, suffering. (*Evangelii Nuntiandi*, s.70, in Paul VI, 1975: 94)

Since the collection of the data for this chapter, Pope John-Paul II has written an Apostolic Exhortation in response to the 1987 Synod of Bishops, in which he has drawn on the parable of the labourers in the vineyard (Matt. 20: 1–7), called by God at different stages in life to 'the vocation of holiness, that is, the perfection of charity' (*Christifideles Laici*, ss.16 and 45, in John-Paul II, 1989: 15, 44).

It is of interest to review the ways in which lay Catholics interpreted their lay roles and the extent to which they regarded their work roles as being vocations, in the light of the sociological conceptualisation of vocation and the recent exhortations by the teaching authorities in the Church as to how lay people should fulfill the obligations of their special calling. In the first place, few felt comfortable either with the concept itself or with the proposition that what they were actually doing might be a vocation in the sense of a specific 'calling' from God to which they had given a conscious and ready response. Thus a lawyer admitted that he was 'suspicious' of the word (Warren, 1988: 205). It may be that such suspicion on the part of lay people is an unconscious result of earlier processes of religious socialisation: differentiating their 'ordinary' lives from the 'real' vocation to the priesthood or to life in a religious community.

The conscious pursuit of a vocation at the onset of adult life was strongest in the accounts of the two social workers. In retrospect, one considered that her early use of the term, 'connected ... with the tradition of the Church's care for those suffering or in trouble ... [and] "doing good" on an individual basis', was naive. Nevertheless, in her account there is a clear sense of development from an original choice (Lynch, 1988: 269). The other suggested that her choice of career was in part a deliberate 'search for justice and love; an expression of my wish to care for and help others less fortunate than myself' (Carroll, 1988: 307).

In the main, however, there was little evidence of any awareness of a conscious choice of vocation or a deliberate response to a sense of calling. This was most obvious in the case of three unmarried mothers, for all of whom unanticipated pregnancy was a disaster which they had to cope with generally on their own and with precious little support. For David Alton (1987), setting out on a teaching career, an interest in, and commitment to, community politics led, rather unexpectedly, to his election to Parliament. In the case of David Ireson (1988) and James Foster (1988), their careers in teaching and highway engineering, respectively, simply emerged as a result of circumstance. Carol Burns remained unsure whether she had a vocation for teaching although it had been a conscious choice at the time of her training. Now she saw her vocation as a journey, a search: 'I have to respond to where I see Jesus, wherever the opportunity presents itself in the community' (1988: 85). It involved looking at her talents realistically and accepting some sort of leadership role in the local community. A retired senior executive admitted that at the start of his career he was just looking for a source of income and that there was nothing high-minded about the choice. Yet it was to become the 'first priority, the main anxiety, the dominating element in personal and family life' (McEvoy, 1987: 259). Nick Warren observed that 'chance or circumstance might have pushed me into a dozen different jobs' (1988: 205).

One conclusion, then, is that for many, perhaps most lay people, there is no sense of a vocation which emerges as an explicit and clear choice as they set out on their adult lives after completing their education. Rather, there is a sense of a journey into the unknown and an openness to the opportunities which beckon but which normally cannot be anticipated. Thus it implies a process of on-going discernment about the individual's talents and gifts, strengths and weaknesses, commitments and constraints – for example to family or community – and about the opportunities or calls on their time, talents and energy which emerge in the normal course of events throughout the life cycle. Thus Barbara Wood admitted that the busy domestic routine of the Catholic housewife had not previously struck her as being a 'vocation' though she had no doubt that it was what God wanted her to do. As for developing her other gifts, such as writing, 'God seems to be taking care of that without my assistance' (1987/8: 297). For women, in particular, there were the unanticipated exigencies of husband's occupations and, in our culture still, the continuing expectation that they would carry the bulk of the burden of child-rearing and family care.

In sum, most lay people do not appear to recognise an obvious 'call' to a particular task or occupation at their entry into adult life or even a process of discernment of God's will and their response to it throughout their lives. Thus lay people frequently give the appearance of 'muddling through' since, as James McEvoy put it, 'once into the job, it was a conveyor belt and there was no chance of jumping off' (1987: 259). It seems likely, therefore, on the basis of these findings, that clerical taken-for-granted assumptions about lay people's sense of vocation are mistaken. It is also possible that a generally weak sense of vocation on the part of lay people not only reflects the dominant role of the clergy in the Church, but also encourages a differentiation between 'religious' and 'secular' aspects of life, and so contributes to the maintenance of clerical control within the Church.

3.3 Coping with everyday dilemmas

The second area explored in this study was the particular difficulties faced by lay people as they tried to live their lives as Christians. It was hoped to include, for example, the problems of businessmen in coping with declining markets for goods and the need, as they might see it, for redundancies or redeployment of employees in the interests of the long-term viability of their enterprise and of the employment it offered; or the financial difficulties and the hurts of stigmatisation by others of the unemployed or single parents; or the increasing demands on, and expectations of, social workers in the face of declining resources; or the ways in which overtired men, anxious about their job security, and their exhausted wives, with finite resources of money, energy and patience, coped with large families or sick children and endless broken nights. The aim was to seek some Weberian *verstehen* or understanding of, and empathy with, lay people as they struggled with such realities in their everyday lives and attempted to attribute to them some sort of religious meaning and significance.

In the first place, in spite of general standards of economic well-being, it cannot be assumed that financial difficulties are unimportant in the lives of lay people. Thus the problems of 'making ends meet' are likely to be particularly acute for young marrieds or at key life-cycle stages such as the suspension of the woman's employment at the first pregnancy. These are well described by the ultimately occupationally successful James McEvoy in his account of coping with money shortages, especially in the early years of marriage, with seven children, camping holidays, clothes from jumble sales, years of 'frantic desperation, and father out of the house twelve hours a day and often two or three nights a week' (1987: 260). Three single parents described how they learned to cope with the frustrations of continual negotiations ('hassles') over social security payments and the 'techniques of neutralisation' (Matza, 1964) used by them to justify unreported part-time earnings because 'they pay you so little that you haven't got any choice but to do it ... I'm doing it to survive' (Kelly et al, 1988: 166).

A second area where difficulty was experienced in coping with everyday needs was that of child-rearing. McEvoy (1987: 260) recounted how he and his wife 'had dependent children for thirty-three years and under-fives for eighteen years. But you don't retire from being a parent' and he described both the joys and the concerns of his present grandparent status. Barbara Wood (1987/8: 299) described the home as 'the battlefront to change the world ... as we make everyday mundane decisions about what to buy and how we should live'. Her account of the vocation of motherhood is a manifesto of the task of passing on a sense of stewardship of God's world 'not just for this generation but for all generations and forever'.

The difficulties of child-rearing were, however, particularly acute in the case of the three single parents. One was fortunate in finding a satisfactory childminder, which enabled her to continue her employment, but she was exhausted by the time she had washed and fed her young son and put him to bed. A second described relentless tiredness with daytime temper tantrums followed by sleepless nights, a problem made all the more acute because there was no partner with whom to share the load. This 'real battle' leaves her feeling 'everything is a chore' so that she is always irritated by her daughter. 'You get a lot of guilt feeling as a single parent'. The third mother stressed the loneliness of the single parent: 'The empty bed seems so empty'. For single parents everything is a hassle and an ordeal to be coped with as best one can.

Nearly all of the lay people in this sample had had to cope with some measure of suffering at some stage in their lives. As Weber pointed out (1966: 108, 138–9, 141), one of the problems for religious belief is the 'difficulty in reconciling the idea of providence with the injustice and imperfection of the social order' (1966: 139), especially suffering. Carol Burns (1988) gave a moving account of how she coped with the knowledge that her baby was not going to live, and again after a subsequent miscarriage. She described the liturgical and burial arrangements made for her dead child in a way which pointed implicitly to a deep religious interpretation of the first major suffering of her life, which she described as changing and deepening her. Especially important were the kindness and understanding of other people, both Christian and non-Christian, which helped her 'to understand how suffering can be a positive force . . . the support you get somehow makes it worthwhile'. The symbolism of how the brokenness of people 'can be unified in the Eucharist' provided her with a heightened sense of the reality of religious beliefs to which she had previously given only notional assent.

In their different ways all three single parents had to cope with suffering in their home lives. The two unmarried mothers had both resisted strong pressures from either the fathers or various authority figures to have abortions, and both subsequently had broken off their relationship with the fathers. One of them also had to cope with the trauma of the sexual abuse of her daughter by the father. The third single mother, now separated from her husband, had coped with his repeated affairs with other women. All three needed some form of supportive contact with understanding people and they were relatively fortunate to have received this either from parish clergy or from groups associated with local churches.

There seems little doubt that the major transformations which are currently taking place in the global economy are drastically affecting the lives of millions of people. Among the greatest problems which people have to cope with as a result of these changes are those which result from unemployment or redundancy. The very word 'redundant' as a description of the social reality of millions of people today is chilling in its social consequences and for the self-respect and identity of those concerned. James Foster, who had lost his job in mid-career, graphically described his near-disbelief that such a monstrous misfortune could befall anyone. He indicated how he and his wife daily reappraised their decisions and prayed 'whatever our age, bring us a real life, where we can all share the work, the leisure, the responsibility and the job' (1988: 55). From these data it seems that one function of suffering and deprivation is to heighten the awareness of a communal dimension to life and the interdependence of people.

Our third area of enquiry concerned the way in which Catholics reconciled moral dilemmas at work or in the determination of priorities in the allocation of time and energies, for example between family, work and parish. Whilst there was some indication of the dilemmas routinely faced by lay people in their everyday lives, in the main these dilemmas, which lay people must resolve with or without clear guidance from their priests or fellow believers in the Catholic community, remain latent and largely hidden and unarticulated on the taken-for-granted grounds that 'this is the way things are'.

The 'techniques of neutralisation' used by a single parent to justify the non-disclosure of additional earnings on the grounds of survival needs have been noted previously. Apart from this, three other examples of work-based dilemmas can be cited. It seems likely that James Foster (1988) was made redundant after a conflict between an older ethic of professional responsibility to take note of the 'public interest', and the commercial ethic of his new masters. Secondly, McEvoy refers briefly to the fact that there were plenty of moral dilemmas at work 'apart from the main one of apportioning time between wife, children and employer'. These were generally resolved 'by weighing the interests of all the other people in the organisation against the interests of one or a few, and by acting as swiftly and sympathetically as possible' (1987: 259).

Thirdly, Loretto Lynch made some telling remarks about the dilemmas of management in Social Services Departments when social workers threatened industrial action:

Whilst once I might have said social workers should not take industrial action since this directly affects people already suffering hardship or stress, I would now reject such a response as over-simple. There may be times, but rarely in my view, when the fight for better resources for services and for reasonable rewards for stressful work would justify strike action ... [Given her] responsibility to ensure that emergency and essential services are provided ... at times this leads to conflict when management action means strike action is countered. (1988: 269)

She also eloquently described how 'in the climate of increasing violence' and following the murder of a colleague by a client, steps to ensure the security of her staff had resulted in a reduction in the quality of user–professional contacts in a situation of:

institutionalised apprehension and mistrust ... the absolute need to protect staff seems to stifle the expression of welcome and acceptance ... [and make] the value of compassion, linked with [her] Christian belief ... harder to express. (1988: 270)

3.4 Lay experiences of support

Our fourth question was concerned with the sources of support lay Catholics relied upon, or derived assistance from, in the resolution of the moral dilemmas in their lives. We wished to explore the extent to which the Catholic community, and especially the local parish, was helpful in providing a coherent system of values for moral decision-making, and also social support for those in need. In the case of the three single parents it was often quite crucial. In a situation of abandonment and loneliness, the parish-based single parent group and its wider contacts through the Family and Social Action (FSA) network and conferences, were vital, and helped to reduce any sense of stigma or exclusion from the local community. But while parishes can be important sources of social support and mutual aid, this is not the usual experience (Willmott, 1986: 69; Hornsby-Smith, 1989: 80–8).

Carol Burns (1988) derived considerable support from parishioners, and also from both Christian and non-Christian friends in the various groups to which she belonged, following the stillbirth of her baby. Barbara Wood described how she found 'Our Lady a great source of strength' and also 'the great central hall of the sacraments' with its 'many doors' ... which [she] knew [she] had a lifetime to open and discover new enriching delights'. Sharing with friends of like mind had helped her and so had the daily prayer meeting with Anglican and Catholic friends to 'keep our appointment with God ... together in the midst of noise' (1987/8: 298, 301). Ecumenical friendships and worship were found to be both enriching and supportive by the Member of Parliament who complained that he did not 'think the Church does enough in its parishes to give prayerful support to the politicians and to encourage prayer about political events or indeed politicians' whose personal and private lives were subject to considerable strains and stresses (Alton, 1987: 225).

The contribution of traditional Catholic organisations was mentioned by a social worker who valued the opportunities 'to share with others in efforts to make the Church's endeavours relevant and effective' in the Catholic Marriage Advisory Council (CMAC) and the Catholic Social Workers' Guild. These provided:

opportunities for shared discussion of the issues raised in [her] professional life, as well as for the study of developments in theology ... shared work and debate, shared worship in small and large groups, have all contributed to [her] development both personally and spiritually. (Lynch, 1988: 271)

The general view among the contributors to the *Everyday Lives* series was that Catholic parishes, groups or associations were not salient for many Catholics but that ecumenical groups were increasing in importance for some. This led us to the fifth question in this exploratory enquiry, lay people's experiences of the Church as an institution. As we have noted, on occasion Catholic institutions did provide support and friendship for the lonely, bereaved or deserted. A family man stressed that the tolerance of noisy children at least at one Sunday Mass was essential. He valued the loyalty and faithfulness of other members of the Church and the traditional symbols of hope to be found in homes in depressed areas of Birkenhead (Warren, 1988). Carol Burns (1988: 87) described how 'it is important to go to Mass on a Sunday ... because it is the community celebration' and because however lacking in inspiration she found it, she thought it important for her children to learn that they were part of a wider community. Unfortunately, money-raising and maintenance issues tended to dominate, and loyalty demanded involvement in parish events.

An unmarried mother reported how unwelcoming a Catholic parish was when she made her first tentative visits while still an Anglican:

I was upset that I was totally ignored ... I've always been a friendly sort of person and I was going for eye contacts, thinking they will say 'hello', but they didn't ... I thought all Catholics had this burning hunger for God and, as they must be experts at it a long time, I couldn't understand why they looked so miserable and were so cold. I felt rejected and put it down to the fact that they didn't like outsiders coming in ... It seemed pointless hanging around at the back in the hope of a 'hello' or a smile ... so I remained in the church till everyone had gone and tried to look as inconspicuous as possible.

In the end she did manage to make a friend 'and for the first time I had a right good grassroots conversation about God'.

The failure of parishes generally to provide support for married people and family life was implied by Barbara Wood:

If healthy Christian family life is to survive and act as a leaven in the community, the parish must take seriously the strains of modern married life and offer greater understanding and support ... Many of us need to be taught to pray together and encouraged to spend time together alone. It is so easy to pass on the stairs on the way to and from meetings. Dedication to Church and community work can put a strain on family and married life. (1987/8: 300–1)

There is evidence here of the problem of the parish as a 'greedy institution' (Coser, 1974; Hornsby-Smith, 1989: 89–92), consuming the discretionary time and energies of active Catholics rather than supporting and facilitating them in their everyday lives. At the same time she asked 'how many families watch with sadness as their teenage children leave the Church because there is nothing to hold them?' As a possible explanation she observed that 'many teenagers have neither felt welcome when small nor find a place during the time when they most need its guidance and support'.

Several of our sample reported that their formative experiences had been outside parish structures. For example, a teacher claimed that 'all too often the parish is too inflexible and too large so that one does not relate to the next person in the pew; and should we be in the pews anyway these days?' (Ireson, 1988: 24). He also strongly objected that his committed Anglican wife 'is made to feel left out' and was not officially permitted to receive Holy Communion. Significant religious experiences for him were likely to be found with the Quakers or the Iona Community. Similarly, a redundant highway engineer reported the positive effects which Marriage Encounter, a structured faith-based marriage-enrichment experience, had had on the lives of his wife and himself: 'the Church had never given me a gift like this before' (Foster, 1988: 55).

The retired executive recorded his increasing concern with 'the entrenched positions and vested interests' of the Church bureaucracy:

One cosy title 'Holy Mother Church' masks this very tough-minded machine, entirely staffed by single-minded men in which women are rarely involved and never given responsibility. There may be built-in checks and balances but secrecy obscures the way they work and when secrecy is broken, the revelations are not reassuring. (McEvoy, 1987: 261)

He continued to voice a number of criticisms felt by many active Catholics who are concerned with the poverty of much contemporary parish life. These clearly indicated that clergy–lay relations, especially at the parish level, may not be as unproblematic as the moderately favourable evaluations of priests in the 1978 national survey of English Catholics might have suggested (Hornsby-Smith and Lee, 1979: 709–2, 108). The data also demonstrated the general finding that compliance with authority figures does not necessarily imply normative consensus (Fox, 1985: 112):

Over the years I have felt a growing alienation from the ordained ministers of the Church. The point has been reached where I find more common cause and shared experience with lay Christians of other faiths than with my own pastors. They are all nice enough well-meaning chaps and do not spare themselves in the service of parish activities. Yet there is a great lack of understanding and few shared concerns between clergy and laity. So they are difficult to talk to or relate to the preoccupations and anxieties [of lay people] ... the disciplines, humiliations and rewards of employment, and the joys and difficulties of family life, do not appear to register with many priests. There have been too many sermons telling me my life is one of self-indulgence, too many examples of priests who can't get up in the morning or keep appointments, too many occasions when I looked for a willing ear and Father looked at his watch ... The sense of separation I have described saddens me but I accept it is unlikely to alter unless some day we have married clergy, worker-priests and even more women priests who do not live as a race apart from the rest of us. (McEvoy, 1987: 261)

In sum, there is evidence from the contributors to the *Everyday Lives* series, that while some had received valuable support and friendship in times of bereavement or loneliness from fellow parishioners, frequently the parish was not very salient for lay Catholics. Some of their experiences had been unsatisfactory and, increasingly, religiously supportive groups were ecumenical. For active Catholics one problem was the opposite one of too 'greedy' demands on their time and energies. This was consistent with a criticism that there was a lack of awareness of the everyday tensions and problems of lay people's lives on the part of many clergy.

3.5 Lay spirituality

In the final area we aimed to explore some aspects of a lay spirituality to meet the everyday realities of life in our form of industrial society as it struggles to make its way in the late twentieth century. Our data showed that, far from simply passively receiving an official spirituality, lay people were in the process of actively *creating* their own lay spirituality appropriate for the 1980s and 1990s. This was deeply scriptural but also resonated clearly with the everyday routines of contemporary lay lives. It was distinct, not only from that of the monastic life, but also in many respects from that of the traditional parish, with its residual ultramontane tendencies, and as it has evolved since the period of rapid growth in the English Catholic community as a result of massive Irish immigration.

It seems that there has been a sudden flowering of different prayer styles following the ending of the defensiveness of the fortress model of the Church and the gradual easing of ecumenical contacts and the sharing of experiences since the end of the Second Vatican Council. Thus David Alton (1987), who tried to read something from the New Testament each day before going to bed, and who was actively involved in the organisation of prayer breakfasts at Liberal Party Conferences and at Westminster, described how a friendship with an Anglican vicar led to a deepening prayer life. The emergence of shared prayer forms in supportive fellowship groups, frequently ecumenical, was mentioned by several people in our sample.

Many regarded themselves as failures in developing private forms of prayer, Lenski's 'devotionalism' (1963: 25–6), yet a rich diversity of forms of prayer were reported. Apart from the traditional obligatory Catholic pattern of 'morning and night prayers', what seems to be emerging is a variety of forms of prayer to fit the particular rhythms and stresses of the daily lives of each individual and to suit their individual temperaments. Thus for David Alton 'the best time to pray is at the beginning of the day but because invariably I'm in such a panic to get somewhere on time, I don't always get the chance to do that. So usually it's at night' (1987: 228).

A similar remark was also made by Barbara Wood, a busy mother and author, who observed that in her ecumenical prayer group, 'there is a special kind of togetherness and a deep level of sharing which our parish Mass lacks' (1987/8: 301). Similarly, one of the single mothers observed: 'I find the readings hard to understand sometimes; they don't seem to make a lot of sense to me. I must admit I find the Mass quite dreary and boring and too long for a small child' (Kelly et al, 1988: 168). On the other hand the redundant man and his wife felt 'almost ineffective without attentive communication with God in a frequent mid-week Mass' (Foster, 1988: 56).

A recurring problem for busy and often exhausted lay people, was that of finding space and time to pray. Thus a busy housewife with numerous commitments in the justice and peace movement and in the local community, confessed sadly: 'I don't really have a set time for prayer. I'm absolutely hopeless about praying. I always say: last thing at night, that will be my time, but I usually fall asleep or something. I never get into a routine so it's something haphazard' (Burns, 1988: 87). A similar observation was made by one of the single mothers. Barbara Wood admitted that 'prayer has often been a central and recurring struggle for me' and described various attempts to hide away quietly only to be obstructed by children. This made her conclude that 'if marriage was really a sacrament and children were a sign of this, then there must be a way of praying with children rather than despite them' (1987/8: 301).

Two people in the sample made interesting observations about confession. The retired executive reported that he had not been to confession for years but articulated a rich theology of marriage which drew deeply on the experiences of everyday lay lives:

In the past, I went regularly, out of pious habit. But it was always such a non-event that the habit faded. In practice married life provides regular experience of confession, contrition, forgiveness and satisfaction so I feel no sense that I am missing these necessary disciplines. (McEvoy, 1987: 260)

One of the unmarried mothers also articulated fears about confession which might well be shared by many Catholics.

I don't like going to confession and haven't been for ages ... My mother always used to make us go to confession every week or fortnight and I always felt I was pushed into something I didn't really understand. Perhaps I am going through a period of trying to understand what it's all about and questioning things I never questioned before ... It's just a problem of trying to understand why it is necessary to go to confession. When I did go in a neighbouring parish once, the priest told me I ought to be ashamed of myself and go at least every six months instead of listening to what I had to say. It's very difficult when you are searching for a reason why you want to go to confession to be suddenly put down by a priest himself. It leads to big question marks, at least it does for me. I don't know if I believe in hell either. Until I came here I used to think of hell as a place where you went if you did something wrong and if you didn't go to confession or you missed Mass on a Sunday and you died, you were gone, you had no chance of getting to purgatory or heaven. They are so brainwashed in Ireland; the priests have them believing what they want them to believe and don't give them the right to question their religion which they do here. (Kelly et al, 1988: 168)

A number of important matters have been raised in this extract. First of all, there is the rejection of an unthinking religious socialisation and the insistence on the right to enquire, question and understand religious beliefs or the disciplines of the institutional Church. Secondly, there is the rejection of authoritarian styles of religious leadership by priests. Traditional forms of religious authority are firmly rejected as inadequate in the contemporary world. Thirdly, there is the 'loss of the sense of hell', so well described by David Lodge in his novel *How Far Can You Go?* (1980). Fourthly, there are, in this unmarried mother's account, strong elements of 'customary religion' (Hornsby-Smith, Lee and Reilly, 1985), with identifiable elements of an earlier Catholic upbringing learned in the socialising institutions of family, school and parish. This is evident in her recall of the traditional penalties for missing Sunday Mass in terms of eternal damnation. Fifthly, nevertheless an enduring religious faith is apparent in her response to difficulties, such as saying *Hail Marys* when she is at the end of her tether. It is also evident in her ultimate trust in God throughout life which is seen as an endurance test:

I think God exists alright. Somebody's up there looking after me. I don't know who He is but He's there when I've been stuck for a decision. And I think that in some strange way He is going to put you through an endurance test ... and it's up to you to come through it in whatever way you can. But irrespective of what you think of Him, He's always there.

A busy social worker admitted that her prayer life was far from organised but described how she made space for it in a busy working day:

My only rule is never to switch on the car radio for my daily journey to work and to snatch amid the morning rush hour at least a few minutes to put myself in the presence of God and to think of the coming day in the light of His plan for me. In my more formal private prayer I find the psalms a rich source of inspiration, with something for every mood, and the Gelineau settings on cassette accompany me on long car journeys. I have also come to appreciate the daily prayer of the Church, and saying alone or with friends the evening and night prayer gives me a sense of being connected to the rhythm of the whole praying Church ... The celebration of the Eucharist is a significant part of the shared experience ... in groups [and] with other Christians I have gained from their contribution in shared prayer. (Lynch, 1988: 272)

Another social worker for whom the psalms were a major source of inspiration, suggested that:

the longing for God can be categorised as the search for truth, justice, peace and love ... We look for [God] in our companions, in the world about us and the opportunities and benefits we receive, in our experiences, in our hearts ... I am caught up in a dynamic process of evaluating, discarding, integrating scientific, psychological, sociological, political, artistic, theological and moral facts, theories, hunches and experiences. There is a constant testing process between idea and reality, theory and praxis. I must strive to become aware of my bias, prejudice, ignorance, weakness and sin which modify my understanding and cloud my judgement ... I must continue the struggle to make sense of all these perspectives. I find, increasingly, as I read and pray that scriptures come to my aid. (Carroll, 1988: 307)

Several of our sample referred to the search for justice in their everyday lives and how that might be expressed in chosen life styles. There was a criticism of the traditional narrow Catholic view of evangelisation 'identifying it with proselytisation, persuading people to accept a certain set of dogmas, making people members of the Church ... [but] a genuine failure among clergy and laity to accept that work for justice and liberation is integral to our faith'. Referring to the Epistle of St James that if faith is not accompanied by good works it is quite dead (Jas. 2: 15–16), Veronica Carroll added:

We are all created in God's image. We are stewards of the universe's resources ... If we fail to share the earth's riches, many millions will reflect only the image of God suffering, crucified. We are impelled to use our time, skills, resources to fight the major evils of our times or we will not 'image' God. Political campaigning, lobbying, letter-writing, marching, fund-raising, fasting, praying, vigils, reading, disseminating information, whatever it takes, we should act. (1988: 308–309)

The importance of the ecumenical dimensions to the development of new forms of lay spirituality has been mentioned previously. After describing how he increasingly guarded his Sunday as a special day and attended Mass in the morning, David Alton commented:

in the evening I attend the Anglican church [where a strong friendship with the vicar had developed over the past decade]. On the first Sunday of each month there's a Eucharist service. It's ten years or more since I first took the Eucharist at that church. It would have been very offensive not to and, indeed, it is very meaningful to me in many ways ... I feel that post-Vatican II the Church has left a lot of its members high. It has failed to maintain the momentum of the ecumenical movement and, as we have met good Christians from other Churches, how can we reasonably be expected to remain at a distance? To encumber us with arcane rules that actually puts limits on how far we can go in reconciliation, seems ludicrous. Ultimately we are all answerable to our Maker. We must search our consciences. Initially I was uneasy about the shared Eucharist but I reflected carefully on the Anglican invitation that any Christian who wished to take part would be welcome. I wish my own Church would say the same. I felt it would have been disingenuous not to take part. It would be like going to dinner and refusing your host's food as unsuitable for your delicate palate. (Alton, 1987: 228)

What is being described here seems to reflect the notion of lower participants being 'warmed up' to ecumenical enthusiasm at the level of ideology while being 'cooled down' when they wished enthusiastically to translate this into praxis (Goffman, 1952; Clark, 1960; Hopper, 1971).

There is clearly a considerable amount of intercommunion taking place quietly and unofficially. Fifteen years ago a member of the bishops' Ecumenical Commission observed that deviance in terms of the Church's rules was necessary if those rules were ever to be changed, and that changed rules followed changed practices rather than the other way round. A teacher married to a committed Anglican was married in her church with a Catholic priest sharing the service with the Anglican vicar. Now he and his family attended a variety of churches including a Quaker service, where he valued the silence, and the Iona community in Scotland, as well as the Lay Fraternity of Charles de Foucauld. It is with some irritation that he observed that at Mass 'the greatest frustration comes when my wife is not able to share in communion' (Ireson, 1988: 25). Like David Alton he felt rather let down that the promise of the Second Vatican Council had not been fulfilled. 'There is a point', he observed, 'where natural caution becomes inertia. Will somebody please pull up the anchor and let's put to sea?' (1988: 27).

3.6 Concluding reflections

The exploratory study reported in this chapter was undertaken in anticipation of the 1987 Synod of Bishops on 'the Vocation and Mission of the Laity in the Church and in the World'. It aimed first of all to explore the ways in which Catholics made any sort of religious sense of their everyday domestic and work routines, and secondly, to test 'taken-for-granted' assumptions about the compliance of lay people, with particular reference to their experiences of parish life and clergy–lay relationships.

The twelve contributors to the *Everyday Lives* series, published in *Priests and People* between October 1987 and October 1988, comprised an opportunity sample of relatively committed and articulate Catholics who agreed to collaborate. There is no claim that the sample was a representative cross-section of all self-identifying English Roman Catholics. All the same, it covered a wide range of experiences, from those of relatively powerful decision-makers to the relatively powerless. They were roughly equally divided between men and women and those living in the north and the south of England. They included both married and single lay people, housewives as well as employed women, and all age groups from the twenties to the sixties.

The study has thrown some light on the six areas selected for exploratory investigation. It has provided evidence for a measure of alienation from existing institutional arrangements in the Church, even on the part of strongly committed Catholics, and a search for more satisfactory forms of communal support, frequently in informal ecumenical groupings, and a much wider variety of forms of prayer and devotionalism than had previously been suspected.

For the Catholics in our sample there was no clear sense of a lay vocation. The fact that few of them admitted to having chosen a vocation in part may reflect the changing social and economic context. In a world experiencing global economic transformations and increasing employment insecurities, there are clearly limits to occupational choice. Rather, our sample focused on processes of discernment of God's will as on-going and unpredictable, a life-long process of 'muddling through'. There appears to be a recognition of this in Pope John-Paul II's interpretation of the labourers in the vineyard who were called at different stages in life (1989: 44–5).

It is in an uncertain world that lay people have to cope with a wide variety of needs, problems, suffering and deprivation. On the whole it seems that they do this substantially on their own. There seems to be a hidden life, not easily articulated, where lay people cope with the moral dilemmas at work or determine priorities in the allocation of their time and energy. A common experience is that some form of social support is sought but that Catholic parishes, groups or associations, on the whole are not very prominent in meeting these needs. This is consistent with the finding from Philip Abrams's study of neighbouring schemes that churches and voluntary organisations were rarely mentioned (Willmott, 1986: 69). In general the testimonies of our sample indicate that in spite of the rhetoric of 'community', the reality is that a great deal of parish life is relatively impoverished. (For a further discussion of this theme, see Hornsby-Smith, 1989: 66–94).

In spite of this, there is evidence of a richly varied devotionalism, ranging from a strong emphasis on the Mass as the communal celebration and thanksgiving, through private participation in the official Office of the Church, an emphasis on scripture reading or shared prayer, especially ecumenically, to a variety of forms of 'customary religion', such as morning and night prayers and a hasty 'Hail Mary' in times of stress. The emergence of a genuine lay spirituality is apparent, for example, in the quiet meditation in the car while travelling to work, in the search for methods of prayer which did not exclude young children, and in the emphasis on the opportunities for reconciliation in the marriage relationship.

With some simplifications, it might be suggested that as recently as the Second World Congress of the Lay Apostolate, Pope Pius XII (1957) regarded the lay apostolate in terms of the participation by a sponsored few lay people in the work of the Church under the direct authority and direction of the bishops. Two decades later, fears were expressed that this handmaiden model was being replaced by a new clericalised model of the laity as a result of the Vatican Council reforms (Barta, 1980). On the basis of this present study, it might be suggested that a third model of the active laity is emerging which stresses the common baptismal calling to transform the world in accordance with the imperatives of social justice. This model emphasises the complementarity of ministries of service and has obvious

implications for the appropriateness of priestly styles and the importance of lay 'formation' within the Christian community for their
everyday lay tasks.

Finally, there is evidence in this study of some deviation from the
official norms of the Church which supports the view that there has
been a transformation in the nature of religious authority in the
Roman Catholic Church in recent years (Houtart, 1969; Koopmanschap, 1978; Mansfield and Hornsby-Smith, 1982). These issues
form the subject of chapters 6 to 9 of this book. We will first explore in
greater detail the religious beliefs of active laity in the following
chapter while the 'customary' religion of nominal Catholics will be
the main concern of chapter 5.

4

THE RELIGION OF CORE LAITY

4.1 Introduction

One of the original purposes of our research was to explore the extent to which there had been a change in the way English Catholics understood the nature of the Church, its relationship to the wider society, and their own roles within the Church, as a result of the reforms promulgated by the Second Vatican Council. In our first interviewing programme in 1974 we regarded the lay members of the bishops' national advisory commissions as core Catholics, sponsored by their bishops or by national organisations or diocesan Churches, and structurally in a position to influence the decision-making processes of the bishops in their determination of pastoral policies and strategies. In our interviews with them, therefore, Penny Mansfield and I anticipated that these matters would be salient for them and that we would be able to discern any signs that there had been a significant shift in the nature of the Church in England in terms of lay participation, lay–clergy relations and new styles of exercising religious authority.

Our interviews with these lay members of the bishops' commissions were conducted as free-flowing conversations focused around four main areas. These included the respondent's interpretation of the current situation in the Church (i.e. in the mid-1970s, nearly a decade after the end of the Second Vatican Council), and in particular their reflections on the teaching of the Church, their images of God and their corresponding views about the nature of religious authority in the Church, areas of tension or conflict in the Church and their experiences of change in the Church at the local level. We also explored the nature of the respondent's Catholicism: their personal religious practices and their reflections on changes in the Church, their reactions to liturgical change, their views on the obligations of religious practice, the clergy, the role of lay people in the Church, questions of faith and morals, the needs of the Church for the future and the role of the Catholic in society. The relevant parts of our interview guide have been given in Appendix 1.

The interviews were generally tape-recorded and subsequently transcribed. Thirteen categories of data were distinguished at the preliminary coding stage. For the purposes of reporting in this book these have been collapsed into two broad areas. In this chapter we will review the responses of these core lay people to questions about their religious and moral beliefs and their images of God. In chapter 7 we will address those parts of the data which bear on our respondents' interpretations of and comments on the nature of religious authority in the Church.

Our analysis is based mainly upon the transcripts of 58 core members of the institutional Church. Of these, 21 were women, 37 married and 2 widowed, 6 were under the age of thirty, 7 were in their sixties, and 13 were converts to Roman Catholicism. In this chapter we will be concerned to outline the views of these core Catholics on the teaching of the Church, in general, and in the areas of social and personal morality, in particular. We wish to identify the extent to which heterodoxy of belief can be detected even among core Catholics. We also wish to explore the ways in which core Catholics might be differentiating between creedal beliefs, which are unquestioned, and issues of social and personal morality, where contestation with the official teaching or rules of the Church might increasingly be regarded as legitimate.

4.2 The teaching of the Church

In this section, we will briefly summarise our findings relating to the personal religiosity of these core Catholics in terms of their responses to questions about the teaching of the Church. Our starting point was the three questions about the teaching of the Church which had been used in a study of Catholicism in Liverpool by Kokosalakis (1971: 27). It will be noted that the context of our investigation was the supposed emergence by Catholic laity from a defensive, fortress model of the Church. In this pre-Vatican Church authority had been exercised bureaucratically from the top down by clerical officials and the official teaching of the Church had been imparted by them using an unashamedly didactic form of pedagogy.

Three distinct stances towards the teaching of the Church could be identified. The first group of respondents adopted a position of substantial *acceptance* of the teachings of the Church. Generally there were no serious doubts or problems about the dogmatic or creedal beliefs of the Church. This is consistent with the findings from the 1978 national survey that there were high levels of creedal beliefs along with considerable divergence on moral issues (Hornsby-Smith and Lee, 1979: 52–4). A stance of acceptance was sometimes attributed to processes of religious socialisation or identity formation:

I am a product of my generation in that I will accept the authority of the Church ... in everything. (c24; Female, 40s)

One has been trained to accept. (c46; Female, 50s)

A few admitted some limited and not very salient doubts, reservations or grumbles:

I don't have any great difficulties, quite honestly. Obviously I react to the sort of ... nit-picking directives. (c33; Male, 50s)

Others coped with uncertainty by means of a strategy of avoidance:

I am sure that if I care to make a great personal, intellectual attack at it ... I might find great difficulty ... and I avoid the attack ... I put a mental block ... that [it] is there and the Church says it ... and I am always pretending that it doesn't. (c27; Male, 50s)

I must admit that when I find things unacceptable I tend to keep away from them ... not to give them much thought because it is more comfortable not to. (c37; Female, 30s)

A second group of respondents remarked on the need for a *modification* in the contemporary formulations of the basic truths or admitted that interpretations of some teachings inevitably changed over time.

It is not so much a question of non-acceptance, more of interpretation ... in other words, I think things out for myself. (c36; Female, 20s)

One respondent suggested that the reason:

why so many people have had so much difficulty over recent changes [was]
because the distinction between the 'essential' and the 'inessential' was never
really made ... [so that] as soon as a few of the inessentials were changed, the
whole thing seemed to collapse. (c57; Male, 30s)

A third group, comprising around one-fifth of the core members,
was characterised by *criticism* of the current emphases in Church
teaching. They tended to refer to specific teachings which they
regarded as in need of modification or more flexible interpretation, on
the one hand, or to appeal to a more pristine form of Christianity,
untainted by the snares of the world and unfettered by the accretions
of centuries, on the other. Some urged a teaching more closely related
to the realities of everyday lives. Several were critical of the
institutional Church for allegedly constraining the growth of freedom
of individuals or:

going beyond its brief ... [which] is to give people a rule of life and to accept
that they are human beings with free wills. (c63; Male, 30s)

I'd like to see a Church which allowed for the growth of individuals [long
pause] I think sometimes some of the pronouncements of the Church really
are ... very limiting ... [and] seen as rather negative. (c23; Female, 30s)

Thus there were criticisms of undue rigidity in the Church's teaching
from core Catholics who admitted that they found no difficulty in
accepting the basic teaching of the Church. One woman instanced in
particular the area of family teaching, regarding *Humanae Vitae* (Paul
VI, 1968) as 'a bit of a disaster', but more especially the too-ready
acceptance of war and violence. The thinking of many was summed
up by one respondent who said:

I don't think I would find difficult anything that I would regard as the
teaching of the Church, but I would find it very difficult to accept some of the
teaching which is given from the pulpit in some churches, for example, some
mariology put over in rather extreme form, or purgatory in rather extreme
form ... I certainly agree with the ideas of (a) hierarchy of truths, and so on,
and I certainly believe that one's understanding of truths can develop so
greatly that, to the outsider, it quite legitimately seems like change. But I
would prefer to see it as development, things like 'transubstantiation'. I'm
quite happy to drop the term and keep the reality, but this particular way of
putting it doesn't seem to be very helpful nowadays. I'm quite happy that it
should be relegated to a footnote in the statement on the Eucharist. But then

I wouldn't regard this as a teaching in the Church. This, I think, is concerned with the 'real presence' rather than any philosophical explanation about it. But it depends there what you mean about the teaching of the Church. I think I am maybe talking about the faith of the Church rather than teaching. Yes, obviously teaching can change and the way in which the faith is presented – this can change, yes, and it could change so much that it looks as if the faith itself has changed. But I don't believe it has fundamentally. (C7; Female, 40s)

In these spontaneous reflections in response to a question about difficulties with the teaching of the Church, this respondent has raised a number of quite distinct, though related, issues. First of all, there is the implicit belief in the fundamental and unchanging truths of the Catholic faith. Secondly, however, there is a hierarchy of truths with differential claims for allegiance. Thirdly, the question of the tenets of belief is distinct from that of its presentation by the official teachers. Fourthly, for these reasons there is considerable scope for the private interpretation of these teachings. Fifthly, the formulations of these teachings are historically contexted and may, therefore, legitimately change and develop according to an evolving understanding of the teachings of the Church. Thus another respondent noted that the problem of formulating the teaching of the Church:

is to go on teaching the same doctrine in words which make sense in the current world ... I suppose we are getting to a culture-free expression of doctrine as far as we can. (C8; Male, 30s)

Finally, there were a number of other issues raised by individual members of the commissions, about which they expressed some reservations. These included over-concrete distinctions between venial and mortal sin; confession; indulgences; homosexuality; the new catechetics; prohibitions about inter-communion in inter-faith marriages; and the role of the laity in sharing the teaching of the Church. From this brief review two conclusions can be drawn. Firstly, while among core Catholics there was a very general adherence to the creedal teachings of the Church, these were by no means interpreted and accepted in a uniform manner. There was general acceptance of the need for doctrinal formulations to evolve over time. Secondly, that there was a hierarchy of truths with differential claims to adherence, was an implicit belief of core Catholics. The further from creedal elements of belief one travelled, the less constrained these core Catholics were in making-up their own minds as to their validity and meaningfulness.

4.3 Images of God

Following our probing of the respondents' interpretation of the teaching of the Church, we explored their views of the causes of tensions or conflicts within the Church. First of all we asked them about their images of God; their responses to these questions will be reported in this section. Secondly, since we hypothesised that there would be a relationship between their images of God and their models of the Church and views about religious authority, we asked them for their views on the nature of authority in the Church. Their responses will be considered in chapter 7. Our study of core members' images of God was inspired by the questions suggested by Houtart (1969: 321; see Question 5, Appendix I of this present book). In particular we invited members to select between a transcendent and an immanent image of God.

We only have data from about one-third of our sample but it is of interest that none of the commission members who answered this question directly selected the transcendent option, though one did say 'that God, through revelation, has shown us the way to live' (c59; Male, 50s). God, the lawgiver, corresponds closely to this image. Five members, however, selected the second, immanent, image of God, though some with qualifications. One, for example, stresses the importance of prophecy which gave man 'certain ideas and concepts which he must fulfil in history ... Man is continually looking for ways to implement the word of God. God isn't dictating exactly how this should be done' (c58; Male, 20s). Another felt the choice was really too academic for most people, adding: 'My immediate reaction is the ... [immanent] alternative but I say that as an unlearned, an uncultured chap ... The average member of the Church is not faced with answering that sort of question' (c61; Male, 60s). A third member suggested that the two alternatives were not exclusive: 'I wouldn't like to take one ... against the other, but I think I would tend to emphasise God acting in history. But I wouldn't want to make these exclusive of one another' (c7; Female, 40s). Similar remarks were made by several members. Some were uneasy at being invited to make a choice while others argued that both images had relevance:

both are true (c8; Male, 30s)

To me they converge (c14; Female, 50s)

It seems to me that the vertical and horizontal views are not really mutually exclusive ... They reflect the Old and the New Testament teaching (c62; Male, 60s)

It's a mixture of both (c68; Female, 40s)

I'm a horrid consensus person ... I don't really like having these questions polarised ... There are moments when I think I want a transcendent God ... when I get too depressed about my fellow humans ... What I do subscribe to, I think, is that God's way of acting in the world is almost certainly purely through people ... I'm afraid I want to have my cake and eat it. But I don't want a transcendent God in the sense of an all-powerful character out here moving people around like things on a chess-board, because I can't see this at all. I can only see [the] actual operation of God within people and within the universe as a whole. (c70; Female, 50s)

Three women stressed the role of the Father in their response:

the loving father relationship ... rather than the Jehovah thing (c19; Female, 60s)

My image of God is of an ever-loving father. I see Him in all of the people around me and all the good I have and the love I have for my husband and my children. (c24; Female, 40s)

I am much more aware of God the Father through the Holy Spirit. (c10; Female, 30s)

Only one member answered in terms of Christ:

I tend to think of Christ far more than of God ... It seems to me that the significance of Christ was to bring God into some sort of meaningful relationship with man ... and to bring God down to earth ... God one approaches through Christ. (c57; Male, 30s)

Another man noted that his image of God had changed over the years and now focused increasingly on the Holy Spirit:

As a child ... one thought of the all powerful God ... Now ... it's more the Holy Spirit acting through mankind that one sees ... one sees God acting through people more ... for change. (c67; Male, 50s)

Finally, some members drew attention to the implications of an image of God for family or parish relationships and for the taking of personal responsibility for our actions. One member was critical of 'a type of paternalism which does not encourage taking responsibility for one's own actions' (c36; Female, 20s). Similarly, a convert stressed the implications for the way the parish priest interpreted his role and suggested that the transcendent image was the one 'we're trying to get rid of ... at the parish level' (c13; Male, 40s).

In sum, while these core Catholics generally resisted the making of a choice between the two alternative images of God, on the whole they felt more comfortable with the immanent image. Furthermore they sensed that this had implications not only for the way they took responsibility in their personal lives but also for the nature of social relationships which should hold in the Church, for example between priests and lay people at the parish level.

4.4 Beliefs and practices

In the course of our interviews about one-quarter of our respondents volunteered information about their religious beliefs and a similar proportion added comments about religious practices. The national survey of English Catholics (Hornsby-Smith and Lee, 1979; Hornsby-Smith, 1987) showed that institutionally involved Catholics generally experienced no difficulties with the doctrinal teachings of the Church. However, several members of the bishops' commissions admitted that they did not entirely understand the theology of the Eucharist and one added 'but perhaps they (Catholics generally) never did' (c20; Male, 60s).

Several commission members reflected interestingly on the nature of their Catholic identity. The crucial issue for these respondents seemed to be whether they were a 'cradle Catholic' or a convert:

Converts have *found* (Catholicism); we've always *had* it. (c24; Female, 40s)

Being a Catholic is not the prime thing in my life ... I am what I am and a Catholic as well ... I couldn't leave the Catholic Church just as I couldn't leave my family. (c54; Male, 60s)

I have over the years suffered many crises of faith ... more than my Catholic friends, and I think that is due to the fact that, as a convert, I am a different sort of Catholic ... You see, when I have doubts, then the very essence of my faith is in the balance, whereas for a 'cradle Catholic', being a Catholic is so much more ... part of their identity. (c4; Female, 40s)

Another member described his traditional upbringing, full of fear and superstition. This conditioning remained with him and he continued to go to Mass out of habit, the early one in order to 'get it out of the way' (c35; male, 50s). There is support in these quotations for the distinctions being made by Hammond (1988) between those with a largely ascribed and inherited identity, with a 'collective–expressive' view of the Church, the result of long processes of religious socialisation, and those with a religious commitment which had been voluntarily chosen.

These core Catholics reported a wide range of religious practices and attitudes towards them which varied from the very traditional to the sometimes deviant. An example of the former was a middle-aged man who noted that simple devotions, such as prayer for a happy death, had been passed on for four generations. He noted, however, that some of the traditional devotions were experiencing trans-formations of meaning:

I still pray for the conversion of England every day, but I don't know what it means any more. In other words I know it no longer necessarily means everyone lines up inside our Church ... but it does mean a society where people do follow out the teachings of Christ, where they do love one another ... but [where] I can no longer conceive the thing in terms of attendance at a particular church. (c29; Male, 40s)

An example of deviance was the irregular Mass attendance by one member only:

because we think that it is good for our children to at least know that the Church exists and ... when they are older they can make a decision themselves ... And then, we have up here on a Sunday evening a sort of *agape* with our own friends ... That's more important to us. [c50; Male, 30s)

Various forms of mild rebellion against the discipline or practice of the Church were indicated in the comments of several members. Thus one reported:

I walk out of more Masses in the middle of the sermon than I would like to admit to because I just can't sit there any longer listening to such twaddle. Because it betrays so frequently an absolutely abysmal ignorance [of] what they are talking about. (c70; Female, 50s)

Some of the most interesting discussions of deviation from the Church's rules concerned the matter of intercommunion in a church of another Christian denomination. One member felt obliged to conform to the prohibition in obedience to the Church authorities: 'ultimately, one is pushed back onto the question of obedience, which is a virtue and which is important' (c57; Male, 30s). Other members responded differently. Thus one pointed out that at a time when ecumenical attitudes had been transformed, 'intercommunion is, of course, something which is strongly felt by inter-Church marriages, the need for it as an expression of family unity in Christ.' She then added the important observation about processes of change in traditional practices that 'the practice is bound to come first', that is before any change in the rule (c7; Female, 40s). In other words, she was suggesting a general proposition about institutional change, that cumulative infractions of the rules of bureaucratic organisations were necessary in order to enforce a change in those rules. Another member married to an Anglican said:

We normally go to church every week, but not always to a Catholic church, sometimes to the local [Anglican] parish church ... I would really like to see a much closer coming together of the Churches ... I think it's important to participate in Christian liturgy but I don't see that ... it is essential for me to restrict my worshipping to [the Catholic] liturgy, particularly in view of my own marital situation. (c51; Male, 30s)

Finally, several members noted that, whatever the institutional rules of the Church, the younger generation of Catholics was much less likely to conform simply because there was a traditional rule. Thus one member contrasted the strong community sanctions against missing Mass in his youth with the contemporary urban situation with its greater mobility and anonymity.

A few members referred to the needs of the Church in the post-Vatican period. One urged that there was a 'need for a new theology of the Incarnation; the world is created, and it is *good*'. He called for a much greater adult education programme 'to help people get away from a very simplistic understanding of God and the Church ... nine first Fridays and semi-magical things' (c33; Male, 50s). For a convert, 'our task is to show people what Christ would have done in our circumstances' (c25; Female, 50s). Another member stressed that 'the Holy Spirit speaks to all sorts of people in the Church ... The hierarchy does *not* have all the insights' (c28; Male, 40s).

Several members were critical of the witness of the institutional Church in social matters. A convert was concerned about the 'profoundly anti-Christian' nature of the materialism of capitalism and affirmed that he would not 'defend the indefensible'. He was, however, consoled by the 'great emphasis upon the sanctity of the individual ... in the Church's teachings' (c40; Male, 60s). Another member was critical of the Church's neglect of slum problems on the grounds that they were 'political' rather than 'moral' issues (c17; Male, 20s). A third member wished 'that the Church would face up to the Christian message' (c36; Female, 20s).

This brief review of beliefs and practices has shown that by the mid-1970s even core members of the Roman Catholic Church in England were articulating uncertainties even about some central elements of the official belief system, and were prepared to indicate only a qualified obedience to the official norms of religious practices and institutional rules. For some, deviance was a necessary stage to the achievement of favoured religious transformations, while for others, particularly younger Catholics, there was a much more insistent demand that rules required more appropriate legitimations than had been available hitherto. The implications of these findings for religious authority will be considered further in chapter 7.

4.5   Social morality

In the course of our interviews, about two-thirds of our sample of lay members of the bishops' commissions referred to various aspects of the teaching of the Church on moral issues. In this section we will report some of the views of these core members of the Church, first of all on socio-economic matters. For several members there was a pronounced bias in the Church's teaching towards issues of personal (and especially sexual) morality with a corresponding neglect of its social teaching. This was expressed in a number of ways. Thus a woman complained about the excessive rigidity in the Church's teaching in the area of the family (very often a euphemism for contraception) while being too ready to tolerate war and violence. A man felt that the Church was too 'other-worldly' and 'counter-progressive' in its teaching while a third member expressed his criticisms in the following way:

I think that ever since the scholastic philosophers a lot of teaching has been in terms of doctrine, that is a more absolute working from principles ... and ... a rigid idea of natural law and no real regard for current situations. I feel that teaching shouldn't be like this. The principles should be there but they should be dynamic principles. The Church is prophetic about [contraception and abortion] ... but refuses to be prophetic about social justice. I would like to see a reversal ... without denying the counsel of perfection ... to be more pragmatic, more willing to listen to human problems involved ... [in the cases of contraception and abortion] and re-emphasise the counsels of perfection on social justice. (c58; Male, 20s)

In this comment there appears to be a criticism not only of the content of the Church's teaching (family morality rather than social justice), but also of the pedagogical style. This is most typically expressed in the conflict between those proponents of the official social teaching of the Church, as articulated in a string of major papal encyclicals issued at regular intervals throughout the past century since Pope Leo XIII wrote *Rerum Novarum* in 1891. These encyclicals have been treated as authoritative and inspired (if not infallible) teaching by traditional Catholics who have often used them deductively and didactically. An alternative, inductive approach has used the 'see, judge and act' pedagogy associated with the Young Christian Worker (YCW) movement and their 'progress-ive' disciples. This latter view was expressed by one YCW-trained member:

the Jesuits' concept of social training was alien to us ... They thought it was social instruction, studying the encyclicals, whereas we believe we *make* the encyclicals ... We get at the job of meeting the problem and *then* we go to the teaching authority in the Church and say 'this is the human situation. What can you do about it?' ... it's telling them the human situation to which the Church has to bring some sort of answer. (c11; Male, 50s)

Another member also stressed that 'we all have the responsibility of formulating the social teaching of the Church'. Unlike the situation on the continent, this had been neglected by the Church in this country. On the other hand, there wasn't much point in waving in front of factory workers a booklet containing this! In his view if it 'just involves the thinkers without the people of action, I think it's [just] going to be an academic exercise' (c67; Male, 50s). Finally, another member complained about the 'lop-sided' character of the Church's concerns in this country and that it did not appear to be on the side of the poor in nearly the same way as in Latin America (c72; Female, 40s).

A number of themes can be drawn from these and similar observations. Firstly, there is the claim that within the Catholic subculture there has emerged a long tradition of Catholic social teaching. Secondly, there is the rejection of deductive, *a prioristic* pedagogical methods for an inductive approach based on lay experiences. Thirdly, potentially the development of social teaching must fuse both theoretical analysis and the experiences and praxis of lay people. Fourthly, English Catholics have lagged behind continental Catholics in this. It seems likely that this was a consequence of the ultramontanist propensities of English bishops over the past century which accorded papal encyclicals a privileged status and uncritical attention. As a consequence, the teachings were not grounded in the everyday experiences of people in this country. Nevertheless, fifthly, because of the Church's active involvement, especially in social welfare issues, Catholics potentially have much to offer to the development of public policy on social matters.

4.6 Personal morality

4.6.1 Contraception

The invitation to the members of the bishops' commissions to discuss difficulties with the teaching of the Church drew forth mainly critical comments on the papal teaching on contraception from nearly two-thirds of our respondents. A common view was that the publication of the papal encyclical *Humanae Vitae* (Paul VI, 1968) had been a disaster. For some, the main problem was that of uncertainty about what exactly was the current official teaching on contraception and the evidence of conflicting advice from different priests:

It is very hard for the ordinary Catholic to know what to do when there is so much divergence. (c4; Female, 40s)

I think the differing opinions on the part of the clergy is confusing ... I certainly wouldn't presume to oppose the teaching of the Church ... I suppose I sin and then look for forgiveness. (c22; Male, 40s)

What the Church teaches about contraception, I might say I find difficult, if I knew for certain at the moment that I knew what it was! (c72; Female, 40s)

A number of members observed that they were unconvinced by the teaching in *Humanae Vitae* or felt that it had got out of proportion when compared to other moral teachings:

I think there is too much concentration on birth control and not enough on the evils of the population explosion. (c44; Male, 50s)

Frankly I don't think that ... even very good Catholics have taken it as a rigid rule ... The question is open to personal interpretation, and that is as it should be. (c54; male, 60s)

I stand on Vatican I (the General Council of the Church which defined the doctrine of papal infallibility in 1870), infallible is infallible and everything else is not infallible! But at the same time, I would give a great deal of weight to a statement put out by the Pope. But as for any statement, I would want to look at the reasoning for it. And it was the reasoning put forward by [Pope] Paul in *Humanae Vitae* which decided me that the whole thing was a mistake. (c43; male, 60s)

Others drew attention to what they regarded as inconsistencies in terms of moral teachings on the matter of intention or on the distinction between the 'natural' and 'unnatural':

I was always taught that the essential part of any action is your intention. The use of the 'safe period' in intention is that you do not have a child ... To talk about differences is simply hair-splitting. (c26; Male, 40s)

To put it simply, as I understand it, you may kill a man if he is about to rape your wife, or in self-defence, and the Church doesn't ask whether you killed him with a knife or your bare hands. It doesn't matter because it is the motivation that matters. But when it gets to birth control, it is not concerned that this is a person who is concerned about the health of his wife, is eager to give his children a good home ... The Church has got to be realistic and it has got to understand the basic psychology of people. (c63; Male, 30s)

A second group of criticisms related to the method of presentation of the teaching and the implications of this for lay participation in the Church and styles of religious authority. One member, for example, who personally thought *Humanae Vitae*, apart from one paragraph, was a magnificent document, was staggered that Pope Paul could set up a commission to study a problem and then completely ignore its findings (Kaiser, 1987). He added:

I don't say he should completely have accepted them but I think he should have given a reasoned argument as to why he wasn't going to accept them, and I thought this was a very bad thing from the point of view of consultation within the Church ... [so that] realistic dialogue within the Church hasn't really got off the ground. (c13; Male, 40s)

Similar remarks were made by two Catholic Marriage Advisory Council (CMAC) counsellors:

I've never been very happy with the way *Humanae Vitae* was promulgated. It was a great difficulty for us in CMAC, and the method by which this was done was very bad as [a] public relations exercise. (c19; Female, 60s)

Half the evening was spent with people ... absolutely black in the face with fury that the Pope had made this edict against contraception when all the Family Commission in Rome had advised him that he must accept it in some form or another ... He had asked for their advice and then hadn't taken it. (c21; Female, 50s)

In the light of the contested nature of the teaching on contraception, it is perhaps not surprising that a third group of members thought it likely that there would be changes in that teaching in time, as there had been in the case of usury. Here, as in the case of intercommunion, the expectation was that deviance from the official norms would precede changes in the rules:

I am sure that eventually ... not in my time ... it will come that the use of contraceptives is allowed simply because people will be doing it ... The way we've lived will be the official way ... I think that people of my generation disagree with the Church in their minds but obey in their practice ... over birth control ... but not so the young ... and I'm right behind them. (c26; Male, 40s)

Well, obviously the birth control question I find very, very, very difficult, but I don't think it's irreversible. I think that a lot more research will go on and perhaps in another generation the Church will come up with something on that. Let's put it this way: the truth can't change, but our knowledge of the truth is changing all the time. And whereas the Church was static, she is now on the move. And the basic teachings ... of the gospels and of Christ will never change, but perhaps the understanding of it will change. (c14; Female, 50s)

Comments from other members indicated elements of uncertainty and ambivalence. A convert said that:

when *Humanae Vitae* burst I felt that the Pope must be raving mad, but now, looking back, I'm delighted he chose against the pill ... [because] it would have put collosal pressure on a lot of women who are physically and emotionally turned off by the pill. (c10; Female, 30s)

About one quarter of those members who raised the issue of contraception or the papal encyclical, either saw nothing wrong with the teaching or expressed their willingness to accept it loyally as the formal teaching of the Church, even if they still hoped for changes or were critical of the presentation of the teaching. One member who described how he had been brought up to be loyal to the Church's teaching, explained this loyalty and argued that a new type of loyalty, appropriate to the contemporary situation and based on participative decision-making, was necessary:

[I]f the doctrine on birth control were changed, I'd get mighty upset, having operated the old system under great difficulty ... I'd murmur: 'the bloody Pope' ... I suppose possibly my generation are the last generation that will feel that way ... The teaching that we received, which was ... relevant to the problems of its day and age, plus the experience we had with the Church, produces loyalty ... Somehow or other people have got to do the same process for another generation in a different situation; not produce the same sort of loyalty or the same sort of attitudes, but something as effective ... I think we must introduce a lot more the notion of people participating, people feeling committed to decisions because they are decisions of themselves rather than something which is merely handed down. (c29; Male, 40s)

Shortly before the interviews with lay members of the bishops' commissions were undertaken, David Martin predicted that with the breakdown of the Catholic ghetto and the emergence of a new Catholic middle class, doctrinal tensions could build up to the point of explosion 'whenever a *single* point of doctrine is undermined simply because a hole in the dyke undermines the complete defensive system' (1972: 187; emphasis in original). The publication of the papal encyclical *Humanae Vitae* in 1968 did in fact create something of an explosion. But on the basis of the evidence we have reviewed here, that explosion was not as catastrophic or as destructive or all-embracing as Martin had anticipated. The bulk of these English core Catholics did in fact regard the teaching on contraception as a mistake. But, in regretting that as an issue it had been given such prominence in Catholic moral teaching, they were in effect re-interpreting it as belonging to an area of life where private judgement was appropriate. Many were more upset by the way in which the traditional teaching had been reaffirmed than by the issue itself because it seemed to indicate a frustration of their expectations and hopes for a new-style, participative Church where due attention would be given by the clerical leadership to lay experiences and advice. The explosion, if such it was, appeared also to be muted by the anticipation of eventual change according to a presumed secular rationality because a once static Church was 'on the move'. The wider significance of contraception was clear. New generations of Catholics would have to struggle to find new but authentic bases of loyalty for themselves. They would not feel obliged to accept meekly, as an earlier generation once had, a religious teaching which did not seem to make sense of their deepest everyday experiences. The issue of contraception is important not only because it affects the lives of so many people, but more particularly because it serves as a touchstone for the much more fundamental issue of religious authority in a changing Church. We will return to this aspect in chapter 7.

4.6.2 Divorce

By comparison with contraception, criticisms of the Church's teaching in relation to marriage and divorce were raised by relatively few members of the bishops' commissions. Where comments were offered, they again indicated a willingness on the part of these core Catholics to seek for teachings and pastoral responses which took greater account of changing social conditions. There were also indications that these were areas where individual moral judgement was more appropriate than strict and inflexible rules. These points are illustrated in the following interview extracts.

A CMAC counsellor suggested that 'people no longer think marriages should be patched-up; they should be allowed to break' (c19; Female, 60s). Another member felt that 'the Church has made a pretty fatal mistake in becoming embroiled in the issue of divorce by confusing civil law, moral law, ... [and] Church law' (c68; Female, 40s). The suggestion that the teaching regarding marriage and divorce and, in particular, the pastoral care of the divorced, needed to be adjusted, was expressed firmly by a young, unmarried woman who mused that:

I suppose I have considered what I would do if I fell in love with a divorced man and wanted to marry him ... My immediate thought is that I would pray very hard and then probably do whatever I thought best ... The thing that would worry most would be having to forego the sacraments, so I suppose that I would accept the authority of the Church ... However, I feel that the attitude to divorced people re-marrying must alter because there are cases where marriages just break down ... I don't believe any longer that all marriages last until death. (c37; Female, 30s)

4.6.3 Abortion

While Catholic deviance in the matter of contraception is well known (Hornsby-Smith, 1987: 111–12), variations in their attitudes regarding abortion tend to be much less apparent. There is a tendency in Catholic circles to regard strict orthodoxy (and inflexibility) on abortion as of absolutely fundamental significance, and as being the key indicator of Catholic loyalty. Those with reservations about the teaching, for example in the light of new biological knowledge, tend to keep them to themselves. Among our sample of core Catholics, however, were several who voiced some uncertainty over the issue. Thus one of the youngest members thought she 'could agree with it on an academic level . . . but I'm not sure about it on a practical level' (c30; Female). A young man was angry about the justification of anti-abortion rallies as being concerned with a moral problem while the Church failed to say anything about the activities of multi-national corporations or inner-city slums on the grounds that these were 'political'. He judged that the Church 'has sold out to the capitalist system . . . and the only vista in which it works is the one on personal morality . . . It criticises sex before marriage, prostitutes and illegitimate children, but it couldn't criticise corrupt companies' (c17; Male, 20s). A similar criticism was voiced by an older man who said: 'of course we all have responsibility to the life of the unborn foetus . . . but that is not the only responsibility . . . Our responsibility is to all life . . . and not just to life itself but [also] to the quality of that life' (c26; Male, 40s). Another member who felt 'very strongly that there is an obsession with abortion, contraception, etc., and not always for the best of reasons' observed that:

in this part of the world we have to live and breath the issue and I feel that the attitude underlying the condemnation of abortion is one of retribution . . . you know the sort of thing . . . these girls have had their fun so let them go through a pregnancy and live with the results of their actions . . . Surely the real way to end abortion is to combat the need, which means offering help to unmarried mothers to see them through their pregnancy and afterwards? (c37; Female, 30s)

Other respondents were more guarded in their observations. While accepting many of the principles, they were nevertheless concerned about the rigidities of theological or biological interpretations and explanations, for example about the initiation of human life. Thus one member who said she was probably a die-hard on abortion, added 'I would agree that it may be necessary at times, but as a method of limiting families, allowing promiscuity, no' (c19; Female, 60s). Another member commented that the Church's teaching needed 'a long, cool look' and observed that in the case of abortion:

I think the arguments put forward are open to a good deal of criticism, which doesn't mean that I am in favour of abortion, but I think we've got to find better arguments than some of the ones we use now ... [But there are] people who are still going about saying: 'on x day a soul is breathed in' ... All these things, to me, belong to a bygone age ... I'm not sure where I stand on this because it's very difficult to separate out one's revulsion on ordinary human grounds from a sort of intellectual conviction. (c70; Female, 50s)

Finally a member who expressed the view that the principal concern should be with 'woman's integral good', was concerned about the traumatic, long-term psycho-medical effects of abortion. She felt there was a need for further research, for example on the 'morning-after' pill. In her view it was wrong to say one was killing anything then as it had not even had time to graft onto the wall of the womb in those four or five hours. She objected to those who claimed such contraceptive methods were forms of abortion. Abortion, as a form of contraception, she regarded as a disaster but 'some contraceptive methods, acceptable to both partners, which will foster their unity in marriage, to me is always immensely preferable' (c14; Female, 50s).

4.6.4 Conclusions

Two final points may be drawn from this brief review of the responses of core Catholics to the moral teaching of the Church. Firstly, it was frequently considered to be too easily diverted into less important issues of personal and private morality rather than the more difficult and controversial issues of social injustice. Secondly, there was a fairly general feeling that the Church was too rule-bound and that it left too little scope for legitimate personal decision-making. These points are illustrated in the observation of a member who suggested that the Church ought to put its moral teaching:

over more often and more simply ... [The] only one clear indication that Christ gave of the day of judgement ... 'I was sick and you didn't visit me ... I was without food ... etc' (Matt. 25) and this is *not* 'did you miss Mass on Sunday?' ... You have got to look after your fellow men ... This is the great message of the Church and this is the sort of message that I can accept ... and to trip over the details is wrong. Charity, that is the great thing ... and even St Paul says this; he has to keep his eyes on the main prize and forget the rules. (c27; Male, 50s)

4.7 Concluding reflections

In this chapter we have reviewed selected parts of our interviews in the mid-1970s with a sample of lay members of the bishops' commissions. We have regarded these members as core Catholics, at the centre of the new national structures of lay participation and advice set up as part of the post-Vatican reform programme. By the nature of their selection and sponsorship, these members are likely to have been well known in the Church and regarded as responsible, committed and articulate lay people. Thus in our classification of Catholics and accounts in chapter 2, we noted that the national advisors were generally attached to the core beliefs of the institutional Church, and scored relatively highly in terms of religious knowledge and the extent to which they were able to offer a coherent and explanatory rationale for their religious beliefs and practices. They therefore represent one pole of a continuum of institutional involvement in the Church.

Five main areas have been considered in this chapter. These include the responses of these core Catholics to the teachings of the Church, especially on the issues of social and personal morality, and also the images of God they hold and their general religious beliefs and practices. Extensive use was made of direct quotations from our interview transcripts in order to convey something of the flavour of their meanings which we have attempted to interpret. Six major conclusions seem clearly to be indicated by the data we have reviewed.

First of all, core Catholics adhere strongly to the creedal beliefs of the Church. These beliefs, however, were not interpreted uniformly nor were they regarded as unchanging in their formulations which needed to evolve over time. Secondly, there was a more-or-less explicit awareness that there existed a hierarchy of truths with differential claims to adherence. The evidence is consistent with the view that the further away from creedal beliefs one moved, the more legitimate it was to employ private judgement in 'making up one's mind' regardless of any official teaching. Thirdly, there was evidence of increasingly overt resistance to some aspects of institutional discipline which indicated that lay compliance is problematic and cannot be taken for granted. Such resistance, which related to such matters as the Sunday Mass obligation and the rules prohibiting intercommunion, was particularly overt in the case of younger

Catholics who insisted on the need for more appropriate forms of legitimation for institutional rules. The view was expressed that deviance from official norms was necessary since rules only changed in response to a general change of practice. Fourthly, it was widely felt that the Church was disproportionately concerned with questions of sexual and marital morality and this was contrasted with the poverty of its concern with issues of social injustice. Fifthly, there was evidence of substantial disagreements with the official teaching of the Church especially in the matter of contraception but also, to a lesser extent, over divorce. Particularly striking was the openness, on the part of a significant minority of members, to search for less absolutist responses in the case of abortion, in spite of the fact that some Catholics regard orthodoxy on this issue as being the major indicator of Catholic loyalty and commitment. Core Catholics considered the Church to be too rule-bound and there was a strong move from deductive to inductive forms of moral reasoning. Finally, while they generally resisted making an exclusive choice between a transcendent and an immanent image of God, there was clear evidence that core Catholics were more comfortable with the latter. In general, religion was seen as an everyday, this-worldly concern.

This chapter has reviewed some aspects of the religiosity of core Catholics. In the following chapter we will review the religiosity of ordinary Catholics in order to emphasise some of the variations to be found among English Catholics in the last quarter of the twentieth century.

5

THE CUSTOMARY RELIGION OF
ORDINARY CATHOLICS

5.1 Introduction

In this chapter we will report some aspects of the religious beliefs of
ordinary Catholics on the basis of focused interviews with random
samples of Roman Catholic electors in the mid-1970s. In contrast to
the national advisors whose religiosity was considered in the previous
chapter, ordinary Catholics, especially those whose allegiance was
simply nominal and who could be regarded as 'dormant' parishioners 'who have in practice "given up" Catholicism but have not
joined another religious denomination' (Fichter, 1954: 22), had lower
attachment to orthodox beliefs, a more limited knowledge of their
religion and of any legitimations for recent changes in the Church,
and their Catholicism was less salient for them in their everyday
lives. The accounts which they gave in the interviews were less
coherent and consistent and they were more likely to offer excuses
than justifications or explanations (Scott and Lyman, 1968) for their
religious beliefs and behaviour (Table 2.1).

Our research was carried out in four parishes: an inner-city parish
(PI) and a suburban parish (PS) in Preston, Lancashire – a city in
northwest England where the proportion of Catholics, between
one-quarter and one-third of the population, is as high as in any town
in England (Bossy, 1975; Gay, 1971) – a London inner-city parish
(LI) where about 15 per cent of the population were self-identifying
Catholics, and a commuter parish (LS) some twenty miles outside
London, where only about 8 per cent of the population identified

themselves as Roman Catholics. The first three parishes each covered an area of about one square mile; the London commuter parish, however, covered an area of some fifteen square miles. In each parish randomly selected samples of electors were interviewed about their social mobility experiences, their religious identification, beliefs and practices, using a structured interview schedule (Hornsby-Smith, Lee and Reilly, 1984).

Second-stage interviews were subsequently solicited from all the once baptised or currently self-identifying Roman Catholics identified at the first stage. (An abbreviated version of the interview guide has been given in Appendix II). A total of 183 focused and generally tape-recorded interviews, which ranged in length from half an hour to two hours, were obtained from the randomly selected Catholic electors in these four parishes, with their different social-class compositions, regional locations and historical memories and contexts. It is these Stage II interviews, focused around four main areas, the socialisation and religious career of the respondent, their religious beliefs and values, their attitudes to change in the Church since the Second Vatican Council, and their experiences of religious change in their own parishes, which provided the data reviewed in this chapter.

We will argue that the variety of heterodox beliefs and practices which were revealed in our interviews can best be conceptualised as 'customary' religion, derived from 'official' religion but without being under its continuing control. It is suggested, on the basis of our interview data, that the beliefs and practices that make up customary religion are the product of formal religious socialisation but subject to trivialization, conventionality, apathy, convenience and self-interest.

5.2 Customary religion

It has long been recognised that religious and/or magical beliefs of a confused and fragmentary kind are to be found widely dispersed throughout British society (Abercrombie et al, 1970; Gerard, 1985; Gorer, 1955; Hay, 1982; Martin and Pluck, 1977; Mass Observation, 1947; Rowntree and Lavers, 1951; Thomas, 1973; Thompson, 1968). There have always been grounds, though, for assuming that such a diffused variety of frequently contradictory beliefs might have been rather less prevalent among Roman Catholics in England. In the first place, as a result of massive immigration from Ireland in the nineteenth century (Beck, 1950: chs. 9 and 14; Bossy, 1975: Part III;

Hickey, 1967; Inglis, 1963: ch. 3; Jackson, 1963; Kennedy, 1973; Lees, 1979; McLeod, 1974: 72–80; O'Connor, 1972; Ryan, 1973; Ward, 1965), Roman Catholicism in England had something of the character of a 'ghetto Church', at least until the 1950s. This, together with a clearly defined authority structure, a co-cultural clergy for the most part, and an extensive system of Catholic schools, might well have been expected to have produced a much greater uniformity of belief and practice among Catholics than among other religious groups. Previous research, however, has led us to suspect that, even if this had been true of English Catholicism in the past, it was less likely to be the case today (Hornsby-Smith, 1987: 20–31).

The first national survey of English Catholics in 1978 had provided some quantitative measures of heterodoxy of belief and practice (Hornsby-Smith and Lee, 1979; Hornsby-Smith, Lee and Turcan, 1982; Hornsby-Smith, 1987: 47–66). However, when we explored the religiosity of ordinary Catholics in the focused interviews in the four research parishes, we found that Catholic heterodoxy was far more complex than even the survey findings had indicated. In general, there was no evidence of syncretism or the 'selective borrowing from two or more distinctive religious traditions' (Robertson, 1970: 103–5, 120). The warning by Worsley, to which reference has previously been made, against imputing 'a spurious unity ... on to other people's belief systems' and attempting the 'over-systematization of belief' (1970: 300–1), seemed particularly appropriate.

The beliefs and practices reported by nominal Catholics came close to what Towler described as 'common religion' (Towler and Chamberlain, 1973; Towler, 1974: 145–62). Like Towler and Chamberlain's respondents, our interviewees conventionally accepted the need for religion as customary and respectable, though voluntary. They also were aware of their early religious socialisation, made use of religious beliefs as a help in life and as a means of explaining their experiences of suffering and perplexity, recognized that religion provided them with a practical ethic, and emphatically stressed that religion was to be regarded as a private matter. On the other hand there are a number of limitations in their treatment which does not clearly distinguish between the definition of 'common religion', a description of its main characteristics and a theory of its transmission through childhood peer-groups prior to any 'systematizing influence of official religion'. There seems to be no reason why the notion of common religion requires a continuity with earlier folk forms of religion or with the content of the informal processes of childhood socialisation. Many of their examples admit of a much greater degree of institutional influence than their definition allows. There seem to be good grounds for distinguishing between magic and superstition, on the one hand, and various beliefs and practices which have tenuous links with institutional religion, on the other (Hornsby-Smith, Lee and Reilly, 1985: 246–7).

The term *customary religion* was proposed to cover this latter area. It consists of those beliefs and practices which are derived from official religion but which are not subject to continued control by the Churches. It was suggested that the term *common religion* be restricted to non-institutionally contexted religious beliefs and practices, particularly of a magical or superstitious nature. *Official religion* was then seen as being made up of the orthodox beliefs and practices of the functionaries (e.g. priests) and activists (e.g. core laity) within a religious institution. We also have a different notion of transmission. Rather than stressing the importance of childhood peer-groups as Towler and Chamberlain did, we would suggest that customary religion results when there is a breakdown in the processes of formal religious socialisation within official religion. In particular we suggest that processes of trivialisation, conventionality, apathy, convenience and self-interest erode and modify the beliefs and practices prescribed by the socialising agencies of official Roman Catholicism and result in current expressions of customary religion.

Before proceeding to the consideration of some of our interview data in the light of our definition of customary religion, a brief reference to related concepts is appropriate. The distinction made by Luckmann (1967) between church-oriented, visible or 'official' religion and 'invisible' or non-Church-oriented religion, fails to allow for the various processes of dilution and erosion of official religion which result in customary religion. Luckmann's concept of invisible religion is more closely related to the notions of 'folk', 'implicit' or 'popular' religion. According to Bailey (1986: 3), the concept of 'folk' religion, which refers to the religion of a people in a corporate sense for Scandinavians or Germans, or to naive, quaint or old-fashioned survivals for Americans, is inappropriate in Britain where religion is individualistic or familial. He proposes the term 'implicit' religion for experiences that seem to transcend the ordinary, run-of-the-mill or everyday. A related concept is 'popular' religion which is used in Southern Europe and the United States and which embraces not only

Mardi Gras phenomena but also spontaneous religious expressions, such as beliefs in reincarnation and superstitious practices like fortune-telling, which survive independently of the official Christian Church and contrary to its teaching. These concepts are closer to Towler's notion of 'common' religion. Finally, Cipriani's concept of 'diffused' religion, which he explicitly distinguishes from 'common', 'popular' or 'folk' religion, seems closer to our view of 'customary' religion since it 'would keep (in a more or less latent form) some sort of link with the church structure' (1984: 33). However, he is concerned with a case of religious monopoly with Catholicism in Italy, whereas in England Catholicism is the religion of a small minority. Thus while the two concepts have some affinity, they relate to quite different structural situations.

In order to convey something of the flavour of the 'customary' religion of ordinary Catholics in our four research parishes, we will focus in particular on interview extracts relating to three main themes: our respondents' images of God; their interpretations of heaven, hell and life after death; and their reflections on personal prayer. Where interview data have been quoted directly, brief details of the social and religious characteristics of respondents will be given in order to locate the extracts in a religious context and to indicate the extent to which aspects of customary religion can be detected among Catholics who may differ significantly from each other in terms of their religious practice or institutional involvement.

5.3 Images of God

The importance of religious imagery has recently been stressed by Andrew Greeley who has claimed that:

The 'sensibility' of Catholics has undergone a rather drastic modification in the last twenty years in the direction of images and pictures and stories of God which are more benign, more gracious, and more affectionate ... The religious imagination seems to have more effect on how people live their lives in this world than any other measure of religion available to us. (Greeley, 1985: 199, 201)

On the basis of survey findings with young adults in North America, Greeley has measured the extent to which different images of God, Jesus, Mary, and life after death are held. Thus God is more commonly described as 'protector', 'redeemer', 'master', 'creator' and 'father' than 'judge', 'lover' or 'mother'. The most popular descriptions of both Jesus and Mary are 'gentle', 'warm', 'patient' and 'comforting' rather than 'stern', 'distant', 'demanding', 'irrelevant' or 'challenging' (1981: 23–9).

These findings have relevance for our own research which, rather than obtaining quantitative measures from attitude scales, addressed itself to the more qualitative exploration of change in the Roman Catholic Church as a result of both post-war social change and the reforms and shifts of religious orientation promoted by the Second Vatican Council. We surmised that there would be a close relationship between the image of God held by Catholics, and their model of the Church and authority relationships within it. We anticipated that, on the one hand, an image of a transcendent God would be associated with a pre-Vatican, 'mechanistic' or bureaucratic model of the Church with a superordinate clergy exercising decision-making power over a subordinate laity. On the other hand, any shift towards a more immanent image of God or one which put less emphasis on the power of God would be more likely to be associated with a more post-Vatican, 'organic' or participative model of the Church where the status differences between clergy and laity were reduced. In the course of our focused interviews, therefore, we invited our respondents to tell us about their image of God in their own words.

In the previous chapter we described how core Catholics were generally able to articulate their views with coherence and consistency in terms of two contrasting images which were put to them. In the case of the four randomly selected samples of ordinary Catholics whose views are the concern of this chapter, it will be seen that there was a much lower level of coherence and consistency. An indication of the range of responses we obtained from ordinary Catholics, from those who attended Mass more than once a week to those who had not done so for many years, has been given in Table 5.1. The twenty-seven selections were obtained from respondents in all four parishes. They have been grouped under twelve categories but do not seem to indicate any consistent variations between the sexes, age groups or social classes, or, perhaps even more surprisingly, between practising and non-practising Catholics.

In general, ordinary Catholics had great difficulty in picturing God and were embarrassed by the question even when they were regular Mass attenders. The first three responses (Table 5.1) illustrate this. Other respondents seemed to squirm uncomfortably and after exclaiming 'that's a very hard one' or 'nobody's ever asked that question before', there would be very long pauses as they struggled to address a concept which seemed not to have entered their consciousness before.

Other respondents seemed to delve deeply into childhood memories to produce answers they had learned at school. This was reflected in the second group of responses (4–7) which drew on holy pictures of God as a man with a beard and long hair. The next five categories of images all had human characteristics to a more-or-less explicit degree: God as having human attributes as a holy man (8–9), as a loving father (10), a caring friend (11–13), specifically identified as Jesus (14–15), or as a judge (16–18). When one put the quotations into a wider context, other aspects of the religiosity of our respondents became more apparent. For example, a mother of two young children, who suggested that it was necessary to give God human attributes explained 'that's how one explains God to children' (PS). A busy student who attended Mass more than weekly, nevertheless admitted that she did not 'think about God that much now; there's so much to do' (PS). It is noticeable that both those who used the image of a friend and those who saw God as a judge, stressed the notions of love or respect rather than fear. This is consistent with a decline in notions of a God of retribution in recent years.

In addition to those images which stressed human attributes, four broad categories saw God as having spiritual characteristics. Thus God was seen as the creator of all things (19), or as a mystical being (20–1), sometimes as a 'sense of strength, tranquillity and peace' (LI), as being everywhere around us (22–3), or as a source of power or energy (24–6). Such views often explicitly rejected notions of God as a person: 'I believe there is a force, but as for defining it as a person or as an aware being, it just isn't on' (LI). We also came across at least one response (27) which could be described as syncretic in that it attempted to embrace several different concepts of God.

To illustrate further some of the inferences we are drawing from the widely differing images of God which were offered by our representative samples of Catholics in four different English parishes in the mid-1970s, the following interview extract indicates the way in which a young mother responded to a series of probes. These commenced by asking her how she would explain God to her young son, continued later to ask specifically what she believed herself, and

Table 5.1. *Classification of images of God (Catholic electors, four parishes)*

A. *Uncertain*
1. That's a very hard one. (pause) Well, I really don't know.
   (LS; female, 38, married; skilled manual; most Sundays)
2. I believe there is something called God, but what it is I've no idea.
   (PS; male, 38, married; clerical; now and again)
3. I don't know, I'm sure I don't ... We were taught to believe in Him and try and live up to Him.
   (PI; female, 84, married; factory worker; weekly)

B. *Childhood*
4. I picture Him as an old man with a grey beard.
   (PS; female, 64, married; manual; weekly)
5. I picture God as an Arab with a beard, long hair, carrying a staff.
   (PS; female, 22, single; non-manual; weekly)
6. Only a traditional one of a bearded, 30ish man.
   (PS; male, 44, married; manager; weekly)
7. Something from my childhood; a holy picture.
   (LI; female, 29, married; programmer; special occasions only)

C. *Human*
8. You really can't conceptualise God; that's impossible. We give Him human attributes because that's the easiest way to think of Him.
   (PS; female, 32, married; non-manual; weekly)
9. I think of God a lot. I think of Him as a holy man.
   (LI; male, 23, single; engineer; weekly)

D. *Father*
10. Like an ordinary man; someone you look up to like your father.
    (PS; female, 40, married; clerical; weekly)

E. *Friend*
11. God's somebody who looks after you.
    (PS; female, 57, married; secretary; weekly)
12. I think of Him as a person, as a good friend ... I think of Him as the boss.
    (PI; female, 23, single; casual worker; infrequent attender)
13. Feeling of warmth, loving and caring. To wear a crown and to be barefooted at the same time. To come down to earth humble.
    (LS; female, 63, separated; inspector; weekly)

F. *Jesus*
14. I have no real picture of God ... I usually think of Christ when thinking of God.
    (PS; male, 38, married; non-manual; weekly)
15. I can't say except that I believe that there is one and that Jesus Christ came to save the world.
    (LS; male, 46, married; inspector; weekly)

G. *Judge*
16. God is somebody you love ... fear Him in the sense of judge and boss, and respect Him.
    (PS; male, 19, single; student; more than weekly)
17. A sort of managing director with a posh suit ... whom one would respect rather than fear.
    (LS; male, 53, married; administrator; weekly)

Table 5.1. *cont.*

18. I think of Him as something good but I've got to play the game as well ... a good person.
    (LS; female, 26, married; clerical; never)

H. *Creator*
19. God is the Supreme Spirit who created all things ... creator of heaven and earth ... creator of the lovely world we live in.
    (PI; female, elderly, single; skilled manual; housebound)

I. *Mystical being*
20. I picture Him in the sky though I know He's not there. He's a mystical being present all the time and with you all the time.
    (LI; female, 20, single; non-manual; now and again)

J. *Immanent*
22. I see God as us; God is in everybody.
    (LI; female, 33, married; secretary; most Sundays)
23. He is just there; He's everywhere; He's in your homes; He's wherever you are.
    (PI; female, 32, married; waitress; less than weekly)

K. *Energy*
24. Some force or power, of a scientific kind, not personal, but has some feelings, a mind.
    (LI; female, 24, single; teacher; weekly)
25. God is really the force behind the universe ... the more you study science, the more you come to believe in an ultimate being.
    (PS; female, 40, married; non-manual; more than weekly)
26. It's a power, some kind of energy.
    (PS; female, 30, married; non-manual; Christmas and Easter only)

L. *Syncretic*
27. I sometimes picture God as a big, strong, old man; sometimes as Christ; sometimes as the wind; you can't see it, but you feel it.
    (LI; female, 49, married; unskilled manual; most Sundays)

Key to respondent characteristics:
Parish; sex, age, marital status; occupational category; Mass attendance.

concluded by asking her how she would respond to a query about God from her next door neighbour:

He was a man, somebody like [her son's] daddy ... in his thirties, who came on earth from His father to ... make reparation for our sins. And because He loved us all so much, he was willing to die for us ...

Jesus came on earth to make reparation for us and He died because that was the only thing He could do to show ... I don't think I'd have had the guts to do it! ... I've come back to childish beliefs ...

Well, there's the three, isn't there? There's God the Father, God the Son, and God the Holy Ghost. See what I mean about having it drummed into you parrot fashion? You don't say one without the other two ...

It's the person in heaven, the creator, the supreme being that watches over us all and He's in heaven ... three persons in one God. As far as I'm concerned, I believe it. I can't prove it to anybody ... But that is what I was taught at school ... and until somebody can show me anything better, that's what I believe ...

He is everywhere, yet you do tend to think of Him as sat up there all the time watching over you ... but He is everywhere and in everything and everybody. And yet it's just human nature. I instinctively feel He is sat up there watching everything. (PS; female, 27, married; clerk; weekly attender)

This extract from a conversation lasting two to three minutes gives something of the flavour of what we have called 'customary' religion. The above respondent three times justifies her response by appealing to her early childhood socialisation or formal religious education at school in terms of 'official' religion. Clearly her current beliefs and concepts, such as 'reparation' and the Trinity, were derived from 'official' religion. But there is also a sense in which they are no longer totally under its control and she remains open to modified beliefs if 'somebody can show me anything better'.

By comparison with this respondent, many of the other responses illustrated in Table 5.1 demonstrated *either* (a) an absence of any conception of God (e.g. 1–3), *or* (b) a failure to develop a mature, adult conception of God beyond childhood understandings (e.g. 4–7), *or* (c) evidence of the remnants of official images of God inculcated during the processes of religious socialisation in childhood (e.g. 14, 15, 23). Whereas the first of these groupings (and particularly extracts 2 and 3) might best be regarded as indicative of an implicit, popular or common religion in the sense described earlier, the second and third groupings seem clearly to indicate 'customary' religion as we have defined it.

5.4 Heaven, hell and life after death

During our early fieldwork in the London suburban parish (LS), we began to realise that ordinary Catholics had a great deal less knowledge of, and attachment to, the official religious beliefs of the Church than the national advisers. Furthermore, their accounts of their Catholicism, as we have noted, lacked the coherence and consistency of the advisers. Accordingly, in the later interviews in the London Suburban (LS) parish and in the remaining three parishes, we began to explore, by means of appropriate probing, other aspects of their religious beliefs. For example, in addition to direct questions about their images of God, our respondents were also invited to comment on related issues such as their beliefs in heaven, hell and the after-life. Considerable amounts of heterodoxy, in terms of official religion, appeared in these areas. That this was generally the case was demonstrated by the 1978 national survey of English Catholics, which showed that around one Catholic in eight did not believe in heaven, life after death, or 'an evil force sometimes called the devil'. As many as one in four did not believe in hell and well over one-quarter thought that the statement 'sometimes people, after they die, come back and live in the world again' was true. In each case the proportions were lower for regular Mass attenders but significantly higher for 'lapsed' Catholics who had not attended Mass for over a year (Hornsby-Smith and Lee, 1979: 193).

In our four research parishes a large proportion of ordinary Catholics, in both manual and non-manual occupations, and including both practising and 'lapsed' or 'dormant' Catholics, did not believe in the devil or hell. Most did not like the idea or were unable to reconcile it with their notion of a good God. Several respondents, including a few practising Catholics, did not believe in an after-life at all. Some felt they would like to believe, or expressed beliefs which appeared to be products of an earlier religious socialisation. However, there was fairly widespread flirting with a miscellaneous range of beliefs including those, such as reincarnation, at odds with official teachings. It seems that, for many ordinary Catholics, concepts such as eternal damnation or hell and the devil, are uncomfortable, unpleasant and inconvenient. We suggest that findings such as these lend support to our interpretation of an official religion which was more-or-less internalised during childhood socialisation, but which has, over the years, been eroded, for example by emphases on convenience and self-interest. What we find empirically is evidence for customary religion no longer directly controlled by the official leadership in the Church.

In Table 5.2 we have illustrated the evidence for customary religion by selecting nine broad categories of response to questions about heaven and hell, the last judgement and life after death. We must stress again that it is not our purpose here to quantify the wide range of responses we obtained but to illustrate our claim that customary religion, as we have defined it, can be discerned among a wide range of ordinary Catholics, including many who are regular

Table 5.2. *Classification of responses on heaven and hell and the after life
(Catholic electors, four parishes)*

A. *Neo-Official*
1. I believe in a day of judgement ... I see heaven as having seen God; and hell as having seen God, having experienced God, without being with Him again.
   (PS; Male, 36, married; engineer; weekly)
2. I believe there is a state of heaven, which is just a mystical state ... There must be a place of punishment, perhaps more purgatory than hell ... I think that God is forgiving.
   (LI; Female, 61, married; non-manual; weekly)

B. *Conventional*
3. I'm sure (heaven and hell) exist ... Heaven is the absence of hell ... Well this is what I was taught and therefore I imagine I really must believe it, but I can't imagine it.
   (LI; Female, 31, married; sales assistant; weekly)
4. That's our belief; that's our teaching ... we believe there's heaven and ... hell ... Regarding the devil, if you're easily led and it's something you know you shouldn't do, you say he's tempting you.
   (PS; Male, 66, married; skilled manual; weekly)

C. *Conscience*
5. Sin is what you do wrong, but it's up to your conscience – if you rob, steal or murder somebody and you think it's O.K. then all right it is. If you think it's wrong, it's wrong.
   (LI; Male, 23, single; engineer; weekly)
6. I believe there's a heaven and somewhere else ... I believe there's some other source of you doing bad ... conscience or something; probably the devil within yourself, type of thing.
   (PI; Female, 31, married; manual; more than weekly)
7. I think there is a heaven and hell, but what there is there, I don't know, like ... what I was taught in them days ... it would be like a kind of earth again.
   (PI; Male, 41, married; manual; weekly)

D. *Childhood*
8. (Heaven is) peace and contentment ... there's supposed to be hell and a devil and shoving coals on fires and we're burning up all the time, that's my view of hell ... that's what we were taught as kids.
   (PI; Female, 29, married; unskilled; special occasions)
9. Heaven, as such, whatever it might be; I mean you look back on what you thought it was when you were little and wonder ... [laughs] lovely wind and cloud and things like that ... it's this eternity.
   (PS; Female, 57, married; secretary; weekly)

E. *Hell on Earth*
10. I feel ... we are living both heaven and hell, that whatever you do wrong, now ... we have to pay for now ... you get some comeuppance.
    (PS; Female, 30, married; skilled; Christmas and Easter)
11. Hell is here on earth ... How can there be a loving God ... when thousands of people, through no fault of their own [suffer].
    (PS; Male, 64, married; skilled; radio and TV only)
12. I think we have a heaven and hell on earth, you know ... I know there is a life after because I have talked to the spirits, and that is a sin for a start.
    (PI; Female, 23, single; casual; occasional)

Table 5.2. *cont.*

F. *Hell is Within You*
13. Well, have you heard the old saying: 'you makes your own heaven and your own hell'? ... People can make your life a misery.
  (PI; Male, 71, divorced; manual; rarely)
14. I don't think I've ever believed in hell ... You don't go down stoking fires or anything like that ... you pay for your sins here ... I don't believe in the devil; I think it's just badness inside.
  (PS; Female, 28, married; operator; most Sundays)
15. I think there are evil forces about ... which give us a prod in the wrong direction ... from our own natural instinct to be disobedient ... in opposition to God's love ... it works within us.
  (LS; Female, 27, married; technician; radio and TV only)

G. *Afterlife and Sex*
16. There'll be no sexuality because sexual is to procreate life and you're not going to procreate life in heaven ... There'll be no sex ... I don't think He'll damn me for one mortal sin.
  (PI; Male, 61, married; skilled; more than weekly)
17. But I don't like the badness ... the pornography ... and the sexual overtures ... reminds me of Sodom and Gomorrah ... I bet that's how the end will come ... through our wickedness and that.
  (LS; Female, 26, married; operator; Christmas and Easter)

H. *Reincarnation*
18. I think that perhaps you do get a chance at another life, you know, reincarnation of some description.
  (PS; Female, 30, married; skilled; Christmas and Easter)
19. Having accepted the idea of an after-life, it must be in some sort of stages ... There's another very good theory, too, which I've often toyed with ... and that is ... reincarnation.
  (LI; Male, 68, married; administrator; weekly)
20. I believe that when we die ... we go to another world that has seven spheres ... and whenever you die in life, you go to the sphere you deserve ... I believe that you are reincarnated in this world.
  (LS; Female, 47, married; clerk; radio and TV only; now self-identified spiritualist)

I. *Other Heterodox*
21. No, I don't believe in heaven and hell; when we die our body disintegrates. There is no life after death ... I don't believe in the devil or any evil force.
  (LI; Male, 23, single; engineer; weekly)
22. I don't believe in hell any more ... [or the devil] ... I find, like, that the phrases I was taught keep cropping up, like conscience and will and so on ... my vague catechism answers.
  (LI; Female, 30, married; professional; monthly)
23. I might believe in a force of evil but not in somebody who goes around tempting people, sort of thing, with a tail ... I think [a struggle] is more between good and apathy than a force of evil.
  (LI; Female, 20, single; student; more than weekly)
24. I don't think there's a devil. I think that was conjured up to try and get people be more religious ... and I don't think there's a hell. I think you pay for your sins as you go through life.
  (PS; Female, 40, married; clerk; weekly)

Table 5.2. *cont.*

25. I can't really believe there is a hell; I can't really believe that people are condemned to hell for ever because I don't think God could do that . . . [I don't believe] in the devil.
(ps; Female, 20, single; student; more than weekly)

Key to respondent characteristics:
Parish; sex, age, marital status; occupational category; Mass attendance.

Mass attenders. Not unexpectedly many responded more-or-less in terms of orthodox teaching (1–2). Even here, though, the first respondent continued to qualify his vision of hell:

but not tormenting, not weeping and gnashing of teeth . . . I think there's a force of evil . . . in opposition to God . . . I'd like to see either of them because one would prove the existence of the other . . . I'd love to see a ghost though . . . the devil's existence would only prove God's existence. (ps; Male, 36; engineer; weekly)

The second respondent continued to refer to 'some bad spirit that tempts us' and of the importance of avoiding the 'occasion of sin', clear evidence of notions learned during childhood socialisation. The first category overlaps with the second group (3–4) which illustrates 'conventional' beliefs about heaven, hell, the devil and temptation.

This relates to the third category of responses (5–7) which refer to the concept of conscience. Thus Respondent 7, after making a conventional observation about heaven and hell, continued by suggesting in connection with the devil, 'your conscience, more or less . . . stealing, temptation, lustful thoughts and things like that and t'other, I think that's where the devil comes in'. The fourth category draws attention to explicit childhood images (8–9), for example of a heaven of eternal peace and contentment and an absence of strife, beautiful, with angels up in the clouds (LI) and where you meet everybody again (PI), and of a hell of fire. Several respondents qualified references to hell by suggesting that hell was here on earth (10–12) or within ourselves (13–15). Sometimes these responses were linked to elements of considerable doubt or aspects of heterodoxy. Respondent 11, for example, who only went to church once every five years or so out of curiosity, asked how there could be a loving God when thousands of people could be killed, through no fault of their own, in an earthquake. A young girl with an unconventional life-style (12) described dabbling with spiritualism and ouija boards.

Respondents in the seventh category (16–17) made some reference to sexuality in commenting on the afterlife. One young woman saw sin in terms of stealing somebody else's husband (PI) and another talked at length about contemporary pornography and associated it with Sodom and Gomorrah and the end of the world. A man who attended Mass more than weekly described his vision of the after-life in the following terms:

I'm sixty one and I'll be like twenty one ... and you'll not need any food, will yer? ... What kind of body? ... I don't know ... but you'll be yourself ... There'll be no sexuality because sexual is to procreate life and you're not going to procreate life in heaven! ... There'll be no sex ... Well, hell, there'll be a certain amount of punishment there but I don't think you'll see God; you'll see Him but you'll never see Him no more ... But whether God will send people to hell; He says He does. He gives them every chance ... But ... I don't think He'll damn me for one mortal sin. (PI; Male, 61; manual; more than weekly)

There is perhaps an element of self-interest, in the contradiction between mortal sin but no eternal damnation, which is one aspect of customary religion. Apart from this, it is of interest to note his pre-Vatican view of sexuality as being primarily for procreation rather than pleasure. This again might be seen to reflect the influence of an earlier religious socialisation without any obvious adjustments in the light of the more developed theology of sexuality of the past two decades or so.

Finally, two categories of responses draw attention to elements of heterodoxy in the expressed beliefs of ordinary Catholics. Among ordinary Catholics generally, considerable reservations were expressed about the notions of hell seen in terms of eternal damnation. Thus one respondent added 'I can't believe in the judgement of what we've done on earth, say whether if you've been good you go to heaven, if you're bad you go to hell; I can't really believe in that' (18). Several people in relation to this indicated that they believed, or had flirted with, the notion of reincarnation as an alternative to notions of eternal damnation (18–20). There were numerous examples of one form of heterodoxy or another. Quotations 21 to 25 in Table 5.2 illustrate this mainly in relation to the existence of hell or the devil, even in the case of people who attend Mass weekly or more frequently. For our present purposes we might also note the references to 'what I was taught' or the catechism (22), that is the references to an earlier religious socialisation no longer under the control of official religion (and concepts like 'conscience' and 'will'), and also a further example of the oft-mentioned view that 'you pay for your sins as you go through life' (24).

Brief reference might also be made to a number of other examples of heterodoxy. One woman, for example, found it difficult to believe in an after-life because 'nobody has come back to prove it' (LI). A similar remark was made by a young manual worker who said that he sometimes believed in the existence of heaven and hell but sometimes did not and so would 'wait 'til he finds out hiself ... seeing is believing' (PI). Another woman stressed 'it is difficult to believe in things that can't be proven' (PI). Finally, several respondents, including some who did not believe in heaven or hell, the devil or sin, claimed not to be superstitious but nevertheless referred to elements of superstition in their beliefs. Thus there were comments about 'touching wood' (PI), not walking under ladders (LI), and an Irish single parent felt she had been dogged by ill-luck and should have had her house blessed (LI). A middle-aged woman wanted to make sure her grandchildren were baptised because 'they wouldn't be protected if they weren't' (LI). Another thought that life was planned for one and there was nothing one could do about it; for example, her daughter had nearly had an accident 'but it wasn't meant for her' (LI).

5.5 Personal prayer

Another area of belief and practice which we explored in our interviews was that of personal prayer. In the pre-Vatican Catechism, prayer was simply defined as 'the raising up of the mind and heart to God' (Anon, 1954: 23). The European Value Systems Study Group (EVSSG) reported that of the people in Great Britain, 'half regularly felt the need for prayer, meditation or contemplation' (Gerard, 1985: 58). For Western Europe as a whole, 68 per cent of Catholics reported that they prayed (Harding and Phillips, 1986: 52). In the 1978 national survey, nearly one-half of English Catholics reported that they prayed daily, one-quarter less frequently and about one in eight in times of crisis only. Among dormant Catholics who had not attended Mass in over a year, the proportion praying in times of crisis only rose to one-quarter and nearly one-third never prayed (Hornsby-Smith and Lee, 1979: 203).

The sociological study of prayer derives from Lenski's classic study of religion in Detroit in the late 1950s. Lenski distinguished devotionalism from doctrinal orthodoxy and regarded the former as 'a more active, behavioural type of religious orientation' which 'emphasizes the importance of private, or personal, communion with God'. Lenski measured this form of religious commitment 'by the frequency with which he prayed and the frequency with which he sought to determine God's will when he had important decisions to make' (1963: 25).

In our focused interviews we did not set out so much to collect quantitative data as to probe for the ways in which ordinary Catholics understood prayer and to identify the variety of ways in which they described their prayer. In general, personal prayer did not seem to be common among ordinary Catholics in our four research parishes, even for those who were weekly Mass attenders. Where prayer was reported, it tended to be either routinised, such as ritual morning and night prayers, or to be a response to personal problems, difficulties or crises, such as bereavement or sickness. Our respondents typically felt the need for prayer on the occasions of death, birth, illness or examinations. It was frequently regarded as a form of therapy to provide relief from worry. Most ordinary Catholics indicated that they were convinced that their prayers were answered.

An indication of the range of responses we obtained to our questions about prayer is given in Table 5.3. The first group of responses stresses the formal prayers (1 and 2), such as the *Our Father*, the *Hail Mary* or the rosary, and formal times of praying such as at the 'morning offering' of the coming day to God and to ask His help with the problems it will bring, and the night prayers with an 'examination of conscience' before going to sleep. These prayers clearly reflected the results of early childhood socialisation. A number of Catholics, especially in the two Preston parishes where we explored this further, indicated that they prayed various combinations of formal and informal prayer, mainly to 'Our Lord', but also to the 'Sacred Heart (of Jesus)', 'Our Lady' and various saints. Thus one man prayed to St Jude when despairing or going through any trouble, St Anthony to find God within his daily life, and St Martin to keep him going (PI). Other saints mentioned included the 'Little Flower' (St Theresa of Lisieux) and St Joseph. The *Hail Mary* was a popular prayer. One West Indian girl, for example, said she prayed to God every day, then Mary and Jesus, because Mary was 'earthly' and Jesus 'a bit of both' (LI).

Table 5.3. *Classification of forms of private prayer (Catholic electors, four parishes)*

A. *Formal*
1. (I pray) every night ... mainly 'Hail Marys' ... don't know why ... it's just something I've done since I were a kid.
   (PI; Male, 28, married; semi-skilled; special occasions)
2. I say prayers every night of my life. If you only say a few prayers every night, you'll not go far wrong.
   (PI; Female, 84, married; skilled manual; weekly)

B. *Conventional*
3. My husband and I have got into the habit of saying prayers together [at night] ... because at school, one of the sayings was 'the family that prays together stays together'.
   (LS; Female, 26, married; operator; Christmas and Easter)
4. I use formal prayers, like the ones that have been passed down.
   (PI; Female, 23, single; casual; occasional)
5. I don't pretend to be religious ... but if you don't say morning prayers, you won't think about the presence of God in your work.
   (PI; Female, elderly, single; skilled manual; housebound)

C. *Informal*
6. I don't get down on my knees and pray but I do say the odd prayer going to work, when the thought strikes me ... and when dropping off to sleep at night ... I don't set aside particular times.
   (LI; Female, 40s, married; nurse; regular attender)
7. [I]f I am thinking about how to deal with a situation with my children, just bringing God into that on an informal level ... and saying please help me sort this out.
   (PS; Female, 40, married; non-manual; more than weekly)
8. It's just hard to get down to talk to God sometimes. And I'll think I'll not bother now ... I just try and ask God to come into my life a bit more and help me be more Christian in outlook.
   (PS; Male, 19, single; student; more than weekly)

D. *Instrumental*
9. Not as much as I did at one time because you haven't got so much to pray for. When your kids are growing up ... it's always there in the background.
   (PS; Female, 57, married; secretary; weekly)
10. I did just after my Maths exams!
    (PI; Male, 18, single; technician; Christmas and Easter)

Key to respondent characteristics:
Parish; sex, age, marital status; occupational category; Mass attendance.

The second group of responses (3–6) points to the conventional or habitual nature of the devotionalism of ordinary Catholics and again indicates persisting elements of an earlier socialisation. One young mother, alone all day with her young daughter, was fulsome about the place of prayer in her life:

I really pray to God every morning to bring [my husband] home safely again to us ... I always say my prayers at night. It's a good habit ... My husband and I have got into the habit of saying our prayers together although he's a non-Catholic ... because, at school, one of the sayings was 'the family that prays together stays together'. I'm so happy, I don't want anything to spoil it ... I'm lucky to have a good family ... In a way [during the day] I've got no other adult to talk to. I do speak to God during the day ... I'm not a religious fanatic or anything. (LS; Female, 26, married; operator; Christmas and Easter)

While being sensitive to the problem of interpretative bias, there nevertheless do seem to be elements of superstition in this extract. Prayer is seen as a bringer of good luck or as a lucky charm, to bring the husband home safely each day and to ensure the continuation of her present familial happiness. At the same time, the relationship to God is a real and personal one; God is the only 'adult' around to talk to during the day when she is confined to home with only a small child for company.

A second woman who does not attend church very often, also clung to elements of an earlier upbringing and also recalled the Catholic slogan about the family praying together:

I don't go [to church] very often. I pray to God in my own way, but if I have a problem, I go ... to church to pray and then I say 'thank You' when He gives me what I want ... and if I need anything. I use formal prayers, like the ones that have been passed down, but I tend to think of Him just as a person that I talk to, like a good friend ... to say 'thanks for helping me along' ... I don't think I have a bad day ... because I have Him to talk to ... You could just walk into a church and there is hundreds of people in there and they are all, in a sense, they are all praying with you ... if you make the effort and you go into church, it's like going up to see Him.

Later in the interview she described how she prayed:

In a way I just lie there and talk to God ... I pray a lot to St Jude now, and St Anthony, and I don't pray so much to God Himself. I just say a couple of *Our Fathers* now and again and talk to Our Lady as well and ... I tell her what's going on in my mind ... So, I ask if I've done something that I think is wrong and tell her and I say, 'Well, can you understand why I did it?' And then I say, 'I know I'm going to be sorry that I've done it later on' and I really am sorry that I've done it later on and ... if I'm miserable, I ask her to stop me being miserable. And I ask St Jude to stop me being miserable, which he does ... So if I want something, I pray to St Anthony and he finds it for me and it's in a most stupid place! So really, me whole life is involved with it, isn't it? ...

me Dad ... gave me this wallet and he says to me: 'You'll be lucky because there's a holy picture in the front ... there's a little prayer here' ... It's like he's giving me a really special gift, giving me something like that because he has nothing else to give me. He has no money and things like that ... And if I set off in my van, me Mum says 'have you got any holy water?', and things like that ... When I came here like, she would search everywhere for a bottle of holy water ... so that I could bless the place ... I feel guilty about ... asking for things all the time, so yesterday, when I went to church, I wanted to say 'thanks'. (PI; Female, 23, single; casual; occasionally)

In this long extract there are numerous points of interest. Firstly, there are elements of both a privatised form of prayer 'in my own way' and of a communal dimension with 'hundreds of people ... praying with you'. Secondly, in addition to prayers of petition, there is also thanksgiving for recognised favours. Thirdly, formal prayers which have been 'passed down' are used. Fourthly, prayer implies a personal relationship with someone 'I talk to, like a good friend'. Fifthly, there is a distinctively Catholic form of devotionalism in the intercessory and mediatory prayer to Mary ('Our Lady') and the saints. Against this, another respondent reported: 'Personally I just pray to God, to Jesus Christ ... It does seem a more direct route' (PS). Sixthly, there is again an element of superstition in the holy picture or holy water as lucky charms. Finally, apart from the convention-ality of the habitual forms of prayer and the elements of convenience and self-interest which can be discerned in this extract, there is also a sense in which official religion is trivialised insofar as its main purpose is the finding of lost objects. A conventional form of Catholic devotionalism is the making of the 'sign of the cross' when passing a church (LS).

A third group of responses stressed informality both in the content of prayer and in its place, time and style (6–8). Several of our respondents indicated that they prayed at various times during the day, in their own words and without 'getting down on their knees' (as if this was the recognised mark of 'real' prayer). Thus respondents prayed when they went to bed (PS), round the house (PS), on the bus to work (LI), in the street (LI), cycling to work (LI), walking to the station (LI) or 'wherever I am' (LI). Typical comments were:

I don't get down on my knees and pray, but I do say the odd prayer going to work, when the thought strikes me. I don't make a habit of setting a half-hour aside for prayer. When I am cycling up the road to work I might 'say one'. And when dropping off to sleep at night I might say a prayer for the dead, my family. I don't set aside particular times. (LI; Female, 40s, married; nurse; regular attender)

Mainly informal, thanks for things going right and thinking about other people, people who are sick, the way you are bringing up your children, whether you are doing the right thing. To me, prayer, to some extent, is if I am thinking about how to deal with a situation with my children; just bringing God into that on an informal level. Not kneeling down and going through all sorts of formal prayers . . . just bringing Him in and saying 'please help me to sort this out'. (PS; Female, 40, married; non-manual; more than weekly)

It seems that informal prayer frequently takes the form of a conversation with God about the domestic and work concerns of everyday life. As such it is much less ritualistic than formal prayer and much more private and personal in its style. A frequently expressed view was that 'you can worship God anywhere . . . at home' (PI) or 'in fields' (LS). This view was typically expressed by those who were not attending Mass regularly and, as such, it took the form of a 'justification'. It was mainly informal prayer which several respondents felt they were 'not good at' (LI) or confessed to 'failing constantly' (LI) to achieve. This sense of guilt at their perceived failure to pray adequately on the part of English Catholics was noted previously in chapter 3.

With a fourth group of respondents the major distinguishing feature is that of petition. Prayer is predominantly instrumental in that it explicitly asks God, either directly or indirectly through a saintly intermediary, for some favour or benefit (9–10). In our interviews references were made to the death of a spouse (PI), times of stress (PS) or trouble (PS), when people are ill (PI), examinations (PI), children's upbringing (PS), a child's disability (PS), or simply 'when it will do some good' (PS). A typical comment was made by a young mother:

I only seem to pray when I want something or when I am frightened, when I need strength. I am more inclined to pray just sitting in church.

She then proceeded to express how difficult it was to talk about prayer even to her children. For her, prayer was a taboo topic, something essentially private and personal:

I find it difficult to . . . talk to my children about prayer, I don't know why. I find it embarrassing . . . Sex I can talk about, but not prayer. (LI; Female, 33, married; secretary; most Sundays)

Finally, some of our respondents admitted that they never prayed and felt no need for it. Usually this was related to a long-standing alienation from religious practice and sometimes also from belief. Thus one man who only attended church on special occasions said that he had 'no real belief in prayer, no sense of communication with this being [God]' (LS). Another associated prayer with superstition (LI). Another weekly attender offered as justification for not really praying the claim that he answered spiritual needs 'by going out and helping people, offering this up to God as [the] equivalent of prayer' (PS).

5.6 Customary and popular Catholicisms

In this chapter we have offered an account of the religion of ordinary Catholics in contrast to the review of the religion of core Catholics given in the previous chapter. Generally we found that ordinary Catholics were less orthodox in their beliefs, knew less about the recent changes in Catholicism, which were in any case less salient to them in their everyday lives. Not infrequently ordinary Catholics, in our interviews with them, gave the impression that they were confronting questions about their religion to which they had never previously given any thought. We have illustrated this by reviewing three main areas: their images of God; their views about heaven, hell and the after-life; and their notions of personal prayer. Other areas on which we have some data but which have not been reviewed in this chapter include comments on various aspects of institutional Catholicism, such as the Sunday Mass obligation and the consequences of 'lapsation', conflicts with priests and resentments about coercive aspects of Catholicism, regular appeals for money and the hypocrisy of churchgoers. In general these data provide further support for the claims we have made in this chapter for what we have called customary religion. We will consider further the responses of ordinary Catholics on issues of religious authority in chapter 8.

We have defined customary Catholicism as those beliefs and practices which are manifestly derived from an earlier Catholic socialisation, mainly in Catholic schools, but which are no longer subject to effective control by the religious leadership in the Church. Among our parish samples of self-identified Catholics we found a number of instances of an absence of any conception of God, which suggests a failure of early socialisation for those without supportive familial commitments in childhood. We also found instances where distant childhood memories were recalled in an unreflective or immature way, or where the remnants of an earlier socialisation appeared to have been eroded or modified in the course of adult life. There were numerous references to religion being 'drummed into you parrot fashion' or 'rammed down their throats when they were young' (Abercrombie et al, 1970: 107). We have sought to demonstrate instances where the beliefs and practices prescribed by the socialising agencies of official Catholicism have been eroded over time and modified by processes of trivialization, conventionality, apathy, convenience and self-interest (Hornsby-Smith, Lee and Reilly, 1985).

Thus, for example, the *trivialization* of Catholicism was demonstrated by the picturing of God as an Arab with a beard, or the devil with a tail, or heaven as a place of peace and contentment and hell as a 'fiery furnace'. Other examples include prayer to saints, primarily to assist in the finding of lost objects.

Conventionality was manifested in unreflective references to the three persons of the Trinity, or to God as a holy man, and catechism notions of mortal sin, conscience and will. It could also be discerned in references to routinised and habitual forms of prayer, such as the morning offering and examination of conscience at night, and in references to such slogans as 'the family that prays together stays together' (LS and PI).

Interestingly, *apathy* rather than evil was contrasted with good by a young student (LI) who attended Mass more than weekly. It seems to be indicated by the absence of personal prayer, or the assertion that you can get on with religion if you like it, or the admission that church attendance is contingent upon feeling in the mood. As Abercrombie and his colleagues pointed out, 'apathy may be mistaken for scepticism, ignorance of the claims of religion or dislike of religious pretension' (1970: 114). On the other hand, it is important to be sensitive to structural constraints on commitment and justifiable and defensive non-participation, and the dangers of *a priori* ways of thinking about ordinary people and distorted expectations of them, and ideological bias (Yeo, 1974). An important contribution of in-depth forms of religious research is the exploration of the experiences of ordinary Catholics with the institutional Church and the avoidance of value-judgements about non-participation which neglect these everyday realities.

Finally, we have argued that for many Catholics, teachings about the final judgement, hell and eternal damnation, and the devil, are uncomfortable, unpleasant and inconvenient. Accordingly our interpretation is that in many cases such teachings are either rejected or modified to suit the *convenience* and *self-interest* of the ordinary Catholic. Other examples seem to be the approval of many of the recent changes in the disciplinary rules of the Church in a rather vague, uncritical and passive way. Other interview data, not presented in this chapter, did suggest that changes in the regulations regarding Friday abstinence from meat, or the length of the period of fasting prior to the reception of Holy Communion, or the easing of ecumenical relationships, have resulted in approval not so much because of any ideological awareness of the new religious insights and possibilities, but mainly on grounds of convenience and self-interest (Hornsby-Smith, Lee and Reilly, 1985: 249).

What we have demonstrated in this chapter, therefore, is evidence of a residual form of Catholicism which has been filtered through personal interpretative processes. This has resulted in customary expressions of official Catholicism.

Apart from the evidence of customary Catholicism, our data also point to the existence of what might better be called 'popular Catholicism', with its close links with 'implicit' religion. In the interview extracts we have reviewed, there are numerous instances of superstitious beliefs in luck, good fortune, fate, and the power of charms and rituals. Respondents 'touched wood', were unwilling to walk under ladders, regarded having their house blessed or their grandchildren baptised as important sources of protection, and used prayers, holy pictures and holy water as lucky charms. A speculative article on popular Catholicism identified a number of other manifestations such as the wearing of 'miraculous medals' or the fixing of a St Christopher medallion in the car, the making of pilgrimages, the saying of prayers of indulgence and the wide variety of almost magical insurance policies employed by Catholics to 'save our souls' and guarantee salvation (Hornsby-Smith, 1986b).

It also seems likely that there is an area of 'popular Catholicism' where the borderline between official religion and its customary forms, on the one hand, and instances of 'implicit' or 'folk' religion, on the other hand, becomes quite blurred. Thus, for example, there is the suspicion in the data we have reviewed that flirtations with reincarnation are derived not only from folk religion but also in the search for more convenient and comfortable versions of what are perceived as unacceptably harsh official doctrines of the final judgement, hell and eternal damnation.

We have now concluded our introduction to the everyday religion of Catholics who differ widely in the salience which their religion holds for them, and on various measures of institutional involvement and commitment. In Part III of this book we will explore some of the consequences of these religious beliefs for the notions of religious authority held by English Catholics.

PART III

TRANSFORMATIONS OF RELIGIOUS AUTHORITY

6

THE POPE'S PARADOXICAL PEOPLE

6.1 Introduction

In the previous three chapters we presented, in outline, aspects of the everyday lives of English Catholics and the way they made some sort of religious sense of them. In addition we explored variations between the religious beliefs of core Catholics and ordinary Catholics. In Part III of this book we will consider interview data from English Catholics relating in particular to questions of religious authority in the Roman Catholic Church. As in Part II we will compare some of the comments made in the mid-1970s by lay members of the bishops' advisory commissions with randomly selected samples of ordinary Catholics in four parishes in the Preston and London areas. Before this, however, we will review in this chapter some findings from an interview programme with people who attended one of the six major public events in 1982 during the first visit of a reigning pope to Britain. Details of the two-stage data collection were given above in chapter 1. The analyses presented in this chapter will be based on the 194 usable ten-minute interviews using the schedule given in Appendix III, and on the 120 responses to the short mail questionnaire completed by our Catholic interviewees four months after the pope's visit. In chapter 9 we will review the evidence relating to transformations of religious authority in the Church from a Weberian perspective.

First, though, it is instructive to summarise some of the relevant findings from recent surveys of English Catholics in order to set the more qualitative data in context. In the study of four parishes it was reported that:

attitudes to authority were found to be associated in a limited way with social mobility experiences of Catholics insofar as the stable middle class is rather less likely to be accepting of authority. There is also a slight but significant association between attitudes to authority and frequency of Mass attendance. (Hornsby-Smith, Lee and Reilly, 1984: 363, fn. 8)

We have previously noted that Catholics registered high levels of assent on creedal matters but much lower levels on issues of personal and sexual morality and on Church discipline. Two questions in the 1978 national survey related to the question of religious authority (Hornsby-Smith and Lee, 1979: 193). Thus well over four-fifths of all Catholics and virtually all regular Mass attenders accepted the teaching on apostolic succession and thought it true that 'Jesus directly handed over the leadership of His Church to Peter and the popes'. On the other hand, only three-fifths of all Catholics and only two-fifths of those under twenty-five accepted papal infallibility and thought it was true that 'under certain conditions, when he speaks on matters of faith and morals the pope is infallible'. As many as 31 per cent considered this to be false. On this question there were considerable differences between weekly Mass attenders, 84 per cent of whom thought it was true, and those who had not attended for over a year (35 per cent). Age differences were striking in that only 43 per cent of the 15–24 age group compared to 83 per cent of the 65 and over age group thought it was true, but social class differences were not great. It is possible that the concept of 'infallibility' is misunderstood by many Catholics (Doyle, 1979) but this cannot be determined from the available survey responses.

Other findings from the national survey indicated that the compliance of English Catholics was less than total. For example, two-thirds of all Catholics thought that 'the hierarchy should share more of their control over the affairs of the Church with ordinary Catholics' and that 'you can still be a good Catholic even if you don't go to church', while nearly three-quarters disagreed with the statement 'the individual Catholic has no right to question what the Church teaches'. One-half thought that 'ordinary Catholics should have a greater say in the choice of their parish priest' and well over one-half wanted more say in money matters. Even so, two-thirds agreed that 'these days people want firm moral guidance from the

Church rather than talk about freedom of conscience'. These some-what conflicting attitudes suggest that, in general, Catholics want firm guidelines from the religious leadership, but the freedom to decide for themselves. Finally, only one-quarter thought that obeying the teaching of the Church was a very important identifying char-acteristic of Catholics. On all these questions there were generally noticeable differences between regular attenders at Mass and non-attenders, and between the youngest and oldest age groups. In general 'Catholics are more likely to be critical of the institutional Church or of its authorities or of its official teachings or regulations the younger they are' (Hornsby-Smith and Lee, 1979: 194–5; 130–1).

It is in their relationship with their parish priest that most Catholics come closest to the issues of religious authority. The 1978 national survey showed that English Catholics rated their priests quite highly on eleven aspects of their work. All the same, they were relatively open to new forms of ministry. More than half would accept married priests and as many as one-quarter women priests (Hornsby-Smith and Lee, 1979: 208–9), both possibilities sub-stantially discounted by the present pope. In sum the survey findings we have reviewed seem to indicate the existence of a considerable body of latent dissent from the official teachings on the nature of religious authority in the Church.

In this chapter we will look at some of the findings from our research at the time of the visit of Pope John-Paul II to England in 1982. We were mainly concerned with the question of religious authority, so that our questions were focused on the reasons for attending the public events, the perceptions of the pope's leadership style, and the pope's teaching, especially in the areas of personal and sexual morality.

6.2 The pope's visit: a special event

In an earlier work (Hornsby-Smith, 1987: 26–31) it was argued that historical evidence from the Victorian period indicated clearly that there was no golden past in post-Reformation Catholicism in England. Survey data for the 1970s showed that a high degree of heterodoxy of both belief and practice persisted, so that it made sense to distinguish different types of Catholics (Hornsby-Smith, Lee and Turcan, 1982; Hornsby-Smith, 1987: 47–55). A variety of Catholic attitudes to papal authority was therefore only to be expected.

Nevertheless, a number of uncertainties remained and the papal visit in 1982 provided a valuable opportunity to explore further the extent of religious change within the Roman Catholic community in England and Wales, particularly as it bore on prevailing notions of religious authority, especially that attributed to the pope.

It would seem that three stages in the historical evolution of English Catholicism in the post-Reformation period can be distinguished. Before the restoration of the hierarchy in 1850, the Catholic gentry wielded authority in the Church at the local level (Bossy, 1975). Following the restoration of the hierarchy, the lay leadership was rapidly replaced by a clerical leadership which was powerfully legitimated following the definition of the doctrine of papal infallibility at the unfinished First Vatican Council in 1870. The judgement of history is likely to be that a one-sided view of papal authority, encouraged by a growing Roman centralism and an English episcopacy with a sycophantic, ultramontane ideology, led to a very marked English loyalty and deference to the pope and to papal pronouncements. Arguably these excesses only began to be corrected after the Second Vatican Council from 1962 to 1965 inaugurated the third stage and proclaimed the countervailing teachings on collegiality, the mission of the whole 'People of God', the right to religious freedom and personal conscience, and so on. It has been suggested that in this third stage, clerical forms of domination are being replaced by new forms of domination by the middle-class, articulate, progressive , activist laity (Archer, 1986; Hornsby-Smith, 1987).

What was uncertain before the Pope's visit was which group of Catholics with what types of loyalties would be most attracted by the uniqueness of the occasion. For example, it was uncertain to what extent the convenience of television coverage was likely to weigh heavily with many traditional Catholics, who a generation previously might have flocked to see the 'sacred' presence of the 'vicar of Christ'. Furthermore, it was not obvious to what extent the maturation of English Catholicism in the previous decade or so, and the emergence from the fortress Church, was likely to manifest itself in a decline in an uncritical adulation of the papacy and a stronger assertion of the rights of the local Church. In general terms, therefore, the first ever visit of a reigning pope to Britain provided a valuable opportunity to confirm and extend the analysis of social and religious change in English Catholicism.

It is worth recalling that the invitation to Pope John-Paul II to visit

Britain had been made by Cardinal Hume and Archbishop Worlock when they presented him with a copy of *The Easter People*, which was the official response of the bishops of England and Wales to the 1980 National Pastoral Congress. This congress, attended by all the bishops, over 300 priests and around 1,700 lay delegates, had generally been regarded by those attending it as a marvellous experience of a 'People of God' model of the Church. In their response the bishops had written enthusiastically about the 'Sharing Church' with lay people regarded as fully participating members (Anon, 1981: 307–28). An earlier, more bureaucratic model of the Church officially appeared to have been relegated to the history books.

However, in spite of its origins, the papal visit bore very little relationship to the N.P.C. At no time did the seven Sector Presidents who had been influential in the planning and execution of the Congress and the writing of its radical, if tactful, reports formally meet the pope. In fact, in spite of all the talk about the 'Sharing Church', organised laity had no opportunity at all to talk with the pope. It seemed that Pope John-Paul II had come to speak *to* the laity, and indeed, during his visit the only people the pope appeared to have the opportunity to *listen* to were representatives of the British Council of Churches at an ecumenical occasion at Canterbury.

Some reservations about the visit, which took place at the height of the Falklands conflict, had been expressed beforehand. There were criticisms of the attempts made to finance the visit and the marketing of souvenirs. Some, perhaps still reflecting the defensive mentality of a fortress Church, feared the visit would simply arouse latent anti-Catholic sentiments. More progressive elements thought it would resurrect an older ultramontanism and re-establish a more traditional and hierarchical model of the Church just when it seemed, in the aftermath of the N.P.C., that English Catholicism was growing to a new maturity and self-confidence. Others were worried that a conservative pope would act to control ecumenical aspirations and collaboration following the publication of the final report of the Anglican–Roman Catholic International Commission (1982), and still others feared the pastoral consequences of yet another condemnation of contraception. In the event, none of these fears was realised.

Around one million people, or perhaps one-third of the numbers hoped for by the Catholic authorities, went to see Pope John-Paul II at the six public Masses or services, over a very warm May Bank

Holiday in 1982, at Wembley, Coventry, Liverpool, Manchester, York and Cardiff. Our interview returns suggest that around five-sixths of them were Catholics. About one-third of the participants were local to one of the events and had travelled under ten miles. Another third came from the region, a distance of up to fifty miles, while about one quarter had travelled further. Why did they go, often travelling uncomfortably through the night to wait for hours with temperatures in the eighties, only to find themselves in the end several hundreds of yards from the pope?

Fourteen distinct reasons for attending one of the events were identified. Most people gave more than one reason. These were analysed using the Guttman Lingoes Smallest Space Analysis to provide a spatial interpretation of the motives (Brown and O'Byrne, 1982). The SSA plot indicated that 'to see the pope' was the central reason for attending for most people. One half of our respondents gave this as their main reason, either as a simple statement of fact:

I wanted to see the Holy Father; it's as simple as that. (Wembley)

I've come because I wanted to come, really to see him. And that's it really. (York)

or qualified by an expression of the desire to see the pope in person:

To see His Holiness, of course. I know you can see him on television, but oh! it's so marvellous seeing him here; seeing him live. I think He's a wonderful man. (Coventry)

Apart from this central reason, three other clusters of reasons were identified. Firstly, there were specifically *religious* motives for attending, such as participating in the Mass. This group of reasons also included the notion, mentioned by one in eight of the participants, that it was one's duty as a Catholic to be there out of a sense of loyalty and identity:

I came because I'm a Catholic and it's my religion and the pope is the leader of the Catholic faith. So we came to see him. (York)

The reason 'came because it is a unique event', mentioned by nearly one-third of our interviewees, seems to belong to this group because people interpreted this in terms of the visible presence of the pope:

Oh! it's such an occasion, I couldn't miss it. And, I mean, we may not have another occasion like this in a life time. (Wembley)

Also belonging to this cluster is the view that the interviewee was unlikely to see the pope in the Vatican:

I've always wanted to go to Rome to see the pope. Many times I've planned a trip like that. We've never made it. So this was ideal. He's coming to me rather than me going to him. (Wembley)

A few participants indicated that they were of Polish extraction and that this particular pope was very special to them:

I'm a Catholic and my parents were born in Poland itself. And this has the extra-special meaning for them, being a Polish pope, you see. (York)

The second cluster of reasons had to do with *participation* in a unique and historical event in community and solidarity with others. One in five of the participants were attending 'to experience the atmosphere' personally by being there:

I'd like to be in the atmosphere when there's so much trouble in the world. There are so many people together on this occasion when they'll be happy together. (Wembley)

The third cluster of motives for attending was labelled *secular*. For example, one participant in ten came with someone else or at their (e.g. their spouse's) request. It also included a few who had come quite spontaneously to participate in a great event:

I mean, I go and see royalty, don't I, and other people that comes, archbishops and that. If they were to come, I would still be here. (Liverpool)

Participants were also asked what lasting effects of the visit they expected. The answers reflected both personal and global concerns. Again, by using the Smallest Space Analysis, three broad clusters of responses were identified. Firstly, just over half the participants expressed expectations regarding *Christian Unity*. Included under this broad heading were the hopes that fellow-countrymen would accept Catholics as ordinary citizens and the overcoming of any remaining prejudices about them:

It's wonderful for England to have him here isn't it? ... Yes, I think it's beautiful because, when you look at all them hundreds of years back, you know there was never a pope allowed in (Wembley)

There was also a strong feeling, expressed by nearly one quarter of the participants, that the pastoral activities of Pope John-Paul II had changed the face of the papacy and the way it was perceived:

Because the other popes were sort of shut away in the Vatican and now this one, he's travelled all over ... it lets people know he's a real human man ... I just hope it's the start of a lot of them now ... that they'll all travel. (Wembley)

A second cluster of expectations of around one quarter of the participants focused around the theme of the *revitalisation* of the Catholic Church and the strengthening of personal faith, mentioned by one in ten, or encouragement to the 'lapsed' to return to full religious practice, referred to by one in fifteen:

Well, what is special is that he is the leader of the Catholic Church, so it's going to be great spiritually for the Catholic people for him coming here. (Coventry)

Perhaps for lapsed Catholics this may ... return back to the Church. (Wembley)

I have total faith in my religion now. Before I was a bit lukewarm, but now I believe he has strengthened my faith and I totally accept the Catholic religion. (York)

The third cluster of expectations expressed hopes for *peace* in general, mentioned by one participant in eight, for some sort of influence in the Falklands conflict, mentioned by one in ten, or generally to represent non-materialistic values, mentioned by over one-fifth of our respondents:

I just hope that, particularly with regard to the Falklands crisis, people are going to ... be a bit ... less aggressive and, well, more thoughtful of others, and in particular, say with regards to the Falklands, perhaps they'll be ... a bit less ... of a hard-nosed approach to the whole thing. (Wembley)

In sum, there seems to be no doubt at all that for those participants at the six different public events we surveyed, the visit of Pope John-Paul II in 1982 was of great historical importance, an event of a lifetime not to be missed. Some attended for this reason alone, drawn by the media interest and the personal attractiveness of a major figure on the world scene. For many Catholics, though, there were, in addition, specifically religious concerns: excitement at the coming of the first reigning pope, as head of the Roman Catholic Church, a focus of special loyalty and attention, to celebrate Mass *with* them. There were in our respondents' comments, shades of a partly defiant assertion of a separate minority religious identity, and partly a hopeful expectation that the years of hostility and suspicion might now, at last, be over. These hopes were partly social, but also partly religious in that ecumenical expectations were prominent. Relief and gratitude that the pope had after all come to Britain in the middle of the Falklands conflict were flavoured with a yearning for peace and the hope that somehow, as a world leader, he might have a pacifying influence in the dispute with Argentina.

Four months after the pope's visit, the Catholic participants we had interviewed were sent a brief mail questionnaire to invite their considered reflections after the euphoria of the event had died down. Our interviewees were asked if the event they had attended had lived up to or exceeded their expectations. On all seven aspects considered, a substantial majority felt that the visit had done so, though one-third did not believe it had been 'a pleasant way of spending a day out'. For our present purposes it is of particular interest that nearly one in four felt that the visit had failed 'as a demonstration of the involvement of the laity in the Church'. On the other hand, only one in thirteen felt that the visit had failed 'as a dialogue between the pope and the people'. About two-thirds claimed to have 'thought seriously about the message of the pope and his sermons since the visit'. In terms of the longer-term impact of the visit, large majorities felt it had been beneficial, especially in encouraging Christian Unity and in showing 'people that Catholics are an ordinary cross-section of British society'. However, over one-third felt that the visit had not helped 'to bring lapsed Catholics back to the Church' and over one-fifth felt it had not informed 'non-Catholics about the nature of Catholic belief and practice'.

6.3 The pope's leadership style

In our interviews we asked people what they thought the main job of the pope was, in general terms, and then what they thought about Pope John-Paul II. While some people answered the first question with reference to the present incumbent, in general people did distinguish between their perceptions of the role and the attributes of the man. This was demonstrated by Smallest Space Analysis (Brown and O'Byrne, 1980) which also distinguished the role of a pope in world terms as well as in terms of a specific function within the Roman Catholic Church.

About half our interviewees saw the pope as the head or representative of the Church. For many people, the prime task of the pope was to hold the Church together:

Well, I think that at the present moment the main job of the pope is keeping all Catholics together. (York)

Related to this was the role of pastoral leadership. Around one-quarter of our interviewees specifically mentioned his role of spiritual guidance and teaching. The model of the shepherd featured in a number of responses:

[To] state, as he has stated, the teachings of the Church. And he has stuck to his ground [on] all the moral issues, which we may not like, but those are the facts and he hasn't given ground on them at all . . . The actual basic teachings he has stuck to absolutely rigidly to them; which I think is right. (Cardiff)

Well, his main job is to be the shepherd of his flock, to lead his sheep, to guide them in the way that he thinks is best. And we are given to believe that he is inspired to help us in that way and if he can. (Coventry)

The Petrine claims were explicitly mentioned by around one in eight respondents while one in six saw the pope as the executive head of a global organisation:

Well, he's . . . like a king, really. He's our ruler, the successor of Christ and St Peter. (Manchester)

The importance of effective communication of his teaching was stressed by several interviewees. In particular, an important role of the pope was that of 'listening more to what is coming from the people' (Liverpool):

I say this about a pope and about many . . . ministers of all religions, that they should mix more with the people. Don't keep themselves aloof from the people. The people like to see them, you know, and they want to be part 'n parcel of them. (Liverpool)

Apart from his role specifically as the religious leader of the Roman Catholic Church, it was considered to be important that the pope promotes Christian Unity. Furthermore, two-fifths or more of our interviewees saw the pope as a significant world religious leader:

I think this is the main job of the pope, to hold the Church together, to bring people together, of all denominations. I think most religions look up to the pope, you know . . . I think that is what it is all about. (Manchester)

To lead the Christian world in the direction that God wants it to go in. (Cardiff)

Finally, the role of the pope was to demonstrate love and compassion for people. Around one-fifth of our interviewees particularly mentioned the role of peacemaker:

Giving love ... he's the leader of the Catholic Church, so we all look up to him. But also he's a shining example of love for people and, er, I think he brings out this love in people in each other. Makes them stop and think what it's all about. (Coventry)

I think, quite honestly, he's a peacemaker, too, because if the pope can't speak on peace, then who can? (York)

When our interviewees were asked to comment on Pope John-Paul II as a person, about two-thirds of them offered overwhelmingly positive evaluations of his personal qualities. We identified over seventy adjectives used to describe him: 'smashing', 'lovely', 'great', 'marvellous', 'tremendous', 'fantastic', 'gorgeous', 'nice', and so on. A distinct group of descriptors related to his ordinariness and humanity; he was likened to a father, grandfather and uncle, but also a 'good drinking partner' (Coventry), and was seen to have the ability to 'create friendship' (Liverpool). Several referred to his 'charisma', his superstar-like magnetic attractiveness, his intelligence and facility with languages:

He's very human; he's not somebody that's on a pillar. (York)

He has this marvellous human quality whereby you look at him and think 'wouldn't he make a wonderful father?' He has this great gift of dealing with people. (Liverpool)

... down-to-earth, homely, more of a man of the people than before, because he does not look aloof. (Manchester)

Well he's human, isn't he? He can yawn and can join in the singing and all this. I think he's lovely. (Cardiff)

Some working-class Catholics saw him as one who, like them, had suffered, and knew from experience the difficulties of life. In this sense he was 'the People's Pope' and they rejoiced in his coming out of the Vatican to visit them on their own ground:

I think because of his background, the fact that he is a Pole and has endured so many hardships ... (Wembley)

This one is a man of the people ... He is also a working man; he's worked for a living, hasn't he? So I don't know. I just think he's great. (Cardiff)

The comments on his humanity contrasted interestingly with comments on his 'Christ-like' qualities as 'a perfect example', and his holiness:

I think he's a very good man and he is doing his best to do what he thinks is right for the Catholic Church. (Cardiff)

One-half of our interviewees also commented on his behaviour, especially his willingness to travel, his not-sticking to protocol, his physical touching of children and the sick.

He was holding some very severely retarded children and he bent down to kiss a very severely retarded little child and I thought that was touching. (Cardiff)

Some saw his election as divinely inspired:

I think he was 'chosen' by the Spirit in a very special way ... I think ... he is certainly sent by God to our times. (Liverpool)

On the other hand, about one in seven of our Catholic respondents felt that the pope was out of touch with the problems facing people and a few specifically mentioned his conservatism:

Perhaps this pope isn't as, um, progressive as people might hope. (Wembley)

In some ways I think he's a very, can be a very hard man. But he has disciplined himself to become that. I just think he is wonderful, the right man for the job. (Cardiff)

In sum, although Pope John-Paul II was regarded in very positive terms as a most attractive person, it was acknowledged with some reservations that he adopted a firm and conservative stance on many issues which concerned ordinary Catholics.

We used the follow-up mail survey to explore further the perceptions of the present pope's leadership style. Respondents were asked to select one of two alternative statements relating to the direction of communication flow between the pope and people, whether or not the pope shared authority in the Church in this country with the bishops, and whether or not he consulted the laity before teaching. In sum, although only one in five of our respondents thought that 'in general lines of communication flow up from the people to the pope', nearly three-fifths thought 'the pope shares authority with the bishops in England and Wales' and well over half thought that 'the pope teaches only after consulting the laity'.

Jennifer Brown (1982; Hornsby-Smith, Brown and O'Byrne, 1983) subjected these data to a faceted model of leadership styles proposed by Shapira (1976). She found that only one in five Catholics viewed the pope's leadership as 'directive', that is authoritarian, on all three measures (behaviour, locus of power, and locus of information). 'The remainder see it in some degree as participative, but disagree in the perceived amount and kind of participation'. These include one-fifth who regard the pope's leadership style as 'negative', one-quarter as 'participative' and one-ninth as 'delegative'. One in six respondents selected what Brown calls a 'reflexive' profile not defined by Shapira but encompassed within her model, and where the 'leader's behaviour is seen as democratic, with the locus of power and information residing with the "boss"'. In further analyses, Brown showed that those selecting the 'directive' profile were least likely to favour married priests; those selecting the 'negotiative' profile were older than the average; those selecting the 'participative' profile were disproportionately female, involved in parish activity and favouring a political role for the Church. Those selecting the 'delegative' profile were disproportionately male, uninvolved in parish activities and sympathetic to married priests, while those selecting the 'reflexive' profile were also disproportionately male. Brown concluded her analysis by noting that 'the most intriguing finding is perhaps that there is not a consensually agreed leadership style to describe Catholics' perceptions of the pope'.

It should be noted in interpreting these results that the respondents were disproportionately involved and committed Catholics. Thus five-sixths of them reported that they attended Mass at least weekly compared to under two-fifths of Catholics generally and one-third belonged to a parish organisation compared to one-eighth of all Catholics. The proportion of orthodox attenders was more than twice that of English Catholics generally. Only one-quarter appeared to be in a manual occupation compared to over one-half of all Catholics, and a disproportionate number had had some form of higher education.

6.4 Papal teaching and authority

Following our invitation to comment on the role of the pope in general and the particular leadership style of the present pope, we introduced two key questions on papal authority. The first asked: 'Do you feel bound to obey all his teachings?' Although five-sixths of the Catholics we interviewed claimed to attend Mass weekly, their responses spanned the whole range from unconditional acceptance of the pope's teaching to outright rejection. While classification of these responses proved to be difficult, two coders working independently reached agreement that one-quarter of the interviewees gave unqualified acceptance to the pope's teaching. Just over one-half gave a qualified acceptance, or appeared confused, or replied that they would 'pick and choose'. The remaining quarter did not accept the pope's teaching. An indication of the nature and range of these unpremeditated comments from all six research sites is given in Table 6.1.

The first groups of responses (1–5) gives something of the flavour of those who gave an unqualified acceptance to the pope's teaching. Response 3 gives a hint that such acceptance is regarded as something inevitable if one wishes to profess a Catholic affiliation. The next response (4) goes further and explicitly pays deference to the charisma of the office-holder as pope. The fifth response is more difficult to categorise since it stresses the notion that the pope's teaching provides guidelines (see also 16–19). In this case the interviewee stresses his view that these guidelines ought to be followed without question by Catholics.

In her analysis of these data, Ann Scurfield observed that most respondents in this category, who were nearly all middle-aged or elderly and stressed their traditional or 'old-style' upbringing, 'felt they had to elaborate, often at some length, at times in an almost apologetic way, the reasons why they felt bound to obey' (1982: 955). Responses 6 and 7 illustrate these almost automatic reactions. They seem to indicate an almost unreflective response of those who have the ascribed status and identity of Roman Catholic. Rather like sex or ethnicity, it is something one is born with, part of one's fundamental identity; one cannot do anything about it. The drift of much of our research into English Catholicism over the past fifteen years is that this type of response is rapidly declining with the dissolution of the distinct Catholic sub-culture as a result of post-war social and post-Vatican religious change (Hornsby-Smith, 1987: 208–14).

The second group of responses all qualify their acceptance of the pope's teaching in some way or other. Six different subgroups might be identified. The first of these (8–11) distinguishes between those

Table 6.1. *Classification of responses to papal teaching*
(Pope's visit; six events)

A. *Unqualified Acceptance*

1. Er, well, I do, yes. I'm quite happy to do so. (Coventry)
2. I wouldn't doubt him or anything (York)
3. Oh yes ... I obey the pope's teachings, every pope. And if we don't go with the pope, we might as well give up our religion (Cardiff)
4. Yes, I do ... and I feel that I, as a lay person, cannot possibly have studied religion in the same way that he has done, to come to the same conclusions. I know we all have our own free will of our own ... But nevertheless, I feel that someone of his stature ... who has devoted his life to religion and so on, that his conclusions, therefore, must be more accurate than mine. (Wembley)
5. I think that the pope is there to give you guidance ... for you to follow and I think ... it's your choice what you eventually decide. But he does give guidelines, which I think ought to be followed if you're a Catholic. (Coventry)

product of upbringing

6. Well yes. I've never thought about it like that. You know, when you're brought up a Catholic you accept ... all that sort of thing, really. You don't ... question it. Perhaps when you are older ... but not me. I just accept. (Coventry)
7. Yes, I'm afraid I do 'cause I suppose I'm a bit old hat ... I've been brought up that way. But, of course, I know that the younger people these days ... look at things in a different light. And I think they're brought up different to we were, you know. (Liverpool)

B. *Qualified Acceptance*

when teaching infallibly

8. Well, this might sound a bit naive, but we think what he does say, when he's speaking for all Catholics in the world, he is divinely inspired. So we believe practically everything he says. (Manchester)
9. Er, if he was speaking *ex cathedra*, yes, as an infallible, on a matter of faith and morals, yes ... Well, there's nothing ... that I disagree with him about. (Manchester)
10. Yes ... in the sense that, um, I believe in the doctrine of infallibility. So in certain aspects of doctrine, where he decides, if you are a Catholic, you have got to accept it. But in other matters, of course, one can make one's own decision. Conscience, to that extent, is very personal. (Coventry)
11. Well, I think if one is putting it into theological terms, when it is speaking *ex cathedra*, I do, because I feel that's almost a definition of being a Catholic. Er, when he's speaking on, er, social and related matters, no. (Wembley)

other contingent

12. In principle, yes, but ... sometimes ... I think some of them are a bit shaky ... if the idea is right, then I'll support it. (York)
13. Well, we do make up our own minds on some things but mostly we believe in the teachings. (Cardiff)
14. That's quite a difficult question to answer. If you say an outright 'no', it looks like you are denying some aspects of your faith. If you say 'yes', it wouldn't be true. (Liverpool)
15. Yes, most of it I feel bound to obey ... there are certain things I'd rather make my own mind up about. (Coventry)

Table 6.1. *cont.*

guidelines

16. Um. Well, I think the commandments are guidelines, I mean, and it's the same for the pope, that they are there for ideals. But you can't always live up to ideals. (Cardiff)
17. Not all . . . He's not saying 'you have to do everything I say'. He's just trying to teach what we should do . . . but leaving it up to yourself whether you do or don't. (Liverpool)
18 No, I wouldn't go so far as to say that. I can think for meself. I've got to admit . . . I'm guided to a very large extent. (Manchester)
19. They're guidelines. I think everybody has their own individual faith . . . Yes, I believe in the Catholic teachings, but . . . I think everybody has different views on all of them. (Wembley)

conscience

20. Um, I think it's up to everybody's personal conscience, and I try to . . . it's a very personal thing. Mm, and really, throughout life you just have to try and do the best you can, following the lines, but if it's impossible, then it's impossible. (Cardiff)
21. I think one accepts the teachings but nobody but the individual can ultimately . . . determine how they might apply to himself at every juncture of life. (Coventry)
22. I wouldn't feel obliged to if it didn't sort of go along with my own . . . I mean if it was my conscience that sort of decided first of all but . . . certainly I would listen to the things he's got to say and take it very much into consideration. (Wembley)
23 No, I have me own conscience on some of the Catholic teaching. But basically his ideas are great to unite all Christians. (Manchester)
24. I don't know that I feel bound to obey them but I feel that they're right and that I should obey them . . . I think that by praying and everything else it helps you to make up your mind. (Wembley)

teaching and practice

25. Well you can try to do them all. Whether you achieve it is another thing, isn't it? (Manchester)
26. Um. I try but, er, strictly speaking the answer is yes, of course. But, um, not without some reservations and misgivings. (Wembley)
27. I think it's up to the individual . . . I don't think that anyone just sticks to the Catholic faith just like that. I mean, they all have their own ways of living their life. (Liverpool)

anticipation of change

28. Er, bound, yes . . . but I think there is a couple that are completely out of date . . . they should try and slightly modernise it . . . . Some principles are completely out of date. (Wembley)
29. Yes, but I do think that many of these things that they talk about are goner change in the future . . . I don't think they're goner be so dogmatical as they've been in the past, you know. (Liverpool)
30. Er . . . infallibility, I think . . . has lost its edge . . . I think it would be unwise if we were ever to make any er rulings, say on doctrine, er with the power of infallibility; I think that is unlikely ever to happen again, er, simply because people are very much more open-minded, um, better educated, and they don't always need this sort of rigid doctrine to show them where to go. (Wembley)

Table 6.1. *cont.*

C. *Rejection*

31. No ... I don't feel bound to go by his 100 per cent word (Coventry)
32. No. No, not at all ... Um. I think ... it's ... a matter of conscience ... He is there to lead you to guide you, but it's down to your own personal conscience. (Liverpool)
33. No ... not in every aspect, I suppose. I use my own conscience where ... I see fit to. (Wembley)
34. No, no. I think there are ... some things that you've got to make your own judgement on. (Manchester)
35. Yes, no, I go my own way really. I ... think I try to think things out. (Wembley)
36. Ar, well, I don't know about that. I think everybody's pleased theirselves, don't they, you know? I don't know ... No. (Cardiff)

cases where the pope claims to be teaching infallibly and those where he does not. Few Catholics had any problems about following the pope in doctrinal matters, but clearly many Catholics – around one-half of those attending the papal events – felt they could use their own conscience 'when he's speaking ... on social and related matters' (11), often a euphemism for contraception, abortion and divorce. The second group (12–15) were similar, though they did not specific-ally refer to infallible teachings and other teachings. A good example of a respondent's attempt to make some sort of distinction is Respondent 14 who is concerned not to give the impression of denying 'some aspect of your faith', that is doctrinal beliefs. As we have previously noted, some respondents specifically argued that the pope's teaching was intended to offer guidelines for action, not invariable rules of behaviour for all circumstances (16–19). These respondents are implicitly arguing their right to make up their own minds, even if in the knowledge of the pope's guidelines. The fourth subgroup specifically articulates this in terms of personal conscience (20–4). Respondent 24 insists that one has to make up one's own mind on all matters and recommends prayer in coping with the dilemma of reconciling this with the pope's teaching. The fifth subgroup distinguishes between the theory and actual practice (25–7), indicating that while there may be no fundamental disagree-ment with the teaching, nevertheless, in the facing of everyday problems, it is necessary to be pragmatic or 'realistic' about one's practice. In the case of the sixth subgroup (28–30), the qualification of acceptance of the pope's teaching is considerable and typically, reference is made to the modification or 'modernising' of teachings regarded as 'out-of-date' (28) with contemporary needs.

The third broad group of responses, offered by around one-quarter of our respondents, was a substantially unqualified rejection of the need to follow the pope's teaching. As Ann Scurfield reported (1982: 955), these Catholics appeared content in many cases simply to reply 'No' or 'No, not at all' without further elaboration. This can be discerned from the relative brevity of the examples given (31–6). Ann Scurfield regarded the combination of overwhelmingly positive evaluations of Pope John-Paul II, with the emphasis expressed by many of our interviewees on 'making up one's own mind', as paradoxical; she concluded that 'most Catholics living and worshipping in England and Wales put greater reliance on private judgement than on Church orthodoxy in many areas of their lives' (1982: 956).

These findings were given quantitative elaboration in the returns from the postal survey of our interviewees four months after the pope's visit. They were asked to select between three pairs of alternatives relating to the authority of the pope. Of those responding, about four-fifths believed that 'the pope's teachings are all directly inspired by God', rather than being 'his personal view of things'. Similarly, about five-sixths of the respondents felt that 'the pope's teachings show that he really understands the problems that face people living in the modern world' while only one-sixth felt he was 'rather out of touch' with them. On the other hand just over one-half considered 'one can question and then disobey some of the pope's teachings and still be a good Catholic' while just under one-half thought that 'as a good Catholic one should try to obey all the pope's teachings without question'.

These findings seem to be consistent with the conclusions that:
(a) Catholics generally accept the pope as an authoritative guide but reserve the right to 'make up their own minds' in most areas of their lives; and:
(b) they distinguish between core doctrinal beliefs, on which they are inclined to accept claims of infallible teaching, on the one hand, and teachings on other matters, for example social and personal morality, and also questions of Church discipline such as the Sunday Mass obligation and rules prescribing a celibate clergy and proscribing intercommunion, on the other hand, where they feel entitled to use their own conscience.

This leads us to the second key question in our interviews with people at the papal events in 1982. We asked: 'Are there any matters you feel entitled to make up your own mind about?' About one-quarter of our interviewees explicitly referred to contraception. As we have suggested earlier, several other people seemed to be using euphemisms for birth control; in longer interviews this could have been explored further. Smaller numbers of respondents also mentioned abortion, divorce, married priests, the role of women in the Church, keeping the Mass attendance obligation, pre-marital sex, and making up their own minds generally.

Our question prompted some defensive sparring from several of our interviewees. Thus a young woman interviewed at Coventry laughed and said: 'Oh! I'm not going into that!' and an older man in Liverpool replied 'You're getting very deep there, aren't you?' A mother interviewed at Wembley said: 'Oh yes there are! My very personal matters', and proceeded to imply that she would have found it difficult to be a good mother if she had any more children. Several comments hinted more-or-less strongly at contraception, such as the man at Manchester who commented: 'the obvious thing, you know. You have to live in the modern age. You have to decide for yourself how many children you are going to have'.

The following extract from an interview with a young woman at Coventry reflects both a generally defensive posture, and also an assumption of implicit, shared understandings with the interviewer of what it is like to be a Catholic:

I. Are there any matters you feel entitled to make your own mind up about?
R. Um. [Pause] Um, I don't know. When you're young it's a lot more difficult to know, um, how far you go to being good, or something. It's easier, I suppose, for older – well, if you get what I mean (laughs). When you're young there are so many pressures around you to conform to what everybody else is doing. A lot of people often question why you are a Catholic and say it's a lot more fun not to be, and, er, but you just have to be strong and so [laughs]. But, er, I try to, you know, live up to the teachings.
I. But you haven't quite said there are any matters you feel entitled to make up your own mind on
R. Um. Well I make up my own mind on all of them, but I bear in mind what I've been taught. There isn't a particular issue I've really ever come to grief over, if you know what I mean. So I suppose, in the main, I would try and agree with all of them, you know. There isn't anything I would really, you know.

There are hints in this extract that the respondent deviates in some respects from the pope's teaching, which she recognises as providing guidelines, but offers 'excuses' ('when you're young there are so many pressures'), in Scott and Lyman's sense (1968), for her implicit behaviour. One can also discern here something of the flavour of the 'customary' religion we discussed in the previous chapter and of the somewhat calculative nature of Catholic moral practice ('how far you go', reminiscent of David Lodge's novel, 1980).

Not all our interviewers probed further when people responded defensively to our question. One respondent at Coventry was pushed by his interviewer to clarify his rather vague comments in response to the same initial question:

R. I think it's a question of definition, really. No, I think there's a question of a teaching and the question of its applicability. I mean, killing, I mean murder is forbidden, but they say there is such a thing as a 'just war'. You know there are a number of defined circumstances, er. One hopes it never happens to one but one could find oneself in a situation when one would say, at this moment, you know, should I, am I justified in killing another person? That's just by way of example. Um, and, er, there are obviously other people who find themselves in regard to particular teachings, you know, doctrines, in the same sort of situation, you know.

I. What have you in mind?

R. Um. Nothing more than anything else. Both of us know what teachings the Catholic Church is most questioned [about] at the moment, um . . .

I. Do you mean contraception?

R. Well the whole range: contraception, divorce, abortion, yes, yes, yes.

There is in this extract something of a Catholic casuistry (the distinction between a teaching and its applicability) as well as a Catholic prudery (the avoidance of mentioning sexual matters explicitly). But there is also evidence that ordinary Catholics, even if they are regularly practising and institutionally involved, are not uniformly rigid in their stance on the issues not only of contraception but also on divorce and even abortion, often regarded as particularly abhorrent to Catholic eyes. Thus a woman at Cardiff replied:

Well yes . . . I mean, not necessarily myself, but as on birth control, if people, I think people do use it, then I think that it is up to them, their own conscience, especially if it's a 'mixed' marriage . . . You know it's a very difficult problem. I do think it's a personal thing and people will make their own minds. Most people anyway . . . But, er, divorce. It's regrettable and very sad, but there again, if people can't live together then, you know, it's very hard to stay together. I think it's just a really very personal [matter of] conscience.

This perhaps indicates something of a pragmatic judgement in the light of everyday realities, not so much as a rejection of the teachings which are still implicitly recognised as legitimate and authoritative guidelines. A common view was that 'it is up to them, really' in these matters. The following extract from an interview at Wembley in response to the same question reflects a general rejection of the official teaching on contraception but also a continuing general (but not universal) opposition to abortion:

I. Do you feel bound to obey all his teachings?
R. Um. I try but, er. Strictly the answer is yes, of course, but, um, not without some reservations and misgivings.
I. Uh hm.
R. And in fact I don't in practice follow them all anyway. But, er, that's something I keep close to my heart [laughs].
I. You wouldn't elaborate on that, would you?
R. No.
I. Fair enough. Are there any matters you feel entitled to make your own mind up about then?
R. Well I think birth control is the, is the basic ...
I. Mm.
R. problem. On things like abortions and that sort of thing, of course I'm totally in agreement with the Church. Um. I think birth control is the one controversial subject that we try to deal with, or the pope's tried to deal with, that I really don't too much agree with the way he's come out.

These extracts have been selected to give something of the flavour of people's response to our questions in a situation where extended probing was not possible. Four months after the interviews we were able to test some of the findings more systematically in the mail questionnaire which was answered by nearly three-quarters of the Catholics previously interviewed. We asked a version of some of the key questions in the 1978 national survey (Hornsby-Smith and Lee, 1979), simplified to require responses of either 'yes' or 'no'. The results parallel those of the national survey when taking account of the fact that those attending the papal events were much more institutionally involved than Catholics generally. Thus six-sevenths of our respondents accepted the official teaching on the consecration but only just under three-fifths agreed that 'under certain conditions, when he speaks on matters of faith and morals, the pope is infallible'. Under one-quarter thought there had been too many changes in the Church recently though seven in every ten respondents did not approve of the reduction in the number of traditional devotions in the Church. Nearly two-thirds did not think the Church was right to condemn birth control but three-fifths did agree with the condemnation of pre-marital sex. Finally just under one-half agreed with the view that 'the Church should become more involved in politics in the pursuit of social justice'.

6.5 Paradoxical Catholics?

It is appropriate to recall the limits of the data we have reviewed in this chapter. Nearly two hundred interviews were conducted with people attending six of the public events during the visit of Pope John-Paul II to Britain in 1982. The respondents were not randomly selected, but we did attempt to ensure roughly equal numbers of both the over- and under 35s in both sexes. Interviews were tape-recorded normally during the long period of waiting prior to the appearance of the pope. Because people were concerned to obtain an optimal position and to participate in the noisy preliminaries before the pope arrived, our interviews lasted no longer than ten to fifteen minutes so that no extended probing was possible.

In spite of these limitations, the results are extremely suggestive. The Catholics we interviewed were generally committed and institutionally involved. Nearly all attended Mass regularly. Even so, while they clearly regarded the pope as both an important world figure and religious leader, and commented overwhelmingly in favourable terms on him as a person, they were nevertheless ambivalent about his leadership style and deeply divided about his teaching and their compliance to it. It was for these reasons that Ann Scurfield wrote that:

it is paradoxical, to say the least, to hear such Catholics evince disobedience to, disagreement with and even in some cases hostility towards, not just the church as an institution but also towards some of the most important and fundamental teachings of the Church, and yet continue in apparently happy and untroubled identification with their faith. (1982: 955)

In a subsequent comment it was suggested that, while Pope John-Paul II was an appealing religious witness, 'Catholics on the whole are not accepting his teaching. They appear to be constructing their own religion and making up their own minds on social and moral issues which confront them in their everyday lives' (Hornsby-Smith, Brown and O'Byrne, 1983: 132). The compliance of lay people is clearly problematic for the clerical leadership in the Church. What does seem to be indicated by our data is that compliance is highly differentiated between doctrinal matters, on the one hand, where adherence is high, and personal morality, on the other hand, where a majority of Catholics claims the right to make up their own minds and often explicitly challenges the legitimacy of clerical authority. The area of social and political morality was rarely raised by our respondents, we suspect because many Catholics take for granted the appropriateness of a differentiation between religion and politics. In the area of Church discipline, there seems to have been a loss of 'the fear of hell' (Lodge, 1980: 113–27) and of the clerical sanctions against those who do not conform to Church disciplinary rules relating to frequency of Mass attendance and reception of the sacraments, mixed marriages, intercommunion, and so on. Several of our respondents underpinned the distinction between Church doctrine, on the one hand, and both morality and discipline, on the other hand, by appealing to the distinction, often quite explicitly, between infallible teaching, which must be followed, and guidelines which are not infallible, which need not be followed.

These issues, introduced in an exploratory way in this chapter, will be considered further for core Catholics in the following chapter and for ordinary parishioners in chapter 8.

CORE CATHOLICS, CONFLICT AND CONTESTATION

7.1 Introduction

In chapter 4 we reported on some of the findings from our interviews with seventy-one of the eighty-three lay members of five of the bishops' national advisory commissions in 1974, and reviewed the religious beliefs of these core Catholics in such areas as the teaching of the Church, images of God, and social and personal morality. The evidence pointed to the existence of a more-or-less explicit sense of a hierarchy of truths with differential claims to adherence, a strong element of private judgement in 'making up one's own mind' regardless of any official teaching, and increasingly overt resistance to some aspects of institutional discipline, on such matters as the Sunday Mass obligation and the rules prohibiting intercommunion, especially on the part of the younger Catholics. In sum, it was clear that as far as these core Catholics were concerned, there was little evidence of a model of a Church with a passive and submissive laity and a homogeneous religious belief system. Rather it was demonstrated that the compliance of these core Catholics within the institutional Church was problematic. These findings raise the issue of religious authority, which is the concern of this present chapter.

A number of commentators have argued that the study of the question of authority within religious institutions has been inadequate from both theological and sociological perspectives (Mansfield and Hornsby-Smith, 1982). Thus McKenzie suggested that the inadequacy of theological studies was due to 'the emphasis placed on authority and the fervour in defending it' (1966: 4) and, according to Kokosalakis:

the reluctance of many sociologists to deal with the question of values and the structures of authority and meaning in religious institutions derives mainly from the lack of a profounder theoretical foundation and/or adequate methodology to cope with the difficulties which these questions imply. (1971: 21)

The Church, like any other social institution, is in a dialectical relation with the society in which it exists. If we are to explain changes in the nature of religious authority, we must take into account both post-war social changes within society generally and the Roman Catholic community in particular, and also religious changes within the Church, especially since the Second Vatican Council. In the first half of the twentieth century two horrendous world wars shattered any tendency to defer automatically to the supposed superiority of the knowledge and wisdom of such traditional authority figures as generals and statesmen. The Church, along with other social institutions, was inevitably effected by the more conditional forms of compliance of 'lower participants' (Etzioni, 1961) in the post-war world.

Advances in science and technology have vastly expanded the knowledge and mastery of the human race over its physical and social environment, and the first tentative steps into space have been taken. In the biological sciences new understandings of the nature of life have been attained. Developments in communications have provided people with a proliferation of information which greatly exceeds that derived from personal experience. All of these developments, however, have posed quite new problems. In the first place the potential for global nuclear annihilation and, more recently, ecological catastrophe, have presented the human race with problems of management and control on a global scale far beyond the experiences and competencies developed in previous historical periods. The emergence of the television interview has exposed many authority figures, including Church leaders, to intimate and penetrating scrutiny for the first time. Such factors have contributed to a desacralisation of authority; its origins have been demystified and the claims of traditional authority figures are no longer considered to be taboo areas.

Furthermore, the post-war world has seen a strong process of democratisation. On the global level this has been demonstrated by the substantial ending of the period of colonialism and the emergence of new nation states. At the national level this could be detected in such developments as the reduction of the age of adult status, schemes for industrial democracy and popular participation in urban planning. The post-war boom provided a material base for the growth of individualism, consumer choice and distinct generational identities and subcultures. Large movements of refugees and migrant workers have contributed to a growing social and cultural pluralism. In sum, social and cultural changes in the post-war world have provided fertile grounds for the reappraisal of all forms of established authority, including religious authority.

Within the Roman Catholic community in England, two factors in particular might be noted. First of all, in the Catholic parish the authority of the priest is likely to have been eroded as ethnic identity (in particular as Irish in an inner-city area with an Irish priest) has ceased to be an important source of cohesion for the Catholic community (Hornsby-Smith, 1987: 208–14; 1989). Furthermore, because Catholics are in general more highly educated than they were a generation ago, their relationship with their priests is less likely to be uncritically deferential. Catholics, like everyone else, have participated in the broad processes of democratisation in industry, universities, schools and homes in the wider society (Hornsby-Smith and Mansfield, 1974).

Secondly, for Catholics the teaching of the Second Vatican Council is likely to have had a profound influence in changing the dominant emphases and orientations which make up the normatively pre-scribed belief and value systems. Houtart (1969) has suggested that the stress placed on collegiality, participation, personal conscience and the importance of cultural differences within the Universal Church, has presented Roman Catholics with a vision of a new and more democratic type of Church organisation. In previous work we have suggested that this represents a shift from a 'mechanistic' to an 'organic' management structure (Burns and Stalker, 1966: 96–125; Hornsby-Smith and Lee, 1979; 27–8; Hornsby-Smith, 1987; 31–32). While we would not wish to deny the extent to which these changes have emanated from within the institutional Church, it is important to recognise that they may have been facilitated, or even necessitated, by developments in the wider society. For example, effective collegi-ality is facilitated when a developed and efficient means of intercommunication exists, and the vast amount of complex information to be assimilated has necessitated the introduction of new structures such as the episcopal conferences and the various commissions (Spencer, 1966).

In his study of a Liverpool parish in the late 1960s, Kokosalakis showed that there was a disparity between the structure of authority and the actual loyalty of some parishioners, and moreover that the gap was much wider and the conflict more acutely felt by those who had been brought up and educated in the post-war years than by the pre-war generations. He inferred from his findings that:

the peak of the crisis is yet to come. As our culture and our society attain a more and more universalistic character, and individuals reach a greater awareness of their individuality and freedom of conscience, these traditional structures will appear more and more unrelated to the lives and direct social experiences of Roman Catholic laity. (1971: 34)

In the course of our focused interviews with core Catholics, we asked the same questions as the Liverpool parishioners were asked in Kokosalakis's study:

Is there anything in the teaching of the Church which you find difficult to accept? Would you be prepared to accept changes in the teaching of the Church? What are the main points in the teaching of the Church which you would like to see changed? (1971: 27)

The relevant parts of our interview guide have been given in Appendix 1. It will be noted that questions on authority followed immediately after those which probed the respondents' images of God, on the assumption that there was a relationship between them. Following Houtart's analysis of 'contestation' (1969), we continued by asking respondents if they thought that authority in the Church was ever questioned or contested, and if so, what was being contested, how and by whom, and what were the reactions of authority figures to any such contestation. We also followed Houtart in attempting to distinguish authority as a *value*, intrinsic in itself, from authority used instrumentally as a *means* to the achievement of particular ends. We proceeded to ask about areas of tension or conflict in the Church, either in general or in the experience of the respondent. This led to a number of illustrations of different authority styles in the Church. In the discussion of the religious beliefs of core Catholics in chapter 4, issues of religious authority were often

Table 7.1. *Model of contestation of religious authority*

Forms of Contestation	Major Categories	Typical Examples
Objects	1. Legitimacy	*Humanae Vitae*; clerical celibacy
	2. Values	Obedience; social justice
	3. Social system	Theologians restricted; bishops' appointments
Types	1. Individual	Contraception
	2. Joint	Cologne Declaration
	3. Social movement	Basic Christian communities
Means	1. Individual	
	(a) private	Unpublished letter; private conversation
	(b) public	Book; TV interview
	2. Collective	
	(a) private	Deputations
	(b) public	Manifesto; demonstrations
Reactions	1. Resistance	Suppression; exclusion; Kung
	2. Limitation	Partial legitimation; nominations; NPC
	3. Acceptance	Total legitimation; Dutch Pastoral Council
Consequences	1. Growth	Increased involvement; enhanced authority
	2. Decay	Loss of credibility; indifference

(Adapted from Houtart, 1969: 319–21)

raised implicitly. In this chapter we will review those data which address these issues more explicitly and comment on the utility of Houtart's framework for their interpretation.

7.2 Houtart's analysis of contestation

For the purposes of our present analysis we have found it useful to follow the conceptual analysis of conflicts of authority proposed by Houtart (1969: 319–21). He begins by proposing the existence of contestation within the post-conciliar Church, and then attempts to interpret this phenomenon through the construction of typologies for the objects, types and means of contestation and the official reaction to it. These typologies have been summarised briefly in Table 7.1.

The first *object* of contestation, according to Houtart, is *legitimacy*, that is the manner in which authority justifies its function or its decisions. This could involve:

the way authority appeals to a divine origin for its justification ... [or] a refusal to recognise the competence of the religious authority's intervention in a specific domain ... for example, the legitimacy of imposing strict norms in the areas of a person's conscience. (1969: 319)

The legitimacy of the authority of the ecclesiastical leadership in the Church has typically been contested over the papal encyclical, *Humanae Vitae* (Paul VI, 1968), and also over the rule concerning clerical celibacy.

The second object of contestation is the *value* hierarchy proposed or practised by the Church leadership. Thus the values of unqualified obedience or loyalty to religious leaders or their decisions may be contested. It may also be objected 'that these values are contradictory to the evangelical norm, or to the values expressed by the Second Vatican Council' (Houtart, 1969: 319). Thus Winter (1973) has protested the emphasis on institutional maintenance in the Church relative to missionary concerns. In a similar vein some activists contest the low priority given to the issues of justice and peace in pastoral policies and practice. Thirdly, Houtart suggests that contestation against the *social system* or the organisational behaviour of the Church can also be identified. Contemporary examples might include protests against the way the Sacred Congregation for the Doctrine of the Faith pressurises liberal or liberation theologians (such as Kung, Curran or Boff), the recent appointment of traditional bishops against the wishes of the local Church (for example in Holland and Cologne), the neglect of human rights in the Church (Sieghart, 1989), and centralising tendencies in the Church.

Houtart next distinguishes three *types* of contestation. In the first place *individuals* may contest the teaching or decisions of the ecclesiastical leadership in the Church. Survey data have indicated clearly that in recent years large numbers of individual Catholics have contested the official teaching on contraception, as outlined in *Humanae Vitae* (Paul VI, 1968). On occasion individuals have grouped together, a recent example being the Cologne Declaration of European theologians (1989) to protest against recent Roman appointments of bishops and constraints on the teaching of theologians. Thirdly, contestation may take the form of a *social movement*. Recent examples might include the charismatic movement, insofar as it reflected a protest against restrictive forms of spirituality in the Church; the basic Christian community movement, reflecting a greater awareness of the social, economic and political concerns of

Catholics in their everyday lives; the justice and peace movement, contesting the low priority given to these issues in pastoral practice; or recent lay movements in the Church contesting many of the post-Vatican reforms.

Houtart next distinguishes *individual* or *collective, private* or *public means* used by the contestants and points to the important role played by the mass media in rapidly transforming individual or group private contestation into a public form. What might have begun as a private letter or conversation or a deputation from a group, for example to a bishop, might easily develop into public means with the full glare of publicity afforded by the television interview or the challenge of a march or demonstration.

Having outlined the objects, types and means of contestation, Houtart offers descriptions of three types of reaction to contestation. The religious leadership can unconditionally refuse to accept the contestation through the suppression or exclusion of the individual (e.g. Kung) or group (e.g. the Lefebvrists), or endeavour to limit or diminish the contestation by giving it some legitimation, or they can accept the contestation. Houtart suggests that initially the Dutch Pastoral Council offered progressive laity 'a channel of expression' in the mid-1960s (Houtart, 1969: 320). It might be argued that the National Pastoral Congress in 1980 was an attempt to provide a partial legitimation for the concerns of lay people as expressed through numerous groups in preparation for the Congress. On the other hand the delegates were generally disappointed by the bishops' response to the Congress in *The Easter People* (Anon, 1981: 307–98; Hornsby-Smith and Cordingley, 1983; Hornsby-Smith, 1987: 36–43) so that in retrospect it seems to have been more an exercise in damage limitation than in acceptance.

Finally, Houtart stresses the variability of the outcomes of contestation in the Church from growth and enhanced moral authority, on the one hand, to loss of credibility and decay, on the other. He suggests that:

the major effect of a 'contestation' which is not reabsorbed is the loss of the authority's credibility ... [which] does not take place without some human cost ... often very high. But for the Church, which is the institution destined to transmit values which are linked to the very meaning of existence, this is translated into an indifference or an abandonment of people's adherence to values and their legitimation ... On the contrary, where 'contestation' has been met positively the result is usually a growth in the moral authority of those who in the Church have a ministerial task. (1969: 320–1)

In an attempt to explain the latent conflict existing in the Church, Houtart hypothesises that there are two groups of people within the Church with opposing concepts of God and the Church. Elsewhere these have been described as the 'traditionalists' with pre-Vatican models and the 'progressives' with post-Vatican models of God, the Church, the priest and parish (Hornsby-Smith, 1989). Catholics in the first group are those who would:

tend to give value to an organisation which places decision and power in the hands of a small group of persons, assuming an uncontested authority ... The institution's cohesion is based on a system of authority, conceived in a vertical way and legitimised by a special divine assistance. Authority is thus seen as a key *value* in the institution. (Houtart, 1969: 321; emphasis added)

According to the second concept of the Church:

the members play an active role ... With regard to the basis of coherence in the institutional Church, it is placed at the level of real participation on the part of its members in its values (that is, in their internalisation), in its internal functioning (in the structures of participation of decisions, in the liturgy, etc.), and in its external functioning (which is evangelisation, in the general sense). Authority is seen according to this perspective as a norm, that is to say a *means* which is more or less efficacious in assuring the pursuit of its goals. (1969: 321–2; emphasis added)

These two groups of Catholics perceive authority differently. For the first group it is seen as a primary *value*, whereas for the second it is only a *means* of achieving efficiency within the institution in the pursuit of its goals. Houtart surmises that the conflicts between the two conceptions of the Church and the corresponding conflicts of authority 'at the level of a certain number of values and legitimations ... probably are irreconcilable'. They can co-exist if an agreement can be 'founded on a certain number of common values and on some practical norms which allow people to live and to act collectively' (1969: 323). However, he believes that where conflicts are situated at the level of values (which might well be the case where there is a huge chasm between those of different theological or political persuasion on the issues of social justice, for example), this kind of solution will not hold in the long run.

This analysis leads to the prediction of an impending crisis within the Roman Catholic Church over the question of ecclesiastical authority. Some commentators have forecast that the conflicts which currently exist in latent form will inevitably result in some kind of rupture. Thus David Martin hypothesised that an explosion of discontent would erupt in the 'total environment' of the Catholic ghetto:

held together by ecclesiastical authority as well as by ethnic identity ... whenever a *single* point of doctrine is undermined simply because a hole in the dyke undermines the complete defensive system. And of course if some limited social mobility creates a Catholic middle class in closer contact with Protestants and humanists of similar status, then this is where the explosion is audible. What becomes audible dissent at this level is often unspoken divergence from Catholic norms at lower levels. Intellectuals begin by inventing verbal subterfuges and, when they can bear these no longer, erupt against authority; the working class either obeys or silently pursues its way in the usual manner of erring humanity. The Catholic system can cope with large-scale divergence, but it cannot brook overt disruption and challenge, and it is precisely this that occurs as more and more climb out of the overlapping ghettos of class and religious separatism. (1972: 187–8)

In this chapter we will explore the utility of Houtart's conceptual framework and analysis and Martin's expectations of an eruption against the ecclesiastical authorities in the Church on the basis of our interviews in the mid-1970s with core Catholics, many of whom had indeed experienced upward social mobility as suggested by Martin. It will be shown that their predictions were only partially supported. A modified analysis of the course of post-conciliar conflict in the Church will be offered.

7.3 Responses to ecclesiastical authority

On the basis of Houtart's analysis we distinguished several categories of response to the exercise of authority in the Church. Firstly there were those who accepted the authority of the Church without question. Secondly we distinguished three categories of value contestation and thirdly, two categories of contestation of legitimacy. We also found it necessary to distinguish a category for those who did not always comply with the Church authorities but who did not regard themselves as contesting that authority (Mansfield and Hornsby-Smith, 1982). In some instances the boundaries between these categories were very unclear but in the analysis of our very rich interview data we have collapsed some categories and distinguished five types of response to religious authority. Examples of these five types of response have been given in Table 7.2.

Table 7.2. *Classification of responses to ecclesiastical authority
(lay members of bishops' commissions)*

A. *Conformists*
  1. Christ left a teaching Church ... left authority with His bishops ...
     (c31; Male, 40s)
  2. One has been trained to accept ... I am all for authority in the Church ...
     I am authoritarian.
     (c46; Female, 50s)
  3. [I give] absolute loyalty to the Church but without the old-type fear ...
     [of] the almighty power of the priest.
     (c35; Male, 50s)
  4. The Church has a monarchical structure ... At the same time it does
     depend on the authority of us all together.
     (c10; Female, 30s)

B. *Accommodators*
  5. Perhaps if I don't ask them then they won't tell me not to do it.
     (c21; Female, 50s; convert)
  6. If there is something I disagree with ... [I] see my task as to influence
     towards its change.
     (c52; Male, 40s)
  7. Authoritarianism is not the same as exercising authority. A parish priest
     who is authoritarian will be challenged by people of all ages. If [a] priest is
     not prepared to talk, listen, he will be challenged. A bishop not prepared
     to consult would likewise be challenged.
     (c20: Male, 60s)
  8. [The] gift given to [the] leader may be more subtly interpreted as [a] gift
     to enable him to bring [the] community to [the] point of agreement.
     (c28; Male, 40s)
  9. It would appear that God is still revealing Himself to us in our search for
     understanding. And this is coming about essentially through discussion,
     dialogue within the Church and with other Churches ... so that ... I think
     we've got to live more adventurously.
     (c33; Male, 50s)

C. *Innovators*
  10. The rules can be bent when you have a loving relationship with God.
      (c3; Female, 50s)
  11. [People are] doing their '[own] thing', whatever it may be ... they've
      thought out their own position and are following it.
      (c14; Female, 50s)
  12. I think some people have to be prepared to act before anything will
      change.
      (c7; Female, 40s)
  13. The bishops cannot, in fact, do everything ... they do rely on expertise in
      the Church ... [and], in a very practical and real way, rely on a consensus
      of the faithful.
      (c55; Male, 30s)

D. *Transformers*
  14. I believe in a democratic Church ... Bishops should be elected ... I don't
      believe in *ex cathedra* authority. So if a guy says something I don't agree

Table 7.2. *cont.*

with, it doesn't cause me any problems ... I just think it's another point of view ... so it doesn't cause me problems in terms of a crisis of conscience. (c50; Male, 30s)

15. I am in conflict with many teachings but I see that this conflict is artificial ... a matter of personal interpretation. So I make my own mind up. (c36; Female, 30s)

16. I do not confront authority. The young are completely different ... they simply do not see authority in those terms ... They appear to have this marvellous confidence to know exactly what is the right, the Christian way of doing things. (c26; Male, 40s)

17. I feel that we are all of us in the most fantastic state of flux and uncertainty but that ... the Spirit works where It will, and at the moment the organised official Church isn't very sensitive to this. (c47; Female, 40s)

18. Certain rules must be there, [but] they are guidelines ... the Church of the future will be a much smaller one ... made up of people who do in fact make their own personal decisions. (c52; Male, 40s)

E. *Opters Out*

19. Catholics tend to opt out if they won't accept the authority of the Church. (c3; Female, 50s)

20. People are contesting authority ... some by getting out ... others by standing up to be counted and these people are suffering because of their sincerity. (c36; Female, 20s)

7.3.1 The conformists

Around one in six of these core Catholics accepted the authority of the official leadership of pope, bishops and priests almost without question, stressing the virtues of loyalty, deference and unquestioning obedience. In our earlier work we referred to these as the 'submissives' (Mansfield and Hornsby-Smith, 1982: 455). This label misleadingly suggests an exclusively passive response to authority and we here prefer the term *conformists* for this category of respondents. At least four distinct elements can be distinguished among the responses of the conformists: the divine origins of religious authority, its habitual nature, the importance of loyalty, and the claim that in the Church authority is shared with members.

A middle-aged woman referred to the authority of Christ who left authority to interpret His teachings to the bishops (1). When people objected to a particular priest or a particular liturgical style it was important to 'take them back to what Christ says and then they will listen'. Several other commission members gave similar responses. A representative of one of the Catholic organisations resented the claims of those lay people who 'by virtue of their superior intelligence or education [claimed they] have a divine right to tell us what to do'. For this respondent the only people who had such a right 'are those who have been commissioned by the Sacrament of Orders so to do'. He saw:

the People of God clustered round their priests and their bishops who are focal points and it is through the Sacrament of Order that God stretches out a helping hand, should we wish to accept [it]. (c59; Male, 50s)

This view interestingly hints at one function of the clergy as being the management of social differences between lay people. An insistence on the authority of the clergy (as 'men apart'), ensures that there are no religiously divisive differences between lay people, even where they do differ in their intelligence or education. Thus another respondent was:

much happier with experts who are priests [who] tell us what we should do ... There are times when I feel that the obligations add up to rather a lot ... but you just live with it ... I am not at all in favour of the layman having to work everything out for himself ... It makes no sense ... I can't see how the individual conscience can work things out ... One's conscience is formed from one's living faith and one's background. (c39; Male, 30s)

Another member insisted there was a need for 'the leadership of priests, bishops and pope' (c24; Female, 40s) and, in the last analysis, 'the clergy are there to inform you of your duty to God and you must obey' (c56; male, 40s).

A second type of conformist stressed the value of the habit of deference and loyalty to authority (i.e. the ecclesiastical leadership in the Church) and of the long socialisation in the discipline of habit in 'home life, family, schooling, teaching, career'. For a middle-aged woman, 'take away authority and you take away all the discipline that keeps the thing together ... I see authority and discipline as being synonymous' (c46; Female, 50s). Similar remarks were made by a middle-aged man who confessed 'I suppose I sin and then look for forgiveness'. He considered discipline to be 'very good for you' and was 'fairly strict' with his children. 'You have to obey rules ... it is character-forming' (c22; Male, 40s).

The third type of response given by the conformists stressed the notion of loyalty but noted a shift in the nature of compliance in the Church. There was no longer a fear of 'the almighty power of the priest' (3). Another middle-aged man noted the link between loyalty to the Church and 'Irishism'. This points to a form of subcultural attachment, common especially in working-class, inner-city parishes in the days of the 'fortress Church'. I have argued elsewhere (Hornsby-Smith, 1987; 208–14) that as a result of post-war social change and post-conciliar religious change there has been a dissolution of this formerly distinctive Catholic subculture. Inevitably, therefore, older forms of religio-ethnic loyalty are dying out. This respondent, however, observed that:

loyalty has lasted longer in this area than others ... There's still a tremendous loyalty to the Church ... I was brought up loyal ... and I would find it very difficult to think of anything that the Church would do which would make me leave her. (c29; Male, 40s)

This respondent also noted changes in the way authority was exercised in the Church and admitted that he was 'so amazed that the Church is willing to consult' now.

A fourth type of conformist response extended this notion of the changing nature of authority and stressed that, to some extent, it was now shared with lay people. This led a convert to observe:

The Church has a monarchical structure with a few people at the top, most of them celibate clerics. At the same time it does depend on the authority of us all together. The pope can't sit in his little ivory tower and produce something that we've all got to believe. This is nonsense. It's something that some Catholics believe but it's not true; it's a caricature of what the thing is. He can only speak with authority when he is speaking for all of us ... The whole question of authority is changing now. There are priests and bishops who honestly want to hear what the laity have to say. There is genuine consultation now ... [However] we've not been prepared for consultation ... and one needs to educate both sides [clergy and laity, to the changing nature of authority in the Church]. (c10; Female, 30s)

7.3.2 The accommodators

There was a second group of respondents, around one-half of the core Catholics, who accepted the authority of the Church but did not always agree with some of its teaching. In other words such respondents were contesting the hierarchy of values in the Church. Three subgroups were identified: those who wished to realise or extend the hierarchy of values (for example, to pay more attention to social teaching on housing rights or more strongly condemn the arms race); those who wished to abandon some values (for example, the traditional teaching on contraception or at least to give it a lower priority); and those who argued that the existing priorities (for example, concerning social justice) were wrong or failing to conform to the gospel or the conciliar teachings. In practice these subtypes were difficult to disentangle.

In our earlier analyses we referred ,to these respondents as the 'doubters' who 'although they complied with authority . . . admitted to experiencing doubts about the content of some of the teachings . . . [or] considered that the hierarchy of values proposed by the [Church] authorities was unacceptable' (Mansfield and Hornsby-Smith, 1982: 455). In the further analyses presented here, we consider it is more appropriate to refer to these respondents as the *accommodators* who adapt 'themselves to the situation . . . and come to terms as best they can with the plausibility problem' of a pluralist society (Berger, 1973; 156). It seems that these respondents were in a process of dialogue, implicit or explicit consultation, and negotiation with the religious leadership in the Church. At least five types of accommodation can be discerned in the responses of these core Catholics: discrete neutralisation, compromising negotiation, participation and collaboration, enabling reinterpretation, and a trusting leap into the unknown (Table 7.2, Nos. 5–9).

In the first place there are those who employ 'techniques of neutralisation' (Matza, 1964) and avoidance in order discreetly to avoid tackling questions of religious authority head-on. At least four of our respondents could be said to have adopted this stance, in particular two people employed by the Church. One admitted:

I am inhibited by my job . . . I can't go out against the authority of the Church . . . I certainly can't speak openly against it on a particular issue . . . I have been so conditioned by my Catholic upbringing that I find it .very difficult to go against the Church's authority without feeling guilty . . . I know in my heart of hearts that I will be unhappy, so I do not confront authority. (c26; Male, 40s)

This man implicitly associated religious authority exclusively with the ecclesiastical leadership in the Church. Another man said that he kept his 'head down and [didn't] go picking quarrels' (c43; Male,

60s). Other respondents seemed to shut their eyes and hope that whatever difficulties they had would simply go away (5). Thus another middle-aged man confessed 'I avoid the attack ... I put a mental block ... that is there and the Church says it ... and I am always pretending that it doesn't' (c27; Male, 50s).

A second type of accommodation stressed the notions of compromise, negotiation and influence towards change or at least adaptation (6). Thus a man with great experience in public affairs who felt the question of birth control was open to personal interpretation and did not consider that the ecclesiastical authorities limited his immediate actions, added:

I am what I am ... I have never known any issue with which I have been connected as having been decisively settled one way or the other. So although I don't accept authority, I accept compromise ... I accept the other side ... I like to change people, but by argument ... by a properly prepared case plus a certain amount of muscle. (c54; Male, 60s).

A third type of accommodation saw lay people as collaborators with the clergy and stressed the need for lay participation in decision-making. Those responding in this way emphasised that they did not reject the legitimacy of ecclesiastical authority but they did object to authoritarian styles of leadership and regarded consultation as a right (7). In the words of one young man:

I think the day has gone ... rightly, when the Church can impose by some edict, a belief or an organisational system, ... It may be that slowing it down (through consultation) is a necessary price, initially, to pay for the end of that authoritarianism. (c9; Male, 20s)

A middle-aged man added wistfully: 'The Church I'd like to be a member of is when you are all working together' (c13; Male, 40s). For a middle-aged woman, the neglect of lay knowledge and experiences was likely to result in poor and uninformed teaching by the clerical leadership in the Church:

A lot of the Roman bishops don't know about the world ... What I don't accept is how they are running the Church ... I do accept the authority of the Church ... I may not accept it very graciously at times ... but they are stopping others from having their effect on the teaching and that's where my arguments lie. (c32; Female, 40s)

Fourthly, a stress on consultation, lay participation and accountable authority was linked to a view of religious leadership in terms of enabling, facilitating or coordinating the gifts and contributions of others, in particular lay people in the Church (8). This is also reflected in the responses of a middle-aged woman who saw authority:

as consulting on every possible occasion, quite genuinely, not just as a gesture, and listening to the responses and taking them into account, but that at the end of the day somebody's got to make the decision which is hopefully based on taking into account of as much as is reasonably possible . . . I should like to think that more of them were getting the authority because of the people they were than because of the post that they hold. But it's an imperfect world! (c70; Female, 50s)

There seems to be here a plea for a charismatic or prophetic form of authority rather than a legal–rational type. Related to this theme of consultation was the view that without dialogue and challenge there would be no room for change, the spontaneous and unexpected, and indeed, for the working of the Holy Spirit:

This dialogue between oneself and the Church: it's not between equals. But one doesn't slavishly follow the teachings of the Church . . . as long as there's continuous dialogue between the two. Otherwise the idea of the Holy Spirit just breaks down completely. (c58; Male, 20s)

This stress on the Holy Spirit was related to the final type of accommodation which invited Catholics not to remain frozen into inaction by a rule-bound timidity. This was expressed by a middle-aged man with a long experience of working in Catholic organisations who saw a developing awareness of God's continuing revelation as an invitation to live trustingly and adventurously (9).

7.3.3 *The innovators*

A third group of commission members 'refused to accept the legitimacy of ecclesiastical authority in an area of their life which they felt was a matter solely for personal conscience. In addition there was the group who felt it was their duty to initiate change by adopting practices which would in time be accepted by the authorities' (Mansfield and Hornsby-Smith, 1982; 456). Unlike the conformists, this group did not always comply with the teaching of the ecclesiastical leadership but unlike the accommodators, they also challenged the legitimacy of this leadership in at least some areas of their lives. Around one in eight of these core Catholics could be designated as innovators of one sort or another (Table 7.2, Nos. 10–13).

For some this implied the selection of 'institutionally proscribed but often effective means of attaining' the prescribed organisational goals of the Church (Merton, 1957: 140–1, 176). This was explicitly articulated by a middle-aged convert who argued that rules could be bent if one had a loving relationship with God and neighbours (10). In practice this was most frequently envisaged in the cases of contraception and intercommunion.

Our interviews with members of the bishops' commissions in the mid-1970s strongly indicated that opposition to the papal encyclical on birth control (Paul VI, 1968) was founded more on the interpretation and exercise of ecclesiastical authority than on the issue of contraception, *per se*. At the start of our work we were advised by the then Social Science Research Council not to antagonise our respondents by raising sensitive personal issues such as birth control. Accordingly we did not mention it directly, but it is interesting to note that almost every commission member used it as a focus for their discussion on ecclesiastical authority. Thus one woman thought that on contraception Catholics had thought through their own position and were 'doing their [own] thing' (11) and a man suggested that the matter 'has been solved by people in their own way' (c11; Male, 50s).

Reflections on the official proscriptions on intercommunion led to some of the most interesting comments on religious authority and the notion, with Durkheimian echos of crime as a normal social phenomenon (1964: 65–75), that deviance against established norms can be conducive to changing those norms. In other words, rules are adjusted to reflect changing patterns of behaviour rather than the other way round. This was well expressed by one member who commented on the growing practice of intercommunion, especially in inter-Church marriages:

I think the practice is bound to come first . . . But I've come to the stage where I can't really regret the unauthorised any more. I used to think this could happen very tidily and at a certain point the authorities would say 'yes' and one could go ahead. But I don't think this is [the] way, in fact, in which things change in the Church. I think some people have to be prepared to act before anything will change . . . I am very cautious and I think I'm a bit glad when others are less cautious. (c7; Female, 40s)

Similar remarks were made by a member who was the Catholic partner in an inter-Church marriage and who had been 'married by an Anglican vicar in an Anglican church with a full papal dispensation'. He did not just consider himself to be a member of a Catholic parish but also frequently attended and received communion in non-Catholic churches. He admitted that his attitude to the Catholic Church was fairly fluid and open but declared:

> I still feel I am a Catholic ... I think it's important to participate in Christian liturgy but I don't see that even though I am baptised into the Catholic Church ... it is essential for me to restrict my worshipping to that liturgy, particularly in view of my own marital situation. (c51; Male, 30s).

A final group of innovators stressed that authority was legitimated to the extent that it was shared with lay people who could contribute their own expertise and experience to decision-making so that official pronouncements more obviously reflected a consensus of Church members (13). This response is similar to that of some accommodators who stressed the importance of consultation. It differs mainly in the emphasis put on the question of legitimacy. Thus a young man warned:

> Before I would accept authority, I would have to be very clear that that authority really was the Church, and I consider that I am as much the Church as the pope ... I believe that he has a special role, a special guidance ... but I feel that we have not really defined clearly what we mean by infallibility ... [and] the principle of collegiality of the bishops. (c63; Male, 30s)

For this respondent, as for several others;

> the Church's role is to preserve what Christ said ... to give people a rule of life and to accept that they are human beings with free wills ... to lay down clearly, as Christ did, basic principles ... but then to accept, as Christ also did, that people have the right to choose.

7.3.4 *The transformers*

We did not find any empirical instances in our final category of people who rejected totally the legitimacy of the ecclesiastical leadership in the Church, but we did identify a fourth category of respondent 'who did not comply with authority in certain matters but who did not feel that they were in any way disobeying the authority or questioning its legitimacy' (Mansfield and Hornsby-Smith, 1982: 456). Around one in seven of the commission members fell into this

category. We called them *transformers* because they appeared to be
reinterpreting the relationship of lay people to the ecclesiastical
leadership in the Church in new ways (Table 7.2, Nos. 14–18).
Recurring themes were those of 'making up one's own mind', with
implicit or explicit references to personal conscience, and the teachings of the clerical leadership in the Church interpreted as guidelines rather than irrevocable injunctions.

The flavour of this type of relationship between lay people and the
ecclesiastical leadership is indicated in the observations of a young
man who believed in a democratic model of the Church (14). He sees
disagreements with official pronouncements as of no more consequence than the expression of different points of view. Similarly, a
young woman who made up her own mind on many teachings, saw
conflicts with official teaching as reflecting no more than differences
of personal interpretation (15). A young person thought that 'you
have got to be true to yourself... to your own values' (c30). In sum,
'as far as the laity are concerned, they are able to make up their own
minds' (c42; Male, 40s) and no especially privileged status was
accorded to the views of the ecclesiastical leadership.

A discrete employee of the Church, whom we have previously
noted was an accommodator who kept his head down and avoided
confrontation with the Church leadership, was nevertheless envious
of the young, for example his own children, who simply did not
regard religious authority in the same way and who seemed to be
perfectly untroubled about following their own consciences or
'doing their own thing' (16). That there were significant generational differences was also attested to by a counsellor of the Catholic Marriage Advisory Council (CMAC) who, in the course of commenting on the current non-directive stance of the CMAC when
teaching about contraception, observed:

I would accept the Church's authority quite happily within the bounds of
my own conscience, and that is my final guide ... I think that this is one of
the difficulties, that the younger generation do not see life as being lived on
'nos' only ... and are not prepared to take it, whereas my generation would
have done ... and we did ... the 'thou-shalt-not generation', which is no
longer regarded as what Our Lord is all about. I very much agree with the
younger generation in this ... I remember in my youth resenting a lot of
this 'Thou shalt not' stuff but doing it because that was the rule ... I
thought this was silly ... or not just ... and I've been very glad to find that

[with] a lot of it, I was right ... We have to make our own decisions more ... I don't think you'll ever have the former [style of authority] any more because people have changed ... I'm not sure about (authority in the Church) being contested; I would think it's being ignored more ... where people have decided they couldn't take it. I suppose it's a contest, really, but rather than stay and fight it, they've just stopped going [to church] ... The younger people have decided that they are not going to sit through this mumbo-jumbo'. (c19; Female, 60s)

For those who 'stay and fight' the situation is one of 'flux and uncertainty' though this can be interpreted as an exciting challenge in the knowledge that the Holy Spirit is at work even if the institutional Church is not very sensitive to what is going on world-wide (17). The transformers do not reject the teaching of the official leaders of the Church so much as interpret them as guidelines to be followed as far as possible but subject to the exigencies of everyday life. In the last analysis people have to make up their own minds.

7.3.5 *The opting out option*

Although none of these core Catholics rejected totally the legitimacy of the ecclesiastical leadership of the Church, a few did refer to those Catholics who did so and whose response to contestation of authority in the Church was to 'opt out' (19). Typically they would become 'dormant' Catholics (Fichter, 1954: 22, 192) but they might also 'switch' to other religious affiliations. Both were regarded as responses to contestation of legitimacy. Interestingly a young woman argued that it was the people who remained in the Church in conflict with the ecclesiastical authorities who suffered most from the contestation (20).

7.4 Transformations of religious authority

Our interview data are very rich and extensive and we have only been able to illustrate our argument selectively. It has been shown that among our respondents there was a significant minority whose attitude to religious authority was traditional, not necessarily un-questioning, but certainly obedient, deferential and loyal. Others, however, complied with the teaching authorities of the Church but not always graciously and resenting some degree of moral coercion. Others explicitly rejected the imposition of rules and regulations and authoritarian styles of leadership. For these there was clearly contestation about such rules and what they would sometimes see as a 'displacement of goals whereby an instrumental value becomes a terminal value', or a form of bureaucratic 'ritualism' which 'interferes with the achievement of the purposes of the organisation' (Merton, 1957: 199).

For many of our core members, contestation and at least a partial rejection of the legitimacy of the ecclesiastical leadership, led to a strategy of 'making up one's own mind'. Included here were those who advocated a policy of 'living adventurously' and trustingly, recognising religious authority as an 'enabling gift'. Some core Catholics recommended deviant behaviour (such as intercommunion) in the expectations that the official rules would in time change to accord more closely with the transformed practices. Many urged the need to take proper account of social and cultural factors in the contemporary situation. Finally, the need for some sort of balance between the guidelines for living taught by the official leadership, and for discretion for autonomous individuals to interpret them in ways which took due note of the realities of their social circumstances, was also stressed. A dialectical form of authority, it was suggested, would leave room for the unanticipated initiatives of the Holy Spirit.

Although there were no instances among our core Catholics of a total rejection of the legitimacy of the ecclesiastical leadership in the Church, this remains a logical possibility. Indeed, several members of the bishops' commissions made reference to those Catholics whose response to contestation in the Church was to 'opt out'. It seems that this rarely relates to the dogmatic teaching of the Church on creedal beliefs, but most frequently to its moral proscriptions on such issues as contraception, abortion, divorce, pre-marital sex and homosexuality, and also its rules of practice, for example the weekly Mass attendance obligation and the proscription of intercommunion.

In this chapter we have explored the utility of Houtart's analysis of the objects, types and means of contestation in the Church and the official reaction to it. We have indicated that there is evidence for some form of contestation among many lay members of the bishops' advisory commissions. However, the use of the word 'contestation' to describe what they see as essentially a 'calling into question' would be disputed by many of our respondents. This results from the use of the word 'contestation' to describe some of the more extreme means which have been employed to express a challenging of authority. As Houtart notes in his article: 'It is this which makes Cardinal Suenens and some other groups of priests say that they refuse to be called "contestants" ' (1969: 325; note 30).

Nevertheless, Houtart's objects of contestation (values, legitimacy and social system) are all identifiable as foci for contestation among our respondents. Several members questioned the values of the ecclesiastical leadership either because they considered that they were inconsistent with those expressed by the Second Vatican Council, or because some of them were underemphasised, or others (typically those relating to personal or sexual behaviour) were overemphasised by the ecclesiastical leadership. Where it was felt that the Church's organisation had not internalised the conciliar values, or that the ways of exercising authority did not correspond to evangelical principles, the social system itself (or the hierarchical organisation of the Church) became a focus for dispute. Finally, on the question of legitimacy, although a number of commission members did not always comply with ecclesiastical teaching, not all of them could be described as contesting the legitimacy of that authority. The majority only questioned the legitimacy of imposing strict norms in areas of personal morality, while only a few went further and disputed the manner in which the religious leadership legitimised its function or decisions.

I would now wish to modify our original interpretation of the three types of contestation proposed by Houtart (Mansfield and Hornsby-Smith, 1982; 457–8). Our interview data provide evidence for all three types. The refusal of many core Catholics to assent to the encyclical *Humanae Vitae* or the admission by a few of discreet intercommunion can be seen as examples of contestation at the individual level. Joint contestation seems to be occurring where Catholics are regarding such actions as a way of applying covert pressure on the official leadership of the Church, for example to internalise the values of Vatican II. The notion that practice precedes legislation was common among several of the commission members who had become frustrated with what they felt was the widening gap between the system of values articulated by the council and the present organisational concerns and practices of the Church. References to the issues of justice and peace testified to an incipient social movement in the Church.

We have concentrated so far on those Catholics who are contesting, but we must not overlook the small group of commission members who accepted unconditionally the content of Church teachings and ecclesiastical authority. These Catholics would accept Houtart's first concept of the Church, that is they valued an organisation which placed power in the hands of a small group of people and whose authority was uncontested. Their reaction to the changes which have taken place within the Church is one of fear that the essential values in the Church are being abandoned. On the other hand, the contestants among our sample would subscribe to the second concept of the Church, where cohesion was based on real participation and authority was built on a horizontal–collegial model and seen only as a means for achieving the goals of the institution.

If, as our findings suggest, contestation does exist within the contemporary Church, is it inevitable, as some writers have predicted, that these contestations will develop into deeper conflicts and even rupture? The answer to this question hinges on two factors: the response of the ecclesiastical leadership to the presence of contestation and the extent to which all the members of the Church accept some kind of pluralism. In general the members of the bishops' commissions felt that there had been a genuine, if slow, development in the processes of consultation by the bishops and of lay participation at both national and diocesan levels. This suggests that in England and Wales the reaction of the ecclesiastical leadership has taken Houtart's second form by giving the contestants a certain legitimation and by promoting the ideology of participation. This strategy seems to have been a reasonably effective exercise in damage limitation but, as Houtart shrewdly notes, this can 'be a means of avoiding the duty of discussing fundamental questions' (1969: 320). It seems that there are two groups of Catholics who differ radically over their interpretations of authority and it is interesting to speculate on the results of this kind of pluralism within an institution noted for the emphasis it has traditionally placed on unity and uniformity.

We have noted that David Martin agreed with Houtart in supposing that those Catholics who are contesting the authority of the ecclesiastical leadership would be a source of an 'explosion' in the Church (Martin, 1972: 187–8). What Martin suggested might have seemed likely in the years immediately after the publication of the encyclical *Humanae Vitae* (Paul VI, 1968). However, by the mid-1970s it was clear that the issue was no longer a matter of feverish debate among Roman Catholics, as several of our informants testified. It seems clear that Catholics had by then in large measure transferred the judgements of contraception from the ecclesiastical leadership to their personal consciences. By doing this the eruption against authority which Martin predicted was avoided but in the process it could be suggested that religion had become more privatised. The consequence, as Martin pointed out, was likely to be that religion would become more vulnerable to secular pressures and the emptying of theological concepts of their power (Martin, 1972: 188–91).

We would suggest that the contestants among our sample of core Catholics are unlikely to 'erupt against authority', because what Martin refers to as 'verbal subterfuge' is, in fact, a transformation and new interpretation of authority which enables the contestants to co-exist with the other members of the institutional Church. Our evidence indicates clearly that more radical transformations are inevitable in the case of the younger generations of Catholics. It is possible that traditional Catholics who are suspicious of the innovations in the Church following the Second Vatican Council may become more defensive and force a split between themselves and the contestants. However, should some form of cleavage occur, it seems quite certain that it would cut vertically across all the strata in the Church and not horizontally separate the laity from the ecclesiastical leadership.

ORDINARY CATHOLICS AND PERSONAL MORALITY

8.1 Introduction

In chapter 5 an account was given of the customary religion of
ordinary Catholics, that is self-identifying Roman Catholics selected
randomly from electoral registers in four English parishes in the
mid-1970s. It was shown that while for many Catholics their religious
beliefs and practices no longer appeared to be under the effective
control of the clerical leadership in the Church, they did frequently
reflect an earlier socialisation in Catholic schools and parishes. We
distinguished their customary religion from the official religion of the
clerical leadership and described in particular their images of God,
notions of heaven, hell and life after death, and their personal prayer.
Implicit in the existence of customary religion is a breakdown, at
least partial, in the authority of the official clerical leadership in the
Church and an indication that the compliance of lay people to this
leadership in the institutional Church is problematic. It is partial,
selective, qualified, accommodating and sometimes defiant. It is the
purpose of this chapter to explore further the question of religious
authority as seen by ordinary Catholics.

Recent survey data have indicated the heterogeneity of Catholic
beliefs and practices. Under one-third of English Catholics in the
1978 national survey both professed orthodox doctrinal beliefs and
conformed to the weekly Mass attendance norm (Hornsby-Smith,
Lee and Turcan, 1982; Hornsby-Smith, 1987: 47–55). Broadly
speaking Catholics expressed high levels of acceptance of key creedal

teachings about God, Jesus and the consecration at Mass, but much lower levels of belief in papal infallibility. Only two-thirds thought that abortion was wrong, while a similar proportion thought Catholics should be allowed to divorce, and three-quarters disagreed with the official teaching on contraception. Generally those who attended Mass regularly and older Catholics conformed much more closely to the official norms of the Church (Hornsby-Smith and Lee, 1979: 192–3). Survey data from four English parishes in the mid-1970s indicated clearly that a considerable amount of convergence of Catholic and non-Catholic beliefs and practices had taken place (Hornsby-Smith, Lee and Reilly, 1984: 357–59) as a result of the post-war dissolution of the defences of the distinctive Catholic subculture (Hornsby-Smith, 1987: 208–14). Evidence of resistance to the official teaching of the Church, especially in the areas of personal morality, was given above for members of the bishops' commissions in the mid-1970s (Section 4.6) and people who attended the public events during the pope's visit in 1982 (Section 6.4).

A note of caution is relevant here. There is a danger that contemporary evidence of overt or covert resistance to the teaching or guidance of the clerical leadership in the Church, especially when comparing older and younger Catholics, will be taken to be indicative of change from a past when Catholics were assumed to have been more compliant. What historical evidence there is, however, suggests that there never was a golden age when lay compliance to clerical authority was not contested, at least by some Catholics (Hornsby-Smith, 1987: 26–31). Thus concern about 'lapsation' rates of Irish Catholics was evident well before the end of the nineteenth century. Interview data and oral histories point to frequent and sometimes bitter conflicts with priests over confession, birth control, marriage to a non-Catholic partner, and marital breakdown. A recurring theme in historical accounts is the authoritarianism of the parish priest in the Catholic community from the middle of the nineteenth century until the 1950s (McLeod, 1981: 128–31). Analysis of the Charles Booth studies of religion in London at the turn of the century indicates that in some cases this resulted in an atmosphere of 'spiritual totalitarianism', and on occasion led to a reaction against 'overbearing ministers' or 'benevolent tyrants' (McLeod, 1974: 74) and revolts against coercive Catholic schools. There seems to be ample evidence, then, for recognising that lay compliance to ecclesiastical authority always has been partial and problematic.

All the same there are good grounds for believing that the new emphasis on the informed personal conscience as the final arbiter in moral decision-making at the Second Vatican Council (in *Gaudium et Spes*, ss.16 and 17, in Abbott, 1966: 213–14) has had a considerable impact on the structure of religious authority in the Church. Thus Kokosalakis has indicated that it 'seems to be in conflict with any type of dictatorial or judicial understanding of authority in religion'. The result, he suggests, is that Catholics 'have become less and less convinced about the importance and/or absolute authority of peripheral doctrines and disciplines of their Church' (1971: 24). In fieldwork in a mainly working-class Liverpool parish in the 1960s he found evidence of a range of views on the authority of the Church. Thus a 60 year old man who accepted the authority of the Church without reservation said:

We can't question these things. You see, for us the Pope says something to the bishops, then the bishops to the priests, then the priests to us. It works that way. We, the Catholics, have no right to question what the Holy Father says. On these matters we just accept what we are told. (1971: 27)

However, younger Catholics especially generally rejected this view, challenged concepts such as papal infallibility, and disagreed with the Church's restrictive attitudes on mixed marriages, divorce, contraception and clerical celibacy. A young grammar school teacher criticised her priests who 'still think that they can tell you what to do even on matters in which the decision should be entirely your own' (1971: 30). Catholics were contesting clerical authority by making up their own minds and ignoring their guidance. Furthermore they were not only coping with conflicts over religious authority by 'opting out' but also by processes of transformation within the Church. Thus a young clerk considered that:

The Church needs reform from inside. It is no good abandoning the Church because you disagree with it ... I have had plenty of disagreements with my Church's teaching, not only on birth control but even on more serious matters, but I think I have solved my difficulties without being unfaithful. (1971: 31)

Other researchers have substantially confirmed this analysis. Thus Joan Brothers, in her study of the impact of post-war educational changes on the traditional Liverpool parish, observed that for former pupils of the extra-parochial grammar schools and universities 'the demands of the parish priest often appear authoritarian' (1964: 161).

In the early 1970s in a mainly middle-class commuter parish near Liverpool, Koopmanschap (1978) found strong evidence among mobile Catholics of 'doing your own thing', 'shopping around' for Mass at parish 'service stations' or 'supermarkets'. His fieldwork led him to stress transformations of beliefs, moral images and authority structures. There was a tension between the Vatican II 'People of God' model of the Church and the traditional tight ecclesiastical social control of Merseyside Catholicism.

About half of his respondents considered 'the Church's function is to advise the people on faith and morals, and not to dictate policies of behaviour', that is 'authority should be exercised in a consultative manner'. One-fifth saw authority as a moral value, essential for the survival of the Church, while one-quarter were more concerned with the instrumentality of authority in the achievement of goals which should take account of changing social conditions (1978: 115–20). For the overwhelming majority of these Catholics there was 'a move away from the magical conception of the priest as the man who acts from the principle of *ex opere operate*' to that of community-builder (1978: 138). The encyclical *Humanae Vitae* (Paul VI, 1968) was said to be 'an important watershed in the transformation of the sacrality of authority' (1978: 147) and nearly four-fifths of these Catholics felt that birth control was a matter of conscience for individual couples. Koopmanschap concluded that:

> whereas the Council intended to transfer some of its moral authority to the people, the encyclical modified this intention and in doing so aggravated the conflict between the teaching authority of the Church and ordinary people. (1978: 149)

Just over one-half of his respondents favoured a change in the traditional doctrine relating to divorce and remarriage (1978: 153). In sum, the sacred symbols appeared to be losing their grip; the embodiment of sacred authority was no longer to be found in the Church, parish or priest, and authority was regarded essentially as an instrument for pursuing parish goals rather than as a value in its own right (1978: 166–7). According to Koopmanschap, what is happening in St Jerome's, with its mobile parishioners, is a form of bricolage, a reshuffling of 'the myths and values of their religious tradition in order to make them fit [their] new experiences' (1978: 233).

In this chapter we will explore further the question of religious authority by reviewing some of the salient issues raised in our tape-recorded focused interviews with randomly selected Catholic electors in four parishes in London and Preston in the mid-1970s. We asked our respondents whether there was anything in the teaching of the Church which they found difficult to accept. In subsequent probing we asked about such matters as contraception, abortion and divorce. We will review the responses of ordinary Catholics on these three issues and consider the implications for religious authority in the contemporary Church.

8.2 Contraception

There seems to be general agreement that in the period immediately after the Second Vatican Council expectations of a change in the official teaching of the Church on the matter of birth control were well-grounded. The final report, the Papal Commission on Population, Family and Birth (*The Tablet*, 22 April 1967) had seemed to pave the way for such a change by providing reasoned arguments (Kaiser, 1987) but in his encyclical *Humanae Vitae*, Pope Paul VI (1968) reaffirmed the traditional prohibitions. Many active Catholic lay people at that time were shattered and rebellious that their expectations had been dashed. While the unrest did not develop explosively in the way that David Martin had predicted, there seems little doubt that it generated a crisis of authority in the Church in ways which are not entirely clear.

Our interviews with 'ordinary' Catholics, that is randomly selected Catholic electors in four parishes in the London and Preston areas, were obtained in the mid-1970s, some six or seven years after the publication of Pope Paul's encyclical. By then the public protests of both priests and lay people were over, the fuss had died down and most English Catholics had adapted to the new situation. In our interviews with them we explored their attitudes to religious authority and the teachings of the Church. More often than not the question of contraception was raised spontaneously to indicate an area where there was explicit disagreement. Where the issue was not directly addressed, we specifically prompted comments about the Church's teaching on such issues as contraception, divorce and abortion. In Table 8.1 we have classified the responses on contraception under twelve main headings. The illustrative quotations have been selected from ordinary Catholics in all four parishes, both sexes,

Table 8.1. *Classification of responses on contraception*
(Catholic electors, four parishes)

A. *Neo-Official*
  1. What you need is to try and get people to control themselves, which can be done through the grace of God.
     (PI; Male, 61, married, skilled manual; more than weekly)
  2. (Some want the Church to say it's alright, when the Church can't say it's alright ... [and] go against God's laws.
     (PI; Female)

B. *Cause of Misery*
  3. This has been one of the unchristian things about the Church, this business of birth control ... It puts tremendous stress on people.
     (PS; Male, 42, married, skilled manual; weekly)
  4. In lots of cases ... all the love and ... affection which was within a marriage wasn't there ... and I think a lot of very good people have suffered quite a lot, and their marriages ... too, because of it.
     (LI; Male, 56, married, non-manual; more than weekly)
  5. It's the nuns and priests who preach, who don't get married ... they think the more babies you have the more little Catholics you'll have.
     (LI; Female, 47, separated; non-manual; never)
  6. I think ... they should have contraception and abortions. I think they should be allowed. They ruin a lot of people's lives without them.
     (PI; Female, 23, single, casual worker; occasionally)

C. *Emotional Strain*
  7. Because some people aren't very good at having babies and it being not very good for them ... and for all sorts of reasons: psychological, emotional, financial.
     (LI; Female, 31, married, unskilled; weekly)
  8. I am inclined to think that for family reasons ... beyond a certain stage, for a particular couple ... I don't think God wants to see a stress situation in a family to the point of it breaking up.
     (LS; Male, 43, married, non-manual; more than weekly)
  9. I've got four children and I think that's enough, so on that line I agree with birth control ... When I had the last child I went through a lot of upset nerves because I [already] had three little ones.
     (PS; Female, 37, married, non-manual; weekly)

D. *Economic Reasons*
  10. Speaking generally, from our point of view, with four children ... it takes a lot of bringing up ... in material terms and in everything else. There's a limit to how far you can stretch yourself.
     (PS; Male, 45, married, clerical; weekly)
  11. If they know they can't afford to have a child ... and young couples today can't find places to live anyway, so why not avoid having any children until they know that they can bring them into the world?
     (LI; Female, 50, married, manual; special occasions)

E. *Overpopulation*
  12. There must be some way of controlling population in places like India without half the population starving.
     (LS; Male, 17, single, student; weekly)

13. World population is obviously one of the things ... The doctrine 'God will provide' has its limitations.
(PS; Female, 40, married, non-manual; more than weekly)

F. *Inadequate reasoning*
14. Obviously you're not killing life because you've no life there in the first place.
(PS; Female, 22, single, non-manual; weekly)
15. I don't really see where God's teaching comes into it.
(PS; Male, 44, married, non-manual; weekly)
16. What the Church does say is that you can use this rhythm method for ... contraception. So the intention is there ... but that you can't use mechanical methods of contraception.
(LI; Female, 30, married, non-manual; monthly)

G. *Incoherent authority*
17. One is not really going against the Church if you use contraception ... I'm going according to the bishops and priests who leave it up to yourself, to your conscience.
(LS; Female, 28, married, skilled; Christmas and Easter)
18. I think it is a worry to have one priest say one thing and another to say another thing because you don't know where you are.
(LS; Female, 29, married, clerk; weekly)

H. *Resented authority*
19. I don't believe what they say ... because they're not going to fetch the kids up. They're not going to give to your family if you have one after t'other ... I think it's nothing to do with them.
(PI; Female, 29, married, manual; special occasions)
20. It's only when you are involved that you start really seriously thinking about these things ... on some of these things one gets the impression that the rules have been made by celibates for celibates.
(LS; Male, 56, married, non-manual; more than weekly)
21. It's up to me, not the Church ... If I want to [use contraceptives] I just go ahead and do it. The Church doesn't come into it. I mean, they can't keep the children for you if you have them one after the other ... It's alright preaching it, but ...
(PI; Female, 32, married, manual; irregular)

I. *Confined legitimacy*
22. I don't agree with a little man sitting in Rome on a golden throne telling me that I can't take the pill if I want to take it or ... for medical reasons because that's a business between me and my God.
(LS; Female, 47, divorced, clerk; never)
23. As far as religious doctrine is concerned, the pope is infallible. As far as practical, day-to-day ... social existence is concerned, I question the pope's infallibility.
(LS; Male, 30, married, skilled manual; occasional)

J. *Appropriated legitimacy*
24. I think on this matter I know better because I am directly involved ... we are supposed to listen to the pope and the clergy because they are God's representatives here on earth ... It's just on something so personal, I know better.
(LS; Female, 29, married, clerk; weekly)
25. This is one of the areas where ... [many Catholics] begin to make up their own

Table 8.1. *cont.*

minds ... I think that, more and more, people are beginning to think things out for themselves ... in a well-informed way.
(PS; Female, 40, married, non-manual; more than weekly)
26. A very large proportion of the Roman Catholic community find it extremely difficult to submit to the authority of the pope in his stand ... In spite of what Rome says, a very high proportion of priests will tell you that it is a matter for your own conscience.
(LI; Male, 68, married, non-manual; weekly)

K. *Redefined legitimacy*
27. [The] Church lays down guidance but I think it's ultimately your conscience whether you practice birth control or not ... I think the Church ... shouldn't be too specific ... [but] guide one's conscience.
(LS; Male, 30, married, skilled manual; occasional)
28. They've not given a definite answer to contraception, have they really? They've given you a guideline that you should take ... and they're against it.
(PI; Male, 53, single, clerical; weekly)

L. *Anticipated transformation*
29. Whether [the Church] will change its outlook, I don't know. People might change it for them ... They can change their ways in things like serving Mass ... Maybe in time they might have to [change] ... It's a bit late in coming, really.
(LI; Female, 52, married, manual; monthly)
30. The teachings of the Church on sex and marriage can't be changed overnight; it would 'rock the boat' too much. They would have to be eroded over time.
(LI; Male, 34, married, non-manual; special occasions)

Key to respondent characteristics:
Parish; sex, age, marital status, occupational category; Mass attendance.

all age groups and social classes. Some of the respondents are committed to the extent of attending Mass more frequently than the weekly norm, while others have only tenuous links with their local parish.

It was in fact very difficult to find one of our ordinary Catholics who was unambiguously in agreement with the Church's official teaching on contraception, and even those who claimed not to have used 'artificial' methods of birth control themselves tended to be sympathetic to the difficulties of young people. The examples given of neo-official comments (1–2) tended to be offered by a tiny handful of regularly practising, elderly people in inner-city parishes and to be rather judgemental. Thus one man in Preston thought that 'people just wanted their own selfish pleasures and to carry on like that' (1). Similarly, an elderly woman in London urged the practice of 'self-control', fearing that 'we are losing all sense of moral control now' (LI)

Around one-half of our respondents volunteered a range of excuses or justifications (Scott and Lyman, 1968: 46) for rejecting the official teaching of the Church on contraception. Categories B, C and D all have the flavour of excuses, in the sense that they appear to admit to breaking the rules of the Church but deny full responsibility. The first of these categories (3–6), mentioned by respondents in all four parishes, stressed that the Church's traditional teaching had been the cause of a great deal of generalised human misery. Thus one man referred to parish gossip between women who had mentioned in confession that their husbands were using contraceptives 'and it has caused very, very great distress' (LI). Two respondents thought that contraception might have been a particular cause of suffering or conflict in their parents' marriages (eg 4). As one woman put it: 'And that whole sex thing could have possibly led to something not quite right in my parents' relationship' (LI). In the case of one respondent (6) there was no distinction made between contraception and abortion; in both cases the teachings of the Church 'ruin a lot of people's lives'.

In the second category of excuses, the focus was more explicitly on the emotional strains resulting from the official teaching. In some cases reference was made to stress specifically on the mother, especially if she already had a number of small children to bring up (9). Thus references were made to 'the circumstances and how the mother can cope' (LI) and one woman observed that she had seen too much suffering and too many 'women old before their time through having too many children' (LI). For a young man contraception was necessary 'to actually protect women ... from having eight or nine children when they can only handle one or two' (LS) and a young mother feared she would be too harrassed to be a good mother if she had more than two or three children (PS). Other respondents referred in general to family stresses. Thus one young woman claimed scriptural support for her view:

In the Bible God said 'go out and love man'. He didn't say 'go and breed like rabbits' ... I don't think they have a right to put a strain on a family with fear of condemnation ... if you don't follow these rules they've laid down for us. Because they are not in the Bible, so they are of no relevance, as far as I am concerned. (LS; Female, 27, married, skilled manual; never)

Economic 'excuses' were also mentioned by a number of ordinary Catholics (10–11). This was particularly felt by those who already had several children and considered additional children would stretch their resources so far (10) that it would be difficult to 'bring children up properly' (LI) rather than 'in hardship' (LS). Others referred to the problems faced by young marrieds in finding appropriate shelter (11).

The next three categories of response (E, F and G) all have the nature of 'justifications' in the sense we have noted before, that is where responsibility is accepted for a breach of the official rules while denying that there is anything wrong with this (Scott and Lyman, 1968: 46). The first of these categories, mentioned mainly by people in the two suburban parishes, involves concern for the rapid increase in the world's population (12–13) with its concomitant problems of feeding it, preventing starvation, finding sufficient space for it, and generally a minimum quality of life. Thus for one respondent 'if they'd had the foresight, they would have realised the dangers of over-population and the doctrine would have been modified before now' (LS).

The second 'justification' identified the reasoning for the official ruling on contraception as inadequate (14–16). A number of quite distinct criticisms were made. Firstly it was argued that, unlike abortion, contraception did not involve the killing of life (14). Secondly, it was doubted that there was a clear indication of God's law (15). Thus one man observed:

You can't find [any] derivation for birth control [in scripture] ... And this makes me think that they're wrong ... I think they know that now ... [but] it's difficult to admit you are wrong; you're on a hiding to nothing ... It just seems ludicrous to let women have children and children ... [I've also come to] the realisation that sexual intercourse is ... not [just] specifically to have children ... [but also] an expression of love and affection and respect for each other. (PS; Male, 36, married, non-manual; weekly)

Thirdly, distinctions between the rhythm method and the use of the pill or mechanical methods of contraception were regarded as inappropriate or unconvincing, especially when questions of intentionality were considered (16). Thus a young woman argued:

I just can't see any reason why it's wrong ... If they can agree with the rhythm method I can't see why they can disagree with the pill ... In a lot of cases people just can't afford to have children; it's just not practical. And it causes a lot of problems in marriage if you've got to be thinking about the right time of the month and everything, you know. You can't regulate the sex life like that. It causes arguments and problems. (PS; Female, 20, single, non-manual; more than weekly)

Finally, a number of respondents commented that the teaching of the Church simply was not clear enough:

They don't give their reasons properly for it. (PI)

I wouldn't say that I'm in opposition to the Church on [contraception] because I don't know what the Church's ... teaching really is. (LS)

A related category suggested that religious authority in the Church on this issue was incoherent (17–18). What was stressed here, particularly by people in the London suburban parish, was that priests differed in their position and advice on the contraception issue. Gossip and conversation networks, especially for women, are probably extremely effective in disseminating such information where it is not a taboo subject. Thus reference was made by our respondents to the fact that 'different priests say different things' (LI) and the suggestion was made that 'priests must know and turn a blind eye' (LS). Under these circumstances the legitimacy of the clerical leadership is inevitably weakened.

For around one-half of our respondents authority appeared to be contested, to use Houtart's expression which we noted in the previous chapter. In the first place clerical authority is resented because priests 'don't have to suffer the consequences' (LI) of their teachings. Here we are concerned with the prohibition of contraception (19–21), but similar remarks were also made in connection with abortion and divorce. Thus a woman sterilised after she had had seven children thought:

they should relax a bit because it's not fair to children ... they don't bring them up for you ... They shouldn't tell people what to do; they don't know anything about married life. (Female, 42, married, manual; weekly)

Another woman remarked 'priests don't have families so don't understand' (PI). A third woman complained that 'a lot of people making the rules are not in a position of having to obey them' (PS) and a fourth that priests 'meddle too much in people's lives' (LI). A fifth described how she tried to reconcile her belief that it was a sin to go against the Church, even if the Church was mistaken, with the realities of her own situation:

to me, if the pope has said such-and-such a thing, then that's it, and if I've gone against the pope ... I'll have committed a sin ... Well I think it would have to be up to me in the end because ... [I] would have to solve the situation ... The priest himself is in a different situation to what I would be ... Supposing it was birth control and he said 'no you mustn't do it that way, you must do it this way'. And supposing I became pregnant again and I couldn't afford to be ... Then he hasn't got to live with that situation, has he? We have to. And who else is going to suffer? The rest of the family. So to me, I'd have to go it on my own ... I would probably ask his advice but if I didn't think he was right then I probably would [go it on my own] ... I usually solve my problems on my own. (LS; Female, 38, married, skilled; monthly)

Something of the flavour of the agonies over the ruling on contraception experienced by older generations of Roman Catholics is apparent in the comments of a man (20) who was active in one of the larger Catholic organisations. He considered that people of his parents' generation had suffered greatly as a result of the prohibition. He explained that he and his wife had 'always conformed to the rules of the Church', adding 'and I tell you one thing it's been bloody difficult!' He continued:

Although I have accepted the ruling of the Church ... nowadays I am not so sure in my own mind that it is sinful, say, to use the pill ... It's only when you are involved that you start really seriously thinking about these things. And what I think is this ... Sex is a part of marriage. It's not all of it, but it's a part of it and sex isn't merely the act of having intercourse ... Everybody ... needs some sort of love and affection ... And I feel if somebody says you mustn't make love to your wife ... (husband) ... or you mustn't give your wife (husband) a cuddle ... because if you do you are going to have some feelings and if you do that you are going to have intercourse, and if you do that you've got to conceive or you've got to leave it whether you conceive or not. I don't think ... that that is right. And I think that with an informed ... and sincere practising Catholic who have a family, you know, they're not being selfish ... in that sense, I don't think that using the pill is wrong.

Turning to his wife, he asked her if she agreed and she, with some emphasis affirmed 'I do, I do'. He continued:

That's what I call Christian marriage ... But what I am beginning to think is that the rules on these sort of things are based purely on the physical aspects of marriage. They're not on the spiritual aspects or love ... I don't think anybody is against the Church and I think in a lot of cases the Church is humane ... But I do think that on some of these things one gets the impression that the rules have been made by celibates for celibates. (LS; Male, 56, married, non-manual; more than weekly)

Two points in particular might be noted here. Firstly, there is in this man's unaggressive deliberations, not only the rebuke that the rules are made by those who do not really understand the situation, but also a reflection of a new emphasis in the theology of marriage on the validity of sexual intercourse in affirming the worth and love for the spouse. Such a shift of emphasis away from procreation has been a constant theme in the writings of lay specialists such as Dr Jack Dominion who sees sexual intercourse as 'a precious gift from God, a recurrent act of body language of love ... a recurrent affirmation of personhood ... confirming each other's sexual identity ... an act of reconciliation ... a continuous experience of hope of being loved ... an act of thanksgiving for our partner's being.' (1989; see also 1975: 165; 1977: 59–65; 1981: 95–7). Such a theology seems much closer to the everyday experiences of married people than the older emphasis on the primacy of procreation.

Secondly, it seems likely that this man is reflecting the agonies of the last generation of lay Catholics to accept the legitimacy of the clerical leadership to teach authoritatively in this area of personal relationships, even if that teaching is found to be unconvincing. Subsequent generations of Catholics seem much more likely to regard contraception as purely a personal matter and to halt 'creeping infallibility' at this point. In other words it seems that since the publication of *Humanae Vitae* (Paul VI, 1968) most lay Catholics have decided that the legitimacy of clerical authority should be excluded from this area. In all probability this exclusion is permanent and irreversible. A number of examples of such confined legitimacy were given by our respondents (22–3). Thus one woman confided that she disagreed with her husband who thought that he couldn't really be a Catholic if he disagreed 'with their ideas on birth control and divorce', adding 'you can disagree with certain things but still agree with Catholicism' (LS). Similarly a middle-aged man 'believed that it wasn't their prerogative to tell me whether I should have three or four children' (LS).

The next category of response explicitly appropriates legitimate authority in this area and stresses 'making up your own mind' on the basis of an 'informed' conscience (24–6). Thus a frequent Mass attender thought that:

the Church has got to change its view on contraception ... perhaps the Church's view of family ... and married life is rather restrictive ... I think the authority of the Church is something which is coming into question and I think that, more and more, people are beginning to think things out for themselves. And I think that if you are a true Christian, a true Catholic, who really believes in God, and so on, you hope that you will make your decisions with His help in a well-informed way ... There are a lot of ... practising Catholics who ... do not follow the authoritarian line of the Church. (PS; Female, 40, married, non-manual; more than weekly)

The final two categories of response focus more explicitly on reinterpretations of authority in this area. For some ordinary Catholics the teachings of the Church were to be regarded as guidelines to action rather than as immutable rules of conduct (27–8). Others anticipated that change in the official teaching would come eventually (29–30), even if the transformation would be painful both for those who previously had struggled to conform and for the clerical leadership which would have to retreat from a former position of certainty and authority. Interestingly, one respondent (29) observed that people might impose change in the rules on the leadership, in ways analogous to those others have suggested might be relevant in the case of intercommunion. A young man acknowledged that the teachings cannot be changed overnight because that 'would rock the boat too much', but also conceded that the rules were right for earlier generations of Catholics and were bound up with the 'Catholic family remaining Catholics and producing Catholics' (30). The suspicion that the prohibition of contraception was a device for ensuring the continued growth of the Catholic community in an earlier, defensive period was voiced by several of our respondents.

In a recent article a theologian has suggested that the way out of the present crisis over contraception may lie in the recognition that a shift of paradigm is taking place (Moore, 1989). The evidence we have reviewed suggests that the significance of such a shift of paradigm, which purports to legitimate the use of contraception within marriage, does not lie with lay people who have largely made up their own minds on this matter, and now regard it as none of the business of the clerical leadership in the Church. Rather such a shift will simply have relevance for the clerical leadership and provide them with a legitimation for a transformation in their own position. In the meantime, lay people will have moved on, possibly to contest the authority of the clerical leadership in other areas of religious life.

8.3 Abortion

The question of abortion is a related but quite different issue. Many traditional Catholics appear to regard it as a fundamental and defining mark of Catholic identity and loyalty. The strong participation of Catholics in pressure groups, such as the Society for the Protection of the Unborn Child (SPUC) and Life, is a measure of the peculiar abhorrence which many Catholics feel for abortion, given their beliefs in the creation of the human person at the point of conception. For these reasons it is rarely possible to have a serious and dispassionate debate about abortion within the Catholic community. All the same, the beliefs and attitudes which ordinary Catholics hold about abortion vary considerably. The assumption of a monolithic Catholic position is a popular myth.

Catholic attitudes and practices have been summarised elsewhere (Hornsby-Smith, 1987: 108–12). Thus in her study of *The People of Ship Street* in Liverpool in the 1950s, Kerr reported that Catholics rejected birth control but tolerated abortion up to three months (1958: 137, 170). When considering seven different circumstances in which abortion might be legalised, in a study of British social attitudes in the mid-1980s, it was reported that Roman Catholics were more resistant than other groups but that 'around a quarter support legal abortion for each of the reasons of preference, and at least 70 per cent support it if the mother's health is endangered or if the pregnancy has resulted from rape' (Jowell and Airey, 1984: 141; see also 136–43, 154–6).

In general, while Catholics usually express more restrictive attitudes towards abortion than other groups, nevertheless a substantial minority indicate that 'they do not have a conscientious objection to termination of pregnancy in virtually all cases' (Cheetham, 1976). In the surveys of ordinary Catholics in four parishes in the mid-1970s, two-fifths agreed that 'it is a good thing that abortion is available legally for those women who want one'. This proportion was under one-half that of non-Catholic electors in the same areas. In the 1978 survey of English Catholics, one quarter disagreed with the statement 'except where the life of the mother is at risk, abortion is wrong' (Hornsby-Smith and Lee, 1979: 192). Finally, in her study of family size and spacing in England and Wales in 1973, Cartwright reported that the proportion of mothers who had considered abortion when they found they were unintentionally pregnant did not vary to any significant extent with the mother's religion (1976: 69–71).

Our purpose in this section is to put some flesh on the bare bones of such survey findings. The ordinary Catholic electors we interviewed in four English parishes in the mid-1970s generally made fewer and briefer comments about abortion than about contraception, perhaps because the issue did not have the same direct impact on most of them in their everyday lives. Seven categories of response have been illustrated in Table 8.2. They did not reflect such overt contestation with religious authority as in the case of contraception, though some of the categories are similar to those identified in Table 8.1 and, in the case of several of our respondents, the two issues of contraception and abortion were considered together when commenting on questions of religious authority.

About one-quarter of our sample of ordinary Catholics expressed their opposition to abortion in a more-or-less unqualified way (1–2). Most of these Catholics saw the issue in absolute terms as the illegitimate and immoral taking of innocent human life. Even in the case of a rape victim, these Catholics saw abortion simply as murder (LI). Hence it should be banned (PI) and the Church was right to speak out against it (LS). Others feared a return to a jungle morality (LI) and argued that just as God had given life, so only God had the right to take it away (PI). A sense of absolute abhorrence is particularly acute in the case of Respondent 2.

While many of the remaining three-quarters of our sample also expressed strong opposition to abortion, they were all prepared, under some restricted and specified circumstances, to accept or even prescribe abortion. A small group of respondents redefined the problem (3–5) in such a way that some forms of abortion could be tolerated. Thus for Respondent 3 the foetus was not a human person until birth, and others did not regard it as murder, at least in the early stages of pregnancy.

A majority of ordinary Catholics was prepared to countenance abortion under some critical circumstances. Generally these circumstances were regarded simply as qualifying a fundamental opposition to abortion. The most frequently mentioned circumstances were medical reasons, particularly concerning the health or life of the mother (6), the victims of rape, particularly if they were under age (7), and if there was strong evidence that a child would be severely handicapped (8). Often several qualifying reasons were mentioned

Table 8.2. *Classification of responses on abortion*
(Catholic electors, four parishes)

A. *Neo-Official*
1. I'm totally against abortion ... under any circumstances because I think it's murder.
   (LI; Female, 61, married, skilled manual; weekly)
2. I think it's terrible ... wrong ... makes me angry ... people just ridding themselves of a child they don't want ... It's the worst kind of self-gratification, I think. They're just stepping outside the natural order of things. And ... Once you do that you're on a slippery path ... to anarchy ... it's just an extension of violence.
   (PS; Male, 36, married, non-manual; weekly)

B. *Redefined*
3. Until the baby is born, it is not a baby.
   (PS; Male, 28, single, non-manual; never)
4. I'm not against abortion in the first six weeks, but after that it's dreadful.
   (LI; Female)
5. I don't accept that abortion is murder.
   (LI; Female, 29, married, non-manual; special occasions)

C. *Mother's Health*
6. At one time I really thought it was sinful to have an abortion, but I think when you get married yourself ... if it's going to make the woman's health any worse or if her husband doesn't get on ... I mean it's not fair to the child.
   (LI; Female, 50, married, unskilled; special occasions)

D. *Rape*
7. I can't see how a girl of fourteen who is raped and who is obviously pregnant, why she shouldn't have an abortion, quite honestly.
   (PS; Male, 38, married, non-manual; weekly)

E. *Handicapped Child*
8. In certain circumstances it's probably better than having a child ... where it can be told in advance that the child is going to be ... a mongol or somebody is going to lead a vegetable-like existence.
   (LS; Female, 31, married, manual; weekly)

F. *Unwanted Child*
9. If somebody makes a mistake and somehow manages not to use contraceptive methods successfully ... then the abortion is better than an unwanted child ... I used to think it murder at one time ... Now, once again, as with so many other things, I'm not so sure.
   (LI; Female, 30, married, non-manual; monthly)

G. *Appropriated Legitimacy*
10. If they find out a woman is not having a perfect child, then she has a right to have an abortion.
    (LI; Female, 50, married, unskilled; special occasions)
11. I think it's wrong for them not to agree with it ... It's everybody to their choice ... I don't think religion should come into it ... the answer should be as the situation lies, shouldn't it?
    (LI; Female, 27, married, semi-skilled; special occasions)

Table 8.2. *cont.*

12. You should be able to give [children] the best or not have them at all. That's why abortion is important ... If I were expecting ... a child now, I couldn't move into a nice area ... and ... it would be spoiling my life ... [and] I would probably blame it.
(PI; Female, 23, single, casual worker; occasionally)

Key to respondent characteristics:
Parish; sex, age, marital status, occupational category; Mass attendance.

by the same respondent. Thus the young woman who would contemplate abortion in the case of severe handicap (8), would also accept it in the 'case of a mother being saved ... where it was the lesser of two evils', and prefaced her remarks by saying 'I'm terribly anti-abortion'. A teenage man who accepted abortion in rape cases where the girl was under age also thought it wrong to have abortion following a casual sexual relationship (PI). Similarly, a man who would accept abortion in the case of rape (7) found it abhorrent to use it simply as a form of birth control. He also expressed fears of a 'domino-effect':

It's not the fact that abortion is on a very wide scale, although that worries me. I think that's the tip of the iceberg, quite honestly. The next thing will be euthanasia ... I might be a pessimist but the next thing will be children at birth who are crippled ... We are tending to reject anything that is not proper. (PS; Male, 38, married, non-manual; weekly)

A fourth qualifying reason related to the case of the unwanted pregnancy, for example as a result of a failure of contraceptive methods. The respondent quoted (9) indicates strong elements of 'customary' Catholicism:

I used to think it murder at one time ... but that was me with my back to the wall and sort of feeling very Catholic ... and say[ing] there was a soul in the body and quoting the teachings of the Church. (LI)

She now no longer feels so sure about the absolutist position. It is here that one comes closest to the theological questioning analogous to what was seen as inadequate reasoning in the case of contraception. In general, though, the articulation of alternative reasoning is not so common in the case of abortion where the absolutist position seems to be regarded as more coherent than in the case of contraception.

The final category (10–12), appropriated legitimacy, mentioned by about one in ten of our respondents, parallels the same category found in the responses in the case of contraception. Again, the key theme is 'making up your own mind' and of the decision being 'up to the individual'. Thus a mother who had had severe problems of handicap with some of her own children, believed it was the right of every woman to have a 'perfect' child and hence to have an abortion where such handicap was anticipated (LI). Similarly, the young woman (11) who did not think 'religion should come into it' asked what a person, who on medical grounds could not have any more children, would do to cope with the predicament of pregnancy. In her view 'the answer would be as the situation lies' (LI). Another example of such a position was given by a young woman (12) who felt that an unwanted child would both spoil her life and also be likely to result in her subsequent resentment of the child.

It seems that while there is evidence that the official prohibition and abhorrence of abortion is qualified by many, perhaps the majority, of ordinary Catholics, unlike the case of contraception, this is not necessarily indicative of an explicit and recognised contestation of religious authority in the Church. While the potential for such contestation might well exist, it seems that the lower salience of the issue in the personal lives of most ordinary Catholics, allows them to express their 'customary' Catholicism with a vague and general condemnation of abortion, while at the same time being quite ready to qualify this in exceptional circumstances. While a large minority of ordinary Catholics emphasise the right to 'make up your own mind' in the case of abortion, adherence to the official position, even though this may be qualified, still appears to be the cultural norm.

8.4 Divorce

Our original question bracketed the three issues of contraception, abortion and divorce. In their replies our respondents commented on divorce rather less frequently than they did on contraception, which was a live issue for almost all ordinary Catholics, and abortion, where culturally based loyalty responses were sometimes expressed. In our four research parishes in the mid-1970s there were few differences between Roman Catholic and other electors on two questions relating to divorce. Just under one-half thought that divorce should be possible where a partner had committed adultery or considered that their marriage had broken down (Hornsby-Smith, 1987: 109). In the

1978 national survey nearly two-thirds agreed with the statements 'two people in love do not do anything wrong when they marry even though one of them has been divorced' and 'Catholics should be allowed to divorce' (Hornsby-Smith and Lee, 1979: 192). Analysis of marital breakdown on the basis of the national survey led to the tentative conclusion that 'overall, Catholics are not any less prone to divorce than members of the population at large' (Hornsby-Smith and Lee, 1979: 117). It seems that marital breakdown was concentrated among those in canonically invalid marriages (which had not been solemnised by a priest) and that those in valid mixed marriages were no more likely to experience breakdown than those in religiously homogeneous marriages (Hornsby-Smith, 1987: 113; see also Hornsby-Smith, Turcan and Rajan, 1987).

In this section we will outline some of the attitudes and beliefs expressed by ordinary Catholics on the matter of divorce. Eight categories of response, similar to those identified for contraception and abortion, have been illustrated in Table 8.3. As was the case with abortion, the responses did not reflect such overt contestation with religious authority as in the case of contraception.

About one-quarter of our responses fell into the first category, which followed the orthodox Catholic position of rejecting divorce (or the implicit right to remarry after divorce) under any circumstances. Some interpreted Christ's teaching (Matt. 19:6) literally and argued that 'there is no such thing as divorce' (1) or that one should 'keep to Christ's doctrine' (LS). A second group stressed the marriage vow 'till death do us part' (2), or insisted that 'if you're married, you're married' (LI). Respondents considered that 'marriage is a binding partnership' (PS) and 'for life' (PS). One respondent in a third group (3) rather gloried in the 'Church's rigidity and authoritarianism' because it meant that it did not 'blow with the wind' and submit to contemporary norms. In the words of a young mother whose parents were divorced, 'the Catholic view at least makes people stop and think and try to make marriage work', even if it was 'perhaps a bit too strict' (PS). Fourthly, there was a group of Catholics who stressed the importance of not breaking solemn vows (4). Thus a young, single man considered divorce was not morally justifiable more for this reason than from a religious point of view (PS). Others argued that because divorce was easy for people, they stopped trying to make their marriages 'work' (PS). This was 'an easy get-out' (PI) which 'lowers the whole standard of human life generally' (PS). As a young

Table 8.3. *Classification of responses on divorce*
(Catholic electors, four parishes)

A. *Neo-Official*

1. There's no such thing as divorce ... I don't believe [in] it. 'What God has joined together, let no man put asunder' ... People can get on if they want.
(PI; Male, 61, married, skilled; more than weekly)

2. Well, I've never agreed with divorce, never. Even the other Churches say 'till death do us part'.
(PI; Female)

3. It doesn't 'blow with the wind' very easily, the Catholic Church ... It's been the teaching of the Church for a long, long time. But it is not only that. It's God and Christ's teaching as well.
(PS; Male, 38, married, non-manual; weekly)

4. Well, if two people can't live together, I suppose they've got to separate ... But ... if you break your vows to that person, if marriage is to have any meaning at all, then in a religious sense I don't think you can marry again.
(PS; Male, 36, married, non-manual; weekly)

B. *Qualified*

5. For myself, divorce would be absolutely unacceptable ... But I couldn't say ... someone is damned for all eternity. I'm sure that God will understand about the problems and difficulties and judge in that way, about people who become divorced and remarried. But I think the Church is right to teach that divorce is wrong.
(PS; Female, 37, married, non-manual; more than weekly)

6. I'm not in favour of divorce from what I see at school ... I don't consider divorce a possibility for myself ... but I've got no qualms about it existing in the society where I'm living because you can't tell other people what to do.
(LI; Female, 24, single, teacher; weekly)

C. *Misery*

7. Divorce ... should be left to the person's circumstances ... If it's necessary to have a divorce and that's the best way out, well, let it be. If nothing else can be done, obviously ... If two people can't bear to live together or can't make it, well, why stay together?
(LI; Female, 27, married, non-manual; radio and TV)

8. It is strange that people should be bound together for life if they don't get on.
(LS; Male, 30, married, non-manual; radio and TV)

9. Where you must know you are not going to get on together ... there is no point in staying together. Then as long as you don't have children ... why ruin ... sacrifice yourself for the rest of your life? Life is there ... is worth living ... They shouldn't be that strict.
(LI; Female, 19, married, student; weekly)

D. *Violence*

10. I think [the Church is] far too strict ... Most people make mistakes ... not just because you get tired or fed up or something ... If your husband starts battering you, or things like that, should be grounds for divorce.
(PS; Female, 20, single, non-manual; more than weekly)

11. I myself wouldn't like a divorce, but again, I can appreciate if somebody's being battered by their husband.
(PS; Female, 41, married, non-manual; weekly)

Table 8.3. *cont.*

E. *Incoherent or resented authority*
12. I cannot go along with ... [the view that] if people have separated they should never live with another man, woman ... And I think there's an awful lot of annulments ... An annulment is nothing more than a divorce ... if you can afford it ... you can get it ... a mockery.
    (LS; Female, 31, married, non-manual; weekly)
13. If they've got divorced ... [and] ... want to marry in the church, why shouldn't they? Why should they have to go to the Registry Office?
    (PI; Male)

F. *Confined legitimacy*
14. I wouldn't like to think I couldn't get a divorce if my husband was beating me ... I don't think [the Church] should concern itself [with these matters] ... I wouldn't like to think the Church was dictating to me what I could do with my life.
    (PS; Female, 28, married, non-manual; most Sundays)
15. Divorce and birth control should be decided by yourself. Priests have no right to interfere; they have no experience of married life.
    (PI; Female, 36, married, manual; now and again)

G. *Appropriated legitimacy*
16. I think it should be up to people to decide for themselves, really ... I think, perhaps, if exceptions were made.
    (PS; Female, 24, married, non-manual; most Sundays)
17. It's up to you, really, for you to decide ... there's nothing wrong with it.
    (LI; Male, 23, single, skilled; weekly)

H. *Redefined legitimacy*
18. The Church does have something to say in this area but should allow people to use their own judgement.
    (LI; Male, 48, married, manual; radio and TV)

Key to respondent characteristics:
Parish; sex, age, marital status, occupational category; Mass attendance.

---

professional woman put it, 'life isn't all roses ... you have to work through the bad times' and be aware that 'expectations are too high' (LI).

Around one in ten of our sample of ordinary Catholics were prepared to qualify their more-or-less total opposition to divorce for themselves by allowing it for other people, or for society generally in some circumstances (5-6). Thus a young African woman thought divorce should be allowed only where there were no children (LI) and a middle-aged man thought divorce was alright for people who did not get on provided it was 'not made too easy' (LI). One young mother in her second marriage observed that the Church was trying to teach an ideal way of life in an imperfect world. While admitting that in the long-run divorce did not solve things, she felt that the Church should widen the scope of annulments. In the meantime she was unable to receive the sacraments but accepted 'her punishment' sadly: 'if you break the rules of the game'. For there had to be rules and it was not good for people to do what they liked (LI). (Strictly speaking it is not divorce which incurs sanctions in the contemporary Roman Catholic Church, but remarriage during the life-time of the former partner, other than in cases of annulments, where the original marriage has been declared to have been null and void.)

Two specific justifications for divorce were repeatedly mentioned: a fundamental inability to get on in ways which sometimes might be harmful to children, and marital violence or wife-beating. Nearly one-third of our respondents felt that marital misery was a sufficient justification for divorce (7–9). (Though it was rarely explicitly stated, the implication generally was that remarriage should be allowed.) The phrases used by different respondents were remarkably similar, referring to cases where marriages 'don't work' (LI and PS), or where the partners 'don't get on together' (PS, PI). Rhetorical questions were repeatedly asked: 'why should people have to suffer a life of misery?' (PS, PI), or 'why should people's lives be spoiled/wasted/sacrificed?' (PS, LI). In almost all such cases it was the marital partners who were being considered, though one young man did refer to the effect of marital conflict on the children (LS).

Nearly one in six of the ordinary Catholics who commented on divorce would allow it where there was serious family violence, usually wife-battering/beating by the husband (10–11). There was very little discussion about such cases; rather such violence was regarded as sufficient justification for a divorce. A mother of four admitted that at school she had accepted the Church's position without question, but observed that 'as you progress into life you become faced with these problems and you get a better understanding and compassion for the people involved' (PS). For reasons such as these, several respondents felt that the Church should 'keep out of these matters' (PS).

The remaining one-fifth of the comments made on divorce were distributed evenly over four categories, which are similar to those identified in the analysis of responses relating to contraception. The underlying theme here would appear to be some form of contestation of the authority of the official leadership of the Church. In the first of these categories, the distinct notions of incoherence and resentment, separated in the analysis of contraception, have been collapsed. Apart from the two cases outlined, one of whom considered that the Church's teaching on divorce and annulments was 'a mockery' which 'doesn't hold much water to me' (12) and the other who resented the prohibition of remarriages in church (13), only one other case was placed in this category. An Italian woman felt that the Church:

can tell them what's wrong, but not to punish them. The Church should never punish anybody. It should tell: 'that is wrong, you shouldn't do it' and tell them the reason why, but then should never punish ... God did teach to forgive ... People decide for themselves ... If they really suffer, then it's best they part ... But it's personal, isn't it? The Church should leave them alone ... It should tell them, not to give them a free hand, but shouldn't interfere, absolutely, should tell it's wrong, that's all. (LI; Female, 49, married, manual; most Sundays)

The key theme of the next category (14–15) is the negative one that the Church, or its priests, should keep out of personal matters. The claim being made here is that this was an area where the everyday knowledge and experience of the ordinary Catholic was a determining consideration because 'they have no experience of married life' (15). One other respondent observed that friends of hers were right to get divorced 'in the circumstances' and that 'the Church should have kept out of these personal matters, not even to give guidelines' (PS). This goes further than the next category (16–17) where the key element is the positive appropriation by lay people of the right to 'make up their own minds' and 'decide for themselves', as best they can 'according to their own criteria' (LI). In the final category (18) the key element is that the Church's teaching is interpreted to be guidelines to action rather than absolute rules. As one young woman put it, on this basis it was possible to disagree with the pope but this was better than the traditional view of an unquestioning adherence to authority (PS). Finally, while there were no close equivalents of the category of anticipated transformation, such as were identified in the case of contraception, one respondent did think that the Church would in time find some way round Christ's teaching because so many people were perhaps dropping out of the Church as a result of its strict stand on divorce (PS).

8.5 The loss of clerical authority

In this chapter we have reviewed the wide range of comments made by samples of randomly selected ordinary Catholics in four English parishes in the mid-1970s on three controversial issues of personal morality. Twelve distinct categories of response were distinguished in the case of contraception, seven in the case of abortion and eight in the case of divorce. There were, however, some clear parallels in the three cases. All included a proportion who expressed neo-official views though in the case of contraception this proportion was minute. When those who offered some form of redefined or qualified orthodoxy are included, around one-third of the responses on both abortion and divorce could be considered neo-official. The bulk of responses on all three issues fell under the broad heading of excuses and justifications (Scott and Lyman, 1968: 47) though the proportion ranged from over two-fifths for contraception and divorce to three-fifths in the case of abortion. The third broad category of response fell under the heading of the more-or-less explicit contestation of authority (Houtart, 1969). Here the proportion ranged widely from one-tenth, in the case of abortion, to one-fifth, in the case of divorce, and over one-half in the case of contraception.

The evidence, therefore, is consistent with a process of contestation with the religious leadership in the Church over what counts as appropriate personal morality for the contemporary Roman Catholic. Direct contestation of the official orthodoxy is found least in the case of abortion. This may well reflect the fact that the direct experience of abortion is relatively rare for ordinary Catholics. Whatever the reason, most Catholics continue to express a strong antipathy towards abortion, even though a majority of them would tolerate it in a limited range of special circumstances, such as the rape of an under-age girl. Some redefined the status of the foetus at different stages to justify their rejection of the official teaching.

Statistically, marital breakdown and divorce is a much more common experience for ordinary Catholics, even though the traditional position on lifetime marriage continues to attract strong support. This appears to be reflected in the larger proportion of Catholics prepared to contest the official position, at least over the treatment of the divorced and remarried.

The case of contraception appears to be different, or at least to have gone a great deal further. Unlike abortion and to a lesser extent divorce, this is a matter which actually or potentially affects the vast majority of ordinary Catholics in their everyday lives. There seems no doubt that by the mid-1970s only a tiny minority was prepared to give unqualified assent to the official teaching. Under one-half of our respondents offered a range of excuses and justifications for their rejection of this teaching, while well over one-half more-or-less explicitly contested religious authority in this case. Some regarded the teaching given by different priests as incoherent or inconsistent, while others resented what they saw as the unwarranted assumption of clerical authority in such a private area of their lives. As many as one in five of our respondents felt that clerical authority ought to be confined to more specifically 'religious' matters while others explicitly appropriated this matter of private morality as one where they were entitled to 'make up their own minds'. Finally some considered a transformation of the official position to be simply a matter of time and the practical politics of not 'rocking the boat'.

This review of the findings of intensive interviewing programmes suggests that there has been a fundamental shift in Catholic attitudes towards the authority of the clerical leadership, at least in the areas of personal morality. What seems to have been indicated by our interview data is a retreat from moral absolutes and the search for some form of 'realistic' adjustment to the perceived complexities, dilemmas and conflicts that are the everyday experiences of lay people. Some have suggested that there has been a paradigm shift, for example in the case of contraception. This might well be the case for the clerical leadership of the Church, as it struggles to maintain legitimate authority over lay people. But our data suggest strongly that the clerical leadership of the Church has lost authority, certainly in the case of contraception, and arguably is in the process of doing so over the less contentious issues of divorce and abortion. In the areas of personal morality more and more Catholics, including those who are institutionally highly committed, are deciding that these areas are not the business of priests, though their guidance may still be acceptable, and that final decision-making must be left to those most concerned to make up their own minds.

9

ENGLISH CATHOLICS AND RELIGIOUS AUTHORITY

9.1 Weberian perspectives

In this chapter we will continue our analysis of the changing nature of religious authority among Roman Catholics in England by exploring the utility of the well-known Weberian typology of legitimate authority (Weber, 1964: 328; 1968: I, 215–16). It will be argued that since the 1950s the Church has experienced a paradigmatic shift (Kuhn, 1970) from a 'mechanistic' to an 'organic' model (Burns and Stalker, 1966). During the period of transition there have been both overt and covert conflicts and contestation between those favouring the earlier and later paradigms. As we have noted previously, these conflicts cross-cut the boundaries separating the clergy from the laity so that there has not been in this country a generalised anti-clericalism.

In order to understand our data it is necessary to place English Catholics in a proper social, religious and historical context. Up to the 1950s a broadly 'mechanistic' model appeared to be appropriate for an unchanging and stable Church. Thus the hierarchical nature of the Church was explicit and pervasive. The pope was Christ's representative on earth, invested with 'sacred' qualities in the popular mind. Below him came the cardinals, the 'princes of the Church', and the archbishops and bishops. At the local or parish level the parish priests and their curates or assistant priests were seen as representative officials of the hierarchy. The priest was considered to be 'a sacred person whose inherent dignity separated him from the laity, over whom he was infinitely superior' (Moore, 1975: 46). The laity were generally regarded as at the base of the pyramid of offices, and they were socialised to a proper deference to clerical super-ordinates whose authority was rarely challenged. For the largely Irish, working-class Catholic community in England and Wales, clerical authority was traditional. But it was also legal–rational in the sense that the processes of Roman centralism, in the century since the restoration of the hierarchy in 1850, had become institutionalised and rule-bound.

The Church in the 1950s was a bureaucratically-administered religious organisation with the pope as the supreme source of decision-making. Decisions were made by the pope and his ecclesiastical subordinates and communicated downwards to the parish clergy and lay people. Religious life was characteristically rule-bound (for example on Mass attendance, fasting, mixed marriages, contraception, ecumenical relations, and so on) and enforced by an imposing battery of religious sanctions (such as the threat of eternal damnation for mortal sin and the pains of purgatory for venial sins). Something of the flavour of this style of Catholicism is conveyed in the appropriately named piece of 'faction' by David Lodge, *How Far Can You Go?* (1980) before what he calls the loss of the fear of hell.

The shift to the post-Vatican Church was paradigmatic in nature (Kuhn, 1970). Considered as a religious organisation, the structure of the Church shifted from the 'mechanistic' to the 'organic' (Burns and Stalker, 1966). The Second Vatican Council endeavoured to reform the Church so that it would be more responsive to the needs of people living in the contemporary world (Butler, 1981). This was reflected in particular in the new theological emphases on the concepts of collegiality, the full participation of the laity as the 'people of God' in the life of the Church, and the pilgrim nature of their missionary task which eschewed absolute or permanent answers to everyday pastoral problems and needs. The reforms were most immediately noticeable in the new styles of liturgical worship. These stressed the full participation of the laity and rejected the spectator model of worship, with the priest as the sole representative mediator between lay people and God. Implicit in the conciliar paradigm of the Church were new models of parish, priest and parishioner (Hornsby-Smith, 1989). New structures were created at the parochial, deanery, diocesan, national, regional and global levels, which allowed lay people at least some opportunities for offering advice on matters on which they had some expertise and sometimes for participation in decision-making.

In his treatment of different forms of legitimate domination, Weber distinguishes the concept of power, which 'is the probability that one actor within a social relationship will be in a position to carry out his own will despite resistance, regardless of the basis on which this probability exists', from that of authority which 'is the probability that a command with a given specific content will be obeyed by a given group of persons' (1964: 152; 1968: 53). This led him 'to classify the types of authority according to the kind of claim to legitimacy typically made by each' (1964: 325; 1968: 213). In particular he distinguished three types of legitimate authority based on legal–rational, traditional and charismatic grounds (1964: 328; 1968: 215). In the following sections of this chapter we will use this typology as a point of departure for the assessment of the nature of religious authority in the contemporary Church in the light of our various data sources.

A number of commentators have drawn attention to a 'missing' fourth type of 'value-rational' authority (Willer, 1967; Satow, 1975; Hammond et al, 1978) in Weber's treatment, and others have suggested various elaborations (Harrison, 1960; 1971). Weber anticipated this when he denied that 'the whole of concrete historical reality can be exhausted in the conceptual scheme' which he developed (Weber, 1964: 329; 1968: 216). It will be suggested that our own empirical data indicate the need to extend or modify Weber's categories.

9.2 Legal–rational authority

The essential features of Weber's ideal-type of legal–rational authority with its rule-bound conduct of official business, its hierarchical organisation of offices, its officials with defined areas of competence and powers, its written records and rules, and so on, are well known. Weber's model has found its expression in classical organisation theory (Rudge, 1968: 26–7) and in the identification of mechanistic management systems appropriate under stable conditions (Burns and Stalker, 1966: 119–20). It is interesting to note that Weber's chief historical example was the Roman Catholic Church with the doctrine of papal infallibility involving claims to universal legal competence in religious matters (Weber, 1964: 334; 1968: 221).

According to Weber, the monocratic variety of bureaucracy is technically the most efficient and rational means of exercising authority over people in terms of its precision, stability, stringency of its discipline, its reliability and predictability (1964: 337; 1968: 223, 1973ff). Weber has, of course, been strongly criticised for his assumption of efficiency and there is a considerable literature on the dysfunctions of bureaucracy and especially its inability to cope with changing conditions (Burns and Stalker, 1966). For religious organisations in particular, there are dilemmas inherent in the institutionalisation of religious experiences and the loss of spontaneity involved in the achievement of stability as a result of the routinisation of charismatic movements (O'Dea, 1970). Thus for Weber, the bishop, the priest and the preacher are no longer carriers of a purely personal charisma, but impersonal officials in the service of the Church (Weber, 1968: 959). The concentration of administration to which Weber refers is evident in the work of the Roman Curia and the increasing centralising tendencies in the global Church.

Weber also makes some perceptive observations about the bureaucratic consequences of processes of mass democratisation, such as the conciliar advocacy of increasing lay participation in the life of the Church, which more often than not result in 'passive democratisation' and the 'levelling of the governed' in the face of an autocratic bureaucracy (Weber, 1968: 985). Indications of such processes are apparent in the increasing involvement of lay experts in the advisory structures in the Church, where decision-making has been strongly influenced by 'bureaucratically articulated' activist, middle-class, progressive elites (Hornsby-Smith, 1987: 133–56; Archer, 1986). Although there clearly is more lay participation in the Church now than in the pre-war years, in many ways it still remains somewhat limited, for example at the parish level, as a result of clerical intransigence or lay passivity (Hornsby-Smith, 1989: 190–6).

While it is clear that there never was a 'golden past' in the evolution of contemporary English Catholicism (Hornsby-Smith, 1987: 26–31), there are good grounds for believing that up to the 1960s the beliefs and practices of Catholics – from frequency of Mass attendance and reception of the sacraments, and fasting and abstinence, to entry into religiously 'mixed' marriages, and so on – were more strongly rule-bound than they are now. Religious sanctions, such as the threat of eternal damnation and excommunication were real, familiar and relatively effective. This rule-bound form of Catholicism was reinforced by a defensive social stance in a relatively hostile environment and a defiantly aggressive religious triumphalism. On the basis of the interview data which we have reviewed in previous chapters, it is apparent that by the mid-1970s these Church rules were no longer so widely known, salient or effective. In the novelist's insightful phrase, there was a loss of the fear of hell:

At some point in the nineteen-sixties, Hell disappeared. No one could say for certain when this happened. First it was there, then it wasn't. Different people became aware of the disappearance of Hell at different times. Some realised that they had been living for years as though Hell did not exist, without having consciously registered its disappearance. Others realised that they had been behaving, out of habit, as though Hell were still there, though in fact they had ceased to believe in its existence long ago. By Hell we mean, of course, the traditional Hell of Roman Catholics, a place where you would burn for all eternity if you were unlucky enough to die in a state of mortal sin. On the whole, the disappearance of Hell was a great relief, though it brought new problems. (Lodge, 1980: 113)

In spite of the evidence of major religious transformations in recent decades, our data do indicate the continuation for many English Catholics of a legal–rational form of authority. Thus when people attending the public events during Pope John-Paul's visit in 1982 were asked what they thought the job of a pope was, around half of them responded in terms of his role as head of the Church:

Well I suppose his . . . divine job is to lead the Church . . . that's the people of Christ on earth. Er, in a more limited way it's to lead the Catholic Church throughout the world. (Wembley)

He is the inheritor of St Peter and from St Peter it has been handed down through popes, and the pope is the head of the Church. (Liverpool)

Subsequently about one-quarter gave unqualified acceptance to the pope's authority and claimed that they did not make up their own minds on any aspect of his teaching. Of those responding to the questionnaire distributed four months after the pope's visit, two-fifths thought the pope's teaching should be obeyed without question, three-fifths agreed with papal infallibility and four-fifths thought his teachings were all directly inspired by God. While in some respects these data may relate to the charisma of the office, it is also likely that they reflect a continuation of a mechanistic, rule-bound model of the Church where the pope, as one of our respondents put it, was the nearest thing to God in a hierarchy of offices, with God as the supreme master and the pope as His 'vicar on earth', the visible head of a clerical bureaucracy.

At the parish level the priest is then seen as the local official responsible for the transmission of 'sacred' commands and the legitimate interpreter of the moral rule book. The persistence of this view of authority is evident in the repeated appeals to 'what Father says' by parishioners unhappy with, or anxious about, the claims and challenges made by 'progressive' Catholics. In spite of the fact that in Catholic theology the parish clergy, like the People of God generally (*Lumen Gentium*, ch. 2), participate in Christ's three-fold office of priest, prophet and king, in practice the role and responsibilities of the priest in Canon Law are expressed very much in legal–rational terms. It is significant that 'only clerics can obtain offices the exercise of which requires the power of order or the power of ecclesiastical governance' (1983; Can. 274 s. 1). Canon 519 specifies that the parish priest exercises the pastoral care of those entrusted to him under the authority of the diocesan bishop and Canons 528–30 specify his duties (Hornsby-Smith, 1989: 130–33).

Before leaving this discussion of legal–rational authority in the Church, it is worth commenting briefly on the modification of it suggested as a result of a study of the American Baptist Convention. Harrison argued that:

the voluntary, anti-authoritarian social groups of the modern world have found it necessary to organise in accord with bureaucratic principles without conferring upon their leaders a rational–legal authority. (1971: 209)

He recognised that people obey leaders for a variety of reasons other than the recognition of legal authority and described the authority of Baptist executives as 'legal–pragmatic' or expediential, and deriving from their religious experiences rather than from their ecclesiastical agencies (1971: 104). This form of authority would seem to have very clear parallels in the case of those staff working in such Catholic organisations as CAFOD (Catholic Fund for Overseas Development) or CIIR (Catholic Institute for International Relations). It seems likely that their authority with justice and peace activists, for example, is legitimised as much by their experience of development issues and the prophetic character of their 'significant others' in the Third World, as from any formal legal–rational status they might have as Catholic agencies recognised by the bishops.

The interview data we have reviewed in previous chapters might also be taken to indicate that many ordinary Catholics regard the authority of the pope or parish priest in a similar light. Thus while there is a recognition of their legal–rational status within the institutional Church, there is also clear evidence that many Catholics regard the official teachings of the clerical leadership to be guides to action, rather than invariant rules to be obeyed without question. In this they appeal pragmatically or expedientially to the Vatican Council's teaching on religious freedom and the primacy of the individual conscience (*Gaudium et Spes*, ss. 16–17; *Dignitatis Humanae*, s. 3; in Abbott, 1966: 213–14, 681).

In sum, the evidence seems to suggest that, with the shift from a 'mechanistic' to a more 'organic' model of the Church in recent decades, there has been a decline in the extent to which religious authority has been legitimated on legal–rational grounds. It is certainly true that these grounds continue to be tenaciously avowed by a significant minority of English Catholics. For these people the pope or their parish priest is a religious 'boss' to be obeyed because he is their lawful superior and they are his subordinates in a hierarchical Church. But there is also much evidence to suggest that many are selecting a Catholic variant of the rational–pragmatic form of authority and are justifying this in terms of the conciliar teaching on the participation of the laity in decision-making (e.g. *Lumen Gentium*, s. 37 in Abbott, 1966: 64) and the primacy of an 'informed' conscience.

9.3 Traditional authority

Weber's second type of legitimate authority is based on claims for 'the sanctity of age-old rules and powers' (1964: 341; 1968: 226–7). It would seem that the claims of the papacy have often been legitimated in these terms. Thus it is claimed that the pope is the successor of Peter, and therefore has the traditional authority of the Keys (to the Kingdom of God; Matt. 16: 17–19). The appeals of Pope Paul VI in *Humanae Vitae* (1968) or of Pope John-Paul II on clerical celibacy or the proper role of women in the Church were couched in the language of the age-old tradition of the Church and the assumed traditional (though in fact historically variable) authority of the pope. Similarly Catholic traditionalists, protesting against the loss of the Latin Tridentine Mass, appeal to the Council of Trent and what they interpret to be the unchanging tradition of the Church as their authority.

In our discussion of the interviews with people who attended the public events during the pope's visit in 1982, we noted that the

Petrine claims were explicitly referred to by around one in eight of our respondents. Furthermore, about one-quarter specifically mentioned the pastoral role of spiritual guidance and teaching, frequently in terms of the traditional model of the shepherd leading his flock and tending the sheep. An ordinary Catholic who was a regular Mass attender, asked to explain her belief that the Church had unlimited authority, observed:

Yes, more or less, because the instructions come from the pope and we have to appreciate that the pope is sort of in place of St Peter . . . Yes, I accept what the Church says, as a ruling . . . I don't think we can do anything because what is to be will be . . . because we are just nonentities who don't know enough about why things should change . . . Who are we to say what the Church should do or shouldn't do? (LS; Female, 56, married, manual; weekly)

As Harrison has indicated, more often than not motives are mixed (1971: 71) and this seems to be indicated in the above extract. The respondent seems partly to imply a legal–rational form of authority but also to take for granted that 'what is to be will be' or that this is the traditional way of things.

Instances of a traditional legitimation of religious authority were found amongst some of the members of the bishops' commissions interviewed in the mid-1970s. Thus one man (c39) who appeared to distrust the competence of lay people in the specialised area of religion and was 'not at all in favour of the layman having to work everything out for himself', appeared to legitimate priestly authority on traditional and deferential grounds. A middle-aged woman observed that a lot of Catholics were afraid of doing anything unless they were told that it was alright (c3). They were puzzled when a priest asked them what they thought and their reaction was 'what's the matter, Father, don't you know?' (c33). A middle-aged man (c35) qualified his 'absolute loyalty to the Church' by adding 'but without the old-type fear and rule' by the priest. Some members urged strongly that the sort of traditional authority of the priest in the parish, which expressed itself in a sense of their ownership of the Church: 'my church, my people . . . my buildings' (c11) and led to lay deference to the fact that 'Father didn't like this', had to be contested.

Several of these core Catholics suggested that traditional, unthinking, deferential forms of loyalty were the product of an older form of socialisation appropriate in former times but quite ineffectual with their children's generation. One man (c29) told the story of a friend, dutifully sitting through a particularly bad sermon, expostulating 'Oh, bloody hell! When is this going to end?' This informant observed that 'people formed in a previous age will submit to it out of a sense of loyalty, but you won't get this with the younger generation'. What seems to be suggested here is that older forms of traditional legitimation of clerical authority, which were appropriate for generations brought up before the 1960s, were either being totally rejected by younger generations or being replaced by new forms of legitimation based on consultation and shared decision-making.

In his analysis of the American Baptist Convention, Paul Harrison refers, in situations lacking 'the usual validity of "long-standing" practice', to what he calls 'mimetic–traditional' authority. This 'indicates a spontaneous effort to mimic tradition in order to establish a legitimate basis of authority' (1971: 214). One example of this would appear to be the post-conciliar quest for 'community' legitimated by the rediscovery of the tradition of the early Church (e.g. Acts, 2: 42–7, 4: 32–5; *Lumen Gentium* in Abbott, 1966, the *Sharing Church* in Anon, 1981; Dulles, 1976; Clark, 1977; Hornsby-Smith, 1989: 66–94). Another example would be the rediscovery of scriptural justice themes articulated by liberation theologians. To some extent, therefore, Harrison's concept of 'mimetic–traditional' does appear to have some value.

Attention has been drawn by Coman (1977: 11–14) to the 'Roman contribution' in the shaping of the English Catholic community, with its assumed particular loyalty to the pope and deference to the Roman central bureaucracy. In the light of this it had been anticipated that the people who would attend the public events of Pope John-Paul's visit to Britain in 1982 would be disproportionately traditional Catholics with a special loyalty to the pope. In the event, as we have shown in chapter 6, only a small minority of our interviewees could be described as traditional Catholics. The evidence indicated either that the traditional authority of the pope has been very much attenuated among English Catholics in recent decades, or that they had never had as strong a personal loyalty to the pope as their Roman-trained bishops. In general we have seen in the detailed analysis of our various data sources that most Catholics, from the core activists on the national advisory bodies to the ordinary Catholics in the parishes, contest the claims of both traditional and autocratic forms of legal–rational authority in the Church.

9.4 Charismatic authority

What then of Weber's third type of legitimate authority? The overwhelmingly positive comments on Pope John-Paul II by Catholics in England and Wales led us initially to describe his authority as charismatic. The concept, however, requires not only personal magnetism but also the following of the teaching of the charismatic leader or teacher. For Weber, charisma refers to the exceptional powers of a 'leader' to induce in his 'followers' a recognition of those powers and to act accordingly:

> From a substantive point of view, every charismatic authority would have to subscribe to the proposition, 'It is written ... but I say unto you ... ' The genuine prophet ... and every true leader in this sense, preaches, creates or demands *new* obligations. (Weber, 1964: 358–61; 1968: 241–3)

In the study which we reported in chapter 6 there were certainly indications that Pope John-Paul II was considered to have exceptional powers or qualities, but what was much more problematic was the nature of the response of his 'followers'. Yet Weber insists that the basis of genuine charismatic authority resides in its recognition in appropriate action. We have seen that only one in four Catholics attending the public events during the pope's visit to Britain was prepared to follow his teaching without question, and that the majority saw him simply as a celebrity who was a 'great guy', but that they made up their own minds on matters of personal and social morality. There was little sense in our interview material that the teaching of the pope had resulted in a 'radical alteration of the central attitudes and directions of action with a completely new orientation of all attitudes towards the different problems of the "world"' (Weber, 1964: 363; 1968: 245).

In Weber's analysis 'charismatic authority repudiates the past, and is in this sense a specifically revolutionary force' (1964: 361–2; 1968: 244). Bureaucratic authority, on the other hand, is bound by rules while traditional authority is bound by precedents from the past (1964: 361–2; 1968: 244). The data we have reviewed in previous chapters appear to suggest a weakening of rule-bound religious authority, whether bureaucratic or traditional, but also the absence of any radical changes in moral attitudes or religious behaviour as a result of the pope's visit. There seems little doubt that, in terms of

Weber's criteria, especially that of the subjection of followers to the teaching of the master, for English Catholics Pope John-Paul II is not a charismatic leader.

Weber argued that if charisma was to persist it had to become 'either traditionalised or rationalised' (1964: 364; 1968: 246). This led him to consider the 'routinization of charisma' and the 'charisma of office' (1964: 363ff; 1968: 246ff). It might be argued that our interview data indicated that, to a limited extent, Catholics in England and Wales recognised the charisma of office of the papacy, and it would seem likely that in its routinisation it has become a combination of both traditional and legal–rational authority. However, as we have previously indicated, our data suggest that, whatever the nature of this combination, for ordinary Catholics, this authority is so attenuated that it appears that the pope in fact has very little religious authority.

A distinction might be made between his authority over his priestly subordinates in the hierarchically-structured Church and his authority over lay people whose compliance is more obviously voluntary and expediential. While for many priests there appears to be a recognition of the pope's legal–rational authority, it seems likely that in the past two or three decades the unconditional nature of their compliance has been transformed, so that even for priests it might be possible to speak of a decline of papal authority (Hornsby-Smith, 1980; 1989: 147–72). For lay Catholics the burden of our data is that in recent years their compliance has become more conditional and pragmatic than in the pre-Vatican period. We have demonstrated that Catholics increasingly make up their own minds, especially on moral issues, so that it appears that papal authority has something of the rational–pragmatic quality suggested by Harrison (1971: 209–12).

Harrison also distinguished a sub-type of charismatic authority. He suggested that a quasi-charismatic leader is a successor to the original charismatic founder who is 'endowed with sufficient qualities of the original leader to warrant obedience'. He also referred to an 'expediential motivation' for this type of authority (1971: 213). Insofar as recent popes have attracted Catholics by their personal qualities, their authority seems to have been quasi-charismatic. Pope John XXIII in particular attracted people because he appeared to be peculiarly endowed with a shepherd-like concern and warmth towards ordinary people. Nevertheless, there is no convincing evidence that this attraction warranted obedience, for example in moral matters. The element of expediential motivation appeared to be prominent in the comments of many of our Catholic respondents, as has been shown in previous chapters. Thus while it might be possible to speak of the quasi-charismatic authority of the pope or parish priest, in reality this authority is very limited and is entirely conditional on its perceived pragmatic rationality or commonsensical characteristics for ordinary people in their everyday moral choices.

Before ending this discussion of charismatic authority, a brief discussion of Weber's treatment of prophecy seems appropriate. In particular, he distinguishes between the personal call of the prophet and the service of the priest in a sacred tradition (1966: 46–7). While it could be argued that Pope John XXIII's call for *aggiornamento* was prophetic and constituted a charismatic-like appeal, there is little sense in which it could be said that the teaching of Pope John-Paul II in Britain was prophetic, except possibly with respect to his strong assertion at Coventry that modern warfare is totally unacceptable as a means of settling disputes between nations (1982: 170). The most that our data would indicate is that the pope's teaching is regarded as a set of guidelines which, to a greater or lesser extent, may be considered in reaching a decision on moral issues. These decisions appear, in the main, to be pragmatic and commonsensical and, as we demonstrated above in chapter 5, frequently characterised by convenience, triviality, conventionality, apathy and self-interest (Hornsby-Smith, Lee and Reilly, 1985).

9.5 Empirical combinations

Two further aspects of Weber's analysis of authority might be mentioned. In the first place, in his discussion of combinations of the different types of authority (1964: 382–6; 1968: 262–6), Weber stresses that the existence of any one of his pure types of authority in a 'ruling organisation' is exceptional, and that in reality various combinations of authority are typically found. For any organisation to continue functioning, 'the habit of obedience' must be maintained and 'solidarity of interest' between the chief and his administrative staff be maximised, given that historically there has invariably been latent conflict between them. There is evidence that where there has been 'systematic habituation to illegal behaviour [which has] undermined the amenability to discipline', this has 'prepared the way for the overthrow of the older authority'. Hence the 'disinterested ideological factor', the commitment to their technical functions by the administrative staff has been crucial.

Applying this analysis to the case of English Catholicism, we have suggested that indeed a combination of Weber's types of religious authority can be discerned, but that these may more closely approximate to Harrison's sub-types: rational–pragmatic, mimetic–traditional and quasi-charismatic. The clerical staff of the Church in England appears substantially to have retained a habit of obedience to, and a solidarity of interest with, the pope. There have been instances of overt clerical disobedience, for example over clerical celibacy (Hastings, 1978), but these are relatively rare. On the other hand, the numerous instances where priests have become formally laicised or have publicly disagreed with the pope on contraception (Hornsby-Smith, 1989: 154–6) indicates a considerable measure of latent conflict. In the case of the laity, the evidence of overt disagreement and non-compliance with the papal teaching on contraception, which we have reviewed in previous chapters, is overwhelming, and suggests the possibility that systematic and unrepentant habituation to proscribed sexual and marital attitudes and behaviour have been conducive to the rejection of papal authority in other areas.

Secondly, Weber continues his analysis of the routinisation of charisma by discussing its transformation in an anti-authoritarian or democratic direction (1964: 386–92; 1968: 266–71). Authority may be limited by various types of collegiality, for example 'functional collegiality with a pre-eminent head' and collegial advisory bodies. The completion of the unfinished business of the First Vatican Council at the Second Vatican Council, and its specification of the collegiality of the bishops (*Lumen Gentium*, s. 22, in Abbott, 1966: 42–4), the periodic Synod of Bishops in Rome, and the emergence of national bishops' conferences may be cited as examples of the former, and the development of various participatory structures at parish, deanery, diocesan and national levels of the Church in England and Wales, may be considered to be examples of the latter.

In the latter case Weber points out that advisory bodies are usually 'made up either of technical experts or of persons of high social prestige or both'. Weber points out that:

Any interest in reviving the principle of collegiality in actual executive functions is usually derived from the interest in weakening the power of persons in authority. This, in turn, is derived from mistrust and jealousy of monocratic leadership, not so much on the part of those subject to authority, who are more likely to demand a 'leader', as on the part of the members of the administrative staff. (Weber, 1964: 398; 1968: 277)

The evidence from studies of Catholic 'elites' in England and Wales bears out this analysis. The lay members of the bishops' national commissions and the delegates to the National Pastoral Congress were overwhelmingly middle-class and middle-aged 'progressives' with an interest in shared decision-making in the Church (Hornsby-Smith, 1987: 133–56). In the meantime the mass of 'underprivileged' lay Catholics is 'oppressed' by a predominantly middle-class style of religion (Archer, 1986) and duly complies with a response which varies from a passive, deferential apathy to a sullen, latent hostility. As David Martin has suggested, 'the working-class either obeys or silently pursues its way in the usual manner of erring humanity' (1972: 188). In other words, as we have seen in previous chapters, they generally make up their own minds on issues which most directly effect their everyday lives.

9.6 Etzioni's analysis of compliance

This leads us to consider the nature of the compliance of Catholics to the decisions and commands of the clerical leadership. In his comparative analysis of complex organisations, Etzioni used the term 'compliance' to refer 'both to a relation in which an actor behaves in accordance with a directive supported by another actor's power, and to the orientation of the subordinated actor to the power applied' (1961: 3). He distinguishes three types of power: coercive, remunerative and normative, and three corresponding, and generally congruent, types of individual involvement in the organisation: alienative, calculative and moral. Religious organisations, such as the Catholic Church, are regarded primarily as 'normative organisations' which rely primarily on the use of 'normative power' to achieve the 'moral involvement' of their members. In Etzioni's ideal-type:

Normative power rests on the allocation and manipulation of symbolic rewards and deprivations through employment of leaders, manipulation and mass media, allocation of esteem and prestige symbols, administration of ritual and influence over the distribution of 'acceptance' and 'positive response' ... Normative organisations are organisations in which normative power is the major source of control over most lower participants, whose orientation to the organisation is characterised by high commitment. Compliance in normative organisations rests principally on internalisation of directives accepted as legitimate. Leadership, rituals, manipulation of social and prestige symbols, and socialisation are among the more important techniques of control used. (1961: 5, 40–1)

The findings from our various data sources, which we have reviewed in previous chapters, suggest that the commitment of most Catholics is partial and complex and rarely approximates to the level of moral involvement envisaged in Etzioni's ideal-type. Only one-third of English Catholics conform minimally to the official norms of Mass attendance and orthodoxy of belief, and at the local level, only about one in eight is a member of a parish organisation (Hornsby-Smith, Lee and Turcan, 1982; Hornsby-Smith, 1987: 47–66). For ordinary Catholics, the Church does not simply employ normative power but also coercive forms such as the threat of eternal damnation for unrepented mortal sin and failure to comply with the full teaching of the religious leadership of the Church.

Etzioni's model, therefore, usefully predicts that the compliance of Catholic 'lower participants' in the face of a variety of types of religious power varies considerably. In the first place, we have noted evidence for a moral commitment on the part of a minority who have been successfully socialised and have internalised the mainly expressive goals of a leadership exerting a 'diffuse and intense normative power, or charisma' (1961: 202). Secondly, the dominant pattern of the beliefs and practices of many ordinary Catholics seems clearly to indicate an instrumental or calculative involvement, insofar as they pragmatically make up their own minds as to 'how far can you go?' in their compliance with the teachings and expectations of the leadership of the Church. Thirdly, there is also evidence of alienative and antagonistic responses from a minority of Catholics who have either experienced coercive forms of power, usually in their relationships with parish priests and over issues of sexual and marital morality or Church rulings on intermarriage, or who regard the attempt of the Church leadership to control such matters as coercive or intrusive and illegitimate.

Thus there is considerable divergence from Etzioni's depiction of compliance in normative organisations, where the 'lower participants are highly integrated' and 'tend to accept the control of organisational elites' so that 'leadership outside the organisational power positions is infrequent' (Etzioni, 1961: 112). An approximation to this model might have been more likely in the era of the 'fortress' Church but is less likely in a reforming post-Vatican 'people of God' Church where lay participation is officially encouraged and where there is a slow emergence of lay leadership in some parishes (Hornsby-Smith, 1989: 186–96; see also Harris, 1969).

Nevertheless, while there has been no serious overt eruption against religious authority, this can perhaps best be interpreted as demonstrating the prevalence of apathy, convenience and self-interest on the part of a passive laity, for many of whom religion is safely segregated from their everyday concerns, rather than as evidence of normative consensus, integration and high levels of commitment. Our data strongly suggest that most English Catholics simply want a quiet life, and are relatively impervious to the blandishments of competing 'progressive' and 'traditional' religious leaders.

Etzioni's analysis is useful here. Thus, unlike the case of adherents to an 'exclusive' sect, for 'cradle' Catholics in a Church with an 'inclusive' membership principle, little 'selectivity' is exercised in recruitment, so that the 'quality' of the participants is relatively low (Etzioni, 1961: 154–9). Empirically, at the local level, the 'scope' or number of activities pursued jointly by members of a parish is 'broad' for only a small proportion of activists and the 'salience', or emotional significance of the involvement of the ordinary Catholic at the parish level, is relatively low. In the same way the 'pervasive-ness', or the range of political or economic activities for which the Church sets norms, tends to be rather small in practice, given the prevalent dualism which rigidly differentiates 'religion' from 'poli-tics' for many Catholics, and despite recent attempts by the Church leadership to extend that pervasiveness, for example in areas of social justice such as unemployment, poverty, definitions of nationality, defence strategies, and so on. In sum, the suggestion by Etzioni (1961: 160–4) that Churches tend to be relatively narrow in scope but highly pervasive, needs considerable qualification in the case of English Catholics.

Finally, Etzioni analyses the distribution of charisma throughout different organisational positions. He regards the Roman Catholic Church as an L-structure, that is one where charisma is functionally required by all 'line' positions (1961: 208–9). Thus he considers that not only the pope, but also bishops and priests, must have charisma-tic authority if the compliance of lower participants is to be achieved.

He suggests that when control over subordinates is relatively lax, charisma is more likely to be developed and sustained (1961: 213), and in L-structures it is functional for expressive elites to subordinate instrumental ones (1961: 217).

Control mechanisms to prevent or reduce deviance and to protect the charisma of official positions, such as those of the parish clergy, are particularly problematic in L-structures. In consequence these develop elaborate preventive and post-factum mechanisms of control (1961: 234–5). Thus the teaching that a sacrament confers grace *ex opere operato*, irrespective of the charisma of the priest, might be regarded as a preventive mechanism, while the various religious sanctions such as excommunication are viewed as examples of post-factum mechanisms for the control of deviant charisma. It might tentatively be suggested, on the basis of the empirical findings we have outlined in previous chapters, that, for many English Catholics, both of these types of mechanisms have become less effective in recent decades. On the one hand, with the paradigmatic shift implicit in the conciliar teaching (Moore, 1975), the charisma of the priestly office is clearly no longer a sufficient warrant for compliance on the part of many Catholics. This is especially the case in the areas of personal morality where, as we have seen, many lay people have been making up their own minds and have regarded their own experiences as having superior legitimacy to the formal teaching of the clerical leadership in the Church. On the other hand, with the loss of the fear of hell, there has clearly been a reduction in the effectiveness of religious sanctions over a wide range of issues from contraception to the Mass attendance obligation.

Etzioni concludes his analysis by suggesting that there is a secular trend towards less coercive and more normative organisations (1961: 311). To the extent that this is the case, one might predict a more committed membership of the Church in the future. However, it is important to note that our interview data have indicated that the compliance of English Catholics is extremely problematic. It seems that habitual forms of obedience are declining, and are being replaced in the main by rational–pragmatic forms of decision-making. It is also possible that a great deal of formal compliance in the more coercive pre-Vatican Church hid a great deal of latent dissent and discontent which has only become more manifest in the more participative environment of the post-Vatican Church. It is important to recognise the general truth that compliance is not necessarily indicative of normative consensus (Fox, 1985: 112).

9.7 Concluding reflections

In his study of Vatican control over lay elites in the Church, Jean-Guy Vaillancourt asked the pointed questions:

Is the present insistence on dialogue and participation an effort to recover ground lost by the necessary abandonment of coercive power, or a willed decision to liberalise and debureaucratise the Church in order to meet the democratic aspirations of contemporary men and women, and of the Catholic laity more specifically? (Vaillancourt, 1980: 6)

His answer was that the Roman Catholic Church is a powerful bureaucracy which is being forced to become more of a voluntary association in order to avoid the alienative outcomes of coercive forms of control. In Berger's terms, the Church has selected the option of accommodation rather than intransigence in a situation of religious and moral pluralism (1973: 156). Developing the work of Weber and Etzioni (1980: 267–8), Vaillancourt suggests that the officials in the Church attempt to retain their grip over the organisation by use of the more manipulative of the normative means of control and in order to avoid grassroots autonomy and internal democratisation (1980: 264–5). In his study of the international delegates to the Third World Congress for the Lay Apostolate held in Rome in 1967, he concluded that:

Many Catholic laymen want more autonomy, freedom and power in all aspects of their lives. They refuse to be passive and obedient members of the clerically dominated Church . . . It is not authority as such which is rejected, but authority exercised as domination rather than as service and love. (1980: 294)

The analyses which we have presented for English Catholics suggest that similar conclusions hold for both core groups of Catholic laity, members of the bishops' advisory commissions and delegates to the National Pastoral Congress, and ordinary Catholics, in the parishes and attending the special events during the pope's visit in 1982. What appears to be new is the loss of the fear of hell (Lodge, 1980). This led many of our interviewees who dissented at least partially from the teaching of the pope, notably on contraception, to do so without any sense of guilt, fear or shame. This is overwhelmingly the case with the youngest cohorts. Arguably this would not have been the case a generation ago, or up to the end of the 1950s.

It seems clear that the threat of religious sanctions which previously intimidated many Catholics into a more-or-less resentful compliance, no longer has the power to convince or persuade. What we initially found 'paradoxical' can better be interpreted as the result of a pragmatic–rational response to the problems of everyday living. The people we interviewed at the public events during the pope's visit in 1982 saw him as a 'great guy' to be welcomed warmly as a celebrity, whose heart was in the right place on some matters, but no more. When it came to responding to his teaching in the absence of any coercive sanctions, the ordinary Catholic might treat him as a guide, but not as an 'ethical prophet' who 'demands obedience as an ethical duty' (Weber, 1966: 55). Our evidence has shown clearly that most Catholics will, in the last analysis, make up their own minds on moral issues pragmatically and common-sensically and, to a greater or lesser extent, in such a way as to favour their own convenience and self-interest.

Three theories of organisational change in the Church might be referred to briefly. Firstly, it might be suggested that the Church is becoming more bureaucratised as a result of the imperatives of a historical process of the increasing rationalisation of social life. This thesis, however, is not entirely convincing. Evidence of centralising tendencies in the global Church might be balanced by a significant decline in rule-making, as indicated by the reduced size of the revised Code of Canon Law (1983) and the increase of collegial and participatory structures at different levels in the Church.

Secondly, it might be argued that the control structures in the Church have shifted from the 'mechanistic', suitable for the stable period of defensive retrenchment in the years up to the Second Vatican Council, to the 'organic', suitable for the changing social and religious conditions in the modern world (Burns and Stalker, 1966). This hypothesis accounts both for the evidence of increased lay participation in the life of the Church and for the greater emphasis on personal freedom and decision-making by informed consciences.

Thirdly, an alternative and somewhat conflicting thesis is that the Church is in a process of transition from a pre-Vatican paradigm to a post-Vatican paradigm, in the course of which old authorities are quietly being discarded and new ones legitimated (Kuhn, 1970). In this view the charisma of Jesus has been institutionalised throughout history and all that is happening is the 'revolution' from the Tridentine Church to a new, and ultimately stable paradigm of the 'people of God', post-Vatican Church. This approach would regard the present period as transitional and to that extent unstable and changing. In due course the new norms can be expected to become more rule-bound; new rigidities will set in and compliance will again tend to the 'habitual obedience' of a passive laity with low involvement in the institutional Church. It remains to be seen which is the more likely alternative.

It is in the context of such formidable changes that we have to consider the transformations of religious authority. It has been argued that our interview data do not correspond at all closely to any one of Weber's three ideal-types of authority. Certainly the pope was accepted as the chief officer in the institutional Church, but this did not result in obedience to directives. To some extent the ambiguous position of the laity may explain this, in that they may more usefully be regarded as clients of the clerical officials than as lower participants in the organisation. Secondly, there was little evidence, either, that Catholics were unduly impressed by the traditional aspects of the papacy. Rather, the dominant drift of our interview material is that Catholics expected to be involved in decisions which closely affected their intimate everyday lives. In this they might be prepared to accept the pope as an official guide, and to this extent there was some charisma of the papal office, but there was little or no evidence that this approximated to the response due to an ethical prophet. In practice Pope John-Paul II was seen as a 'nice guy' but this had few implications in terms of obedience to his teaching.

It is perhaps possible to refer to the concept of 'selective' charisma in two senses. Firstly, the pope was adopted as an ethical prophet by specific groups in restricted areas. For example, justice and peace activists (but not necessarily Catholic conservative politicians) saw his teaching on warfare (but not on marital sexuality) in this light. Thus one can only refer to the influence of the pope in a very diffuse way with many reservations on specific issues. Secondly, there appeared to be a general acceptance of the contemporary model of the visiting pope, in that it demonstrated the respectability of the Roman Catholic Church in the eyes of its political leaders, and of religion as a significant voluntary cultural activity in Britain today. But beyond this, our interview data demonstrated clearly that papal authority was minimal.

PART IV
CONCLUSIONS

RELIGIOUS PLURALISM AND SECULARISATION

10.1 Introduction

This book has explored the transformations which have taken place over the past three or four decades in the religious beliefs of English Catholics, and in the ways in which they have responded to the issues of religious authority. In this final chapter we will review the evidence which has been presented and consider whether or not it can best be considered in terms of the secularisation thesis.

In this study we have drawn on four main data sets arising from focused interviews, usually tape-recorded, with different samples of English Catholics: 'core' Catholics or lay members of the bishops' national advisory commissions; representative samples of Catholic electors in four different parishes; Catholics attending one of the public events during the pope's visit in 1982; and contributions made by relatively articulate and involved Catholics in an enquiry into the everyday lives of lay people. Our main concern has been to 'flesh out' with our qualitative interview data the analysis of structural changes in English Catholicism presented in an earlier study (Hornsby-Smith, 1987).

Four main issues have been addressed: the changing nature of Catholic identity and religious belonging and the meaning which their religion holds for English Catholics, the range and nature of Catholic beliefs and the extent to which these are differentially acknowledged by different types of Catholics; the salience which their religion holds for English Catholics towards the end of the twentieth century; and the nature of religious authority, its shifting boundaries and patterns of legitimation.

The strengths and limitations of our study were indicated in chapter 2. Our data were obtained from focused interviews with Catholics, the overwhelming majority of whom were unknown to the interviewers, within a relatively short period of time, rarely more than two hours. Our data therefore reflect whatever limited amount of trust and openness we were able to achieve, the extent to which the research purposes were understood and shared, the salience of the issues for our respondents, and the extent to which they felt threatened in any way by the issues we wished to raise. With some respondents, particularly the 'core' Catholics, there was a clear understanding of the purpose of the investigation and a readiness to respond to our probing and to collaborate with us in the pursuit of what they interpreted to be our research purposes. It is also not unlikely that they used the opportunity our interviews provided to air some of their grievances with the Church.

With other Catholics, particularly 'dormant' Catholics with little direct contact with the institutional Church, our probes were often less clearly understood, partly because the appropriate knowledge base was absent. Nominal Catholics who had not been to church for many years were not only unfamiliar with recent changes in the Church, for example the growing participation of lay people in the parish liturgies, but were also frequently unable to articulate clearly any response on religious matters. In order to explore further any 'implicit' or 'invisible' religion which such Catholics might have had, an even more intensive form of investigation than we were able to undertake would have been necessary. We reflected on these methodological issues in our discussion of Catholic 'accounts' in chapter 2.

In sum, the quality of the accounts, which were our primary source of data, varied considerably. In the analyses of our data we have been conscious of these variations and have endeavoured to allow for them by selecting illustrative quotations from a wide range of Catholic types. In one sense such variations are instructive and a firm reminder that our research agendas are not necessarily shared by those whom we were investigating. It is necessary to give due weight to this in our interpretations of what the research data mean. In another sense, however, these methodological problems did not concern us over-much, since our purpose was not to present a statistical statement of the probabilities of different views being held. Rather, our primary purpose was to use our qualitative data, with all its limitations and variability, to illustrate the range of positions held by people who identified themselves as Roman Catholics, whatever the strength of their current institutional affiliation. At the very least we have been able to demonstrate repeatedly that the religious beliefs of English Catholics do not comprise a neat, coherent and consistent system, subject only to occasional instances of deviation from the official orthodoxy. Our data have shown clearly that the religious beliefs of English Catholics vary over a very wide range in ways which seem rarely to have been acknowledged.

What our data have indicated is that there is a pluralism of Catholic beliefs and practices which point to a distinct 'hierarchy of truths' in the minds of most Catholics. In the absence of directly comparable data over a significant time span it is perhaps hazardous to comment on probable changes over time. But it seems likely that up to the 1950s Catholics differentiated relatively little between creedal beliefs, non-creedal beliefs such as papal infallibility, teachings on moral issues (whether dealing with personal sexuality such as contraception, or socio-political issues such as the nuclear defence strategy or racism or development issues), and disciplinary rules (such as the Mass attendance obligation, the prohibition of inter-communion or frequency of confession). In a strongly rule-bound and guilt-ridden Church, where notions of mortal sin and eternal damnation were strongly emphasised, it seems likely that Catholics were just as likely to feel coerced to conform on matters of abstinence (or what was generally referred to as 'fish on Fridays'!) as they were to avoid contraception or to believe in the Trinity. It also seems likely that with the 'loss of the fear of hell' from the 1960s, this is much less true today.

It is, therefore, a reasonable inference from our data that beliefs have become more differentiated in recent decades, and that from a relative uniformity of beliefs in a fortress Church there has emerged a more pluralistic set of beliefs in the more voluntaristic, post-Vatican Church. Such a pluralism of beliefs has been reflected in the plurality of responses to clerical, and especially papal, authority in the Church. The evidence we have presented in this book has shown clearly that very few English Catholics confer an unqualified legitimacy on the teaching of the pope. Rather our data have indicated a considerable degree of pluralism and a clear propensity to differen-

tiate between 'religious' matters (where the clerical leaders still have
legitimate authority, though even here, in a participatory 'people of
God' model of the Church, some committed lay people feel perfectly
entitled to a share in that authority), and 'moral' and 'regulatory' or
'disciplinary' issues (where the individual in a human context
familiar only to him or her has the legitimate authority in the last
analysis to make up his or her own mind). In the rest of this chapter
we will review the evidence for both types of pluralism and conclude
by considering their significance for the debate about secularisation.

10.2 Pluralism of belief

In earlier work (Hornsby-Smith, Lee and Turcan, 1982; Hornsby-
Smith, 1987: 47–66) the evidence from the 1978 national survey of
English Catholics was used to demonstrate not only a striking
heterogeneity of beliefs, in terms of doctrine and morality, but also
noticeable differences between different types of Catholics. This
pluralism of belief was replicated in the other surveys to which
reference has been made: Catholic electors in four English parishes
(Hornsby-Smith, Lee and Reilly, 1984); delegates attending the
National Pastoral Congress in 1980 (Hornsby-Smith and
Cordingley, 1983; Hornsby-Smith, Procter, Rajan and Brown, 1987);
and people who had attended one of the public events during the
pope's visit in 1982 (Brown, 1982; Brown and O'Byrne, 1982;
Hornsby-Smith, Brown and O'Byrne, 1983). The evidence for differentiated structures of belief is overwhelming.

A major aim of this book has been to explore further the range of
meanings encapsulated in this heterogeneity of belief by drawing on
evidence from interview transcripts with a wide range of English
Catholics. The three chapters of Part II of this book pointed to a rich
mosaic of qualitative variations in their beliefs. A limited study of the
everyday lives of lay Catholics (chapter 3) suggested that few of them
had a very clear sense of vocation, and that the existing institutional
arrangements in the Church, in particular the parish, often failed to
provide them with effective support in their attempts to make
religious sense of their everyday lives with all its difficulties, conflicts
and moral dilemmas. However, out of their struggles, new forms of
lay spirituality were emerging which were more in tune with the
rhythms of their daily lives.

In order to demonstrate both similarities and differences between different types of Catholics, the beliefs of 'core' Catholics (chapter 4) and 'ordinary' Catholics (chapter 5) were compared. We noted, first of all, that this contrast was clearly not simply one between ortho-doxy, conformity and deference to clerical authority, in the first instance, and heterodoxy, deviance and resistance to authority, in the second. The way our 'core' Catholics were selected and sponsored to be members of the bishops' advisory commissions, suggests they were regarded as responsible, committed and articulate lay people. Yet in their interviews, while there was little or no evidence of deviation from creedal beliefs, there was a strong awareness of a hierarchy of truths with differential claims to adherence. Thus the further they moved from creedal beliefs the stronger became their acceptance of private judgement and 'making up one's own mind' regardless of any official teaching. When questions of ecclesiastical discipline were addressed, it became clear that lay compliance was highly problem-atic, especially amongst the younger members. In the areas of sexual morality, too, there were substantial disagreements with the official teaching of the Church, and core Catholics demonstrated clearly a search for less rule-bound, absolutist and deductive forms of moral teaching.

In our investigation of the religious beliefs of 'ordinary' Catholics, that is random samples of self-identified Roman Catholics in four English parishes, we focused on responses in three main areas: the images of God held by these Catholics; their beliefs about heaven, hell and life after death; and personal prayer. Twelve different categories of response to questions about God were identified. A few respondents were uncertain and unable to articulate any image. The views of others reflected childhood depictions, God was human, a father, a friend, incarnated in Jesus, seen as a judge, creator, or mystical being, as an immanent being or form of energy, or some combination of different images. Interestingly, as the examples given in Table 5.1 illustrate, these different images were not systematically patterned in terms of differential religious practice, and many of them were articulated by both regular and infrequent Mass attenders.

The responses which ordinary Catholics gave on heaven, hell and life after death were rather more clearly differentiated in terms of religious practice, though again there was evidence that similar beliefs were held by Catholics who differed widely in terms of their institutional involvement (Table 5.2). Nine categories of response were distinguished. Some replies approximated closely to the official orthodoxy while others were more obviously conventional. Some responses stressed the importance of conscience. Some offered childhood images of heaven and hell, while others, perhaps most revealingly, saw hell as being here on earth, or 'within you'. A number of respondents associated sex with their responses and there were a significant number of heterodox responses including beliefs in reincarnation. Questions about private prayer generated four broad categories of response (Table 5.3), some of which were again articulated by Catholics who differed significantly in terms of their institutional involvement.

Our early studies originated in the attempt to identify the responses of ordinary Catholics to post-war social changes and to the reforms and shifts of theological orientation arising from the Second Vatican Council. We concluded, on the basis of early analyses of our interview data that:

there has been very little coherent ideological opposition to that renewal. This is not to say, however, that its absence betokens a widespread commitment to renewal. We suspect that the official functionaries within the official Church have too often assumed that lay Catholics have been effectively socialised, are ideologically committed, have a coherent belief structure, and are responsive to direction by the institutional leadership and that they have interpreted the absence of a widespread and coherent negative reaction to the post-Vatican changes as a sign that they have been substantially accepted. (Hornsby-Smith, Lee and Reilly, 1985: 249; 1977)

It was quite clear from our interview data that all of these assumptions were problematic. In the first place, recent changes in the Church were unlikely to have had much impact on the majority of self-identified Roman Catholics with little institutional involvement. Secondly, the changes were unlikely to produce passionate opposition where the involvement in the institutional Church was of an essentially conventional kind. Many of our 'ordinary' Catholics failed to see the liturgical changes of the past two or three decades and the increase of lay participation as anything other than a 'nice idea'. They demonstrated no awareness that these changes might signify a fundamental new self-awareness of the Church as the 'people of God' and a dynamic religious community on pilgrimage rather than as a static, hierarchically structured religious organisation with a subordinate laity deferential towards clerical officials (Abbott, 1966; Dulles, 1976).

The evidence from our interviews with ordinary Catholics suggested that their previous experiences of religious socialisation had inclined many to judge the various changes selectively. For example, some disliked the emergent forms of liturgical pluralism because they stressed such notions as the universality of the Church, while others recalled, uncritically, catechism answers learned in childhood. It seems that the religious involvement of many Catholics is coloured by apathy and self-interest so that changes which tended to make religion easier or less unconventional in a pluralist society, were welcomed. Such passive or negative reasons were found, for example, in the approval given to the ending of Friday abstinence; the eased fasting regulations; the elimination of sanctions against, and the relaxation of the granting of dispensations for, religiously mixed marriages; the vague and unreflexive approval of ecumenism; and so on. The widespread disbelief in evil or in hell might also be interpreted as an aspect of the apathy and self-interest which characterised much of the religiosity of ordinary Catholics.

It was the accumulation of such evidence that led us to distinguish between the official religion of the clerical leadership in the Church and the customary religion of ordinary Catholics. We confined the term to those beliefs and practices which were derived from official religion, normally through the processes of religious socialisation in the home, school and parish, but which were no longer subject to the control of the clerical leadership. We saw customary religion as resulting where there was a breakdown in the processes of formal socialisation, particularly in the post-school years. Current expressions of customary religion resulted from processes of trivialisation, conventionality, apathy, convenience and self-interest, which had eroded and modified the formally prescribed beliefs and practices of official Roman Catholicism. We found numerous examples of such processes in our interview transcripts, as we indicated in chapter 5. We have argued that what was expressed by our respondents was a residual form of Catholicism filtered through personal interpretative processes.

Apart from instances of customary religion, there were also numerous examples of superstitious beliefs in luck, good fortune, fate, and the power of charms and various rituals. We referred to such examples of 'popular' Catholicism as occurring on the borderline between official religion and its customary forms, but as likely to have a closer affinity to 'implicit', 'folk' or 'invisible' religion.

In sum, what our qualitative investigation of the beliefs of English Catholics has shown is that there is a pluralism of Catholic types, such as 'core' Catholics and 'ordinary' Catholics, or 'nuclear' and 'dormant' parishioners, which differ from each other in terms of doctrinal and moral beliefs, and levels of practice and institutional involvement. There is also a pluralism of beliefs ranging from 'official', through 'customary' to 'implicit' or 'popular' Catholicism, and these beliefs are at least partially cross-cut by levels of religious practice. We have demonstrated how various beliefs – official, customary or popular – are frequently espoused, both by regularly practising Catholics and by those with little direct contact with the institutional Church.

Secondly, we have suggested that in the defensive, pre-Vatican, fortress Church, relatively little differentiation existed in the attachment accorded to the complex battery of Catholic beliefs. They were relatively 'all of a piece' so that it was not surprising that David Martin had anticipated the collapse of the whole system 'wherever a *single* point of doctrine is undermined simply because a hole in the dyke undermines the complete defensive system' (1972: 187). We have argued that in fact no such total collapse did occur, but that what has emerged over the past two or three decades, is a much more explicit and recognised 'hierarchy of truths' on the part of ordinary Catholics.

The whole burden of our research evidence is that English Catholics in the 1970s and 1980s differentiated significantly between creedal or core beliefs (which continued to attract very high levels of assent), non-creedal or more peripheral beliefs (including papal infallibility), personal and social morality (where many Catholics considered the clerical leadership to lack both credibility and legitimacy), and institutional rules and regulations (which were regarded as no longer incurring effective religious sanctions, and to which conformity was largely dependent on such pragmatic considerations as convenience and self-interest). Increasingly Catholics, most especially the younger generations, made up their own minds on an increasing range of issues.

Thirdly, it is appropriate to recall the discussion of consistency, coherence and salience in chapter 2. The religious beliefs of English Catholics, especially those we have referred to as 'ordinary' Catholics, are rarely uncomplicated, consistent and theologically coherent. Rather, they are typically characterised by contradictions (Harris,

1980: 84–6), ambiguity and ambivalence (Merton and Barber, 1963), and incoherence. One example of a contradiction might be the advocacy of 'responsible parenthood' along with the prohibition of contraception; another might be the teaching about the 'priesthood of all believers' while regarding women as being, in the words of one seminary professor, 'unsuitable sacramental signs for ministry'! Ambivalence might be said to characterise the attempt to reconcile the proscriptions against the remarriage of divorced people with considerations of pastoral care. The evidence from our research interviews, only a fraction of which has been reported in this book, suggests that their Catholicism was salient in their everyday lives for only a small proportion of mainly 'core' Catholics. Our findings are consistent with the conclusions of Melanie Cottrell (1985): religion has no significant place in the lives of most Catholics and, even for many regular Mass attenders, churchgoing is largely a habitual social action with few consequences for everyday social behaviour at work or in the political realm.

Two further comments extend our analysis. First of all, what seems to have happened is that over the past two or three decades attachment to the Church has shifted from the 'collective–expressive', with its largely involuntary Catholic religio-ethnic identity and attachment to a whole battery of beliefs which are relatively undifferentiated, to the 'individual–expressive', with its essentially voluntary identification and differential attachment to different elements of belief (Hammond, 1988). In this process the 'loss of the fear of hell' has played a major part. Secondly, Grace Davie (1989a; 1989b) has pointed out that the paradox of residual belief without belonging, or institutional involvement, is a phenomenon not only of religion in contemporary Britain but also, more generally, in Western Europe. She has also interestingly suggested that there may be sociological similarities between the 'customary' religion of English Catholics and French Protestants, both minority religions subjected to assimilationist processes in societies characterised by a decline of religious hostility and an increase of religious indifference (1987: 35; 136, fn. 9).

10.3 Pluralism of legitimations of religious authority

Apart from the pluralism of Catholic beliefs, this book has also addressed the emergent plurality of ways in which religious authority is legitimated. The four chapters of Part III of this book were concerned to explore transformations of religious authority in the case of English Catholics in the 1970s and 1980s. Besides the groundswell of democratising forces unleashed after the Second World War, for Catholics the new theological emphases on the participating 'people of God' at the Second Vatican Council held out great promise for more collaborative patterns of clergy–lay relations and less autocratic clerical leadership styles in the post-Vatican Church. Some commentators have gone so far as to suggest that we are entering an age of democratic authority and at least the partial demise of Max Weber's rational–legal form of legitimation. Thus Peter Abell has argued that:

Just as Weber, at the turn of the century, was able to claim a general tendency toward what he termed 'societal rationality' and the concomitant rational bureaucratic administrative structures, we can detect a tendency toward democratic authority structures. Weber was able to document a decline in the importance of traditional and charismatic sources of legitimation, so, likewise, we can chart the decline in rational–legal forms of legitimation. (1979: 142)

Our interview data have certainly confirmed that the authority of the clerical leadership in the Church, from the pope to the parish priest, is by no means accepted unreservedly. Rather, contestation and conflict are frequently found on specific matters. There is also evidence to suggest that new forms of legitimation are emerging. The indications are that, at least to some extent, some lay people are struggling towards more democratic forms of decision-making in what has traditionally always been defined as being intrinsically, from its origins, a religious community of believers with divinely instituted, hierarchical forms of clerical authority (Canon Law Society, 1983; Cans. 330–572).

As we indicated in the previous section and as far as one can judge, on the basis of the research evidence we have reviewed in this book, recent decades have seen the emergence not only of a differentiation of religious beliefs, but also of corresponding forms of legitimation of religious authority. It might be speculated that this is an instance of a more general resistance to centralised authority. At the macro level, this has manifested itself in the struggles of local Churches against Roman centralism, as illustrated by the remark of one of the bishops of England and Wales around 1980 when he observed that 'it was time the local Churches took on Rome!'

We commenced our exploration of the transformations in religious authority by reporting our findings from the interviews we conducted with around two hundred people who had attended one of the public events during the pope's visit in 1982. Although the bulk of our interviewees were regularly practising Catholics, and although they were virtually unanimous in their positive evaluation of Pope John-Paul II as a person, their responses to his teaching spanned the whole spectrum from unqualified acceptance to complete rejection (Table 6.1). For some the pope had to be obeyed, otherwise 'we might as well give up our religion' (Wembley). Such beliefs were sometimes recognised as being the result of their Catholic upbringing. Others were prepared to accept the pope's teaching when he was speaking *ex cathedra* on doctrinal issues but not on social or moral issues. Most Catholics in practice made up their own minds on most matters, recognising the pope's teaching as offering authoritative guidelines to action. On certain issues, such as contraception, some Catholics anticipated that change would come but recognised that this would create difficulties for the religious leadership. It was evidence such as this which led us at first to refer to the 'paradoxical' pope's people (Scurfield, 1982; Hornsby-Smith, Brown and O'Byrne, 1983).

Further evidence for the heterogeneity of Catholic attitudes to religious authority were given on the basis of our interviews with core Catholics (chapter 7) and ordinary Catholics (chapter 8). In chapter 7 we employed Houtart's model of contestation of religious authority in the Church (1969) in the analysis of our interviews with members of the bishops' advisory commissions. This enabled us to distinguish five types of core Catholics in terms of their responses to ecclesiastical authority (Table 7.2): the conformists who accepted the clerical leadership even if with some provisos; the accommodators who took up a negotiating stance towards bishops and priests and who had a sense of practical possibilities; the innovators who felt that rules could be bent or that deviance was necessary to change them; the transformers who envisaged inevitable changes, often resulting from pressure applied by younger generations of Catholics who 'have this marvellous confidence to know exactly what is the right, the Christian way of doing things'; and those who contested authority by opting out of the institutional Church.

Finally, in chapter 8 we reviewed the responses of ordinary Catholics from four English parishes on the controversial issues of contraception, abortion and divorce. Twelve distinct categories of response were reported in the case of contraception (Table 8.1), seven in the case of abortion (Table 8.2) and eight in the case of divorce (Table 8.3). We noted that in all three cases a proportion of respondents expressed neo-official views, though whereas in the case of contraception this proportion was very small, around one-third of responses on both abortion and divorce could be regarded as redefined or qualified forms of the official orthodoxy. Around two-fifths to three-fifths of responses on all three issues offered excuses or justifications for rejecting the official teaching. A third broad grouping of responses indicated a more-or-less explicit contestation of authority by around one-tenth of Catholics, in the case of abortion, to one-fifth in the case of divorce, but over one-half in the case of contraception. The evidence from our interviews suggested that the clerical authorities in the Church have almost completely lost authority in the case of contraception, and may well be on the way to losing it in other areas of personal morality where there is a growing sense that, in the final analysis, decisions should be left to those most concerned.

The empirical data on which this book has been based were derived from around 500 hours of focused interviews with a wide range of different Catholics including 71 lay members of the bishops' advisory commissions (our 'core' Catholics), 183 Catholic electors in four English parishes covering both regional and social class variations (our 'ordinary' Catholics), and 194 people who attended one of the public events during the pope's visit in 1982. As far as is known, this comprises the largest set of qualitative research data relating to English Catholics between the mid-1970s and the mid-1980s. (Analysis of the interviews carried out with 77 parish activists have not been included in this present study in which attention has been drawn to both the similarities and differences between the two polar groups of 'core' and 'ordinary' Catholics.)

As in the case of religious beliefs, Catholic attitudes to clerical authority in the Church show considerable heterogeneity. On the one hand there is evidence of differentiation between issues. It seems that there is a decline of, and contestation of, clerical legitimacy roughly corresponding to the differentiation between creedal, non-creedal, social and personal moral teachings, and the disciplinary rules and regulations of the institutional Church. As in the case of religious beliefs, views on religious authority are also cross-cut by different types of Catholics. This is most obviously the case over contraception, where both practising and non-practising Catholics reject the official teaching, but least obvious in the case of abortion. Apart from the contestation of clerical authority in the areas we selected for particular attention, there is also some evidence that progressive, middle-class Catholics are contesting older forms of clerical domination, especially at the parish level (Archer, 1986).

The broad patterns of our empirical findings, therefore, lead us to the clear conclusion that there have been significant transformations in the ways in which a whole range of English Catholics have legitimated the exercise of religious authority in the Church, from the pronouncements of the pope to the everyday realities of priest–lay relations in the parishes. In chapter 9 we reviewed the evidence, taking Weber's typology of legal–rational, traditional and charismatic authority as our starting point. Like Harrison (1971), we found that it was necessary to introduce some modifications to this typology. In particular we noted a decline of habitual forms of obedience and their replacement especially by rational–pragmatic forms of decision-making.

Our findings seem to be entirely consistent with those of Melanie Cottrell (1985) in the sense that their religion had salience for only a tiny minority of our ordinary Catholics, even where they were regular Mass attenders. Their outlook was also generally this-worldly and pragmatic, and this was reflected in the strength of the movement towards 'making up your own mind', especially on the issues of personal morality. There was a strong sense that popes or priests were lacking in credibility as putative authorities in these areas where the individuals themselves were the only ones capable of weighing all the circumstances of their everyday lives realistically and pragmatically. It is of some considerable interest and relevance that at the Synod on the Family in Rome in 1980, Cardinal Hume referred to the 'special authority in matters concerning marriage' of married couples (Catholic Information Services, 1980: 6).

Although we did not explore the matter in depth, it is clear that similar views about the lack of credibility and legitimacy of the clergy as authorities on political and economic issues were widely held. Thus there were strong negative reactions to comments made by bishops on trade unions and industrial disputes. A number of ordinary Catholics expressed a strong preference for the separation of religion and politics such as might well inhibit any strong pastoral concern with the issues of socio-economic justice.

A number of final observations might be made on the basis of our interview data. Although there is no evidence of a generalised anti-clericalism in England, there are indications of a fair amount of discontent which usually expresses itself in grumbling about the local parish priest. A close reading of our transcripts and a focusing on the question of religious authority in the Church, however, does seem to indicate a fairly diffuse and latent awareness of the distinctions between 'us', lay people, and 'them', the clergy. Insofar as there really is a democratic imperative, the likelihood is that there will be growing contestation of clerical authority in those areas where lay people feel they possess relevant knowledge and experience, while the clergy lack credibility.

Secondly, our respondents seemed in general to be opposed to absolutist moral rules. They very strongly emphasised the importance of circumstances which might alter or determine their response to any moral dilemma. This was particularly apparent in some of the comments made on abortion where large numbers of Catholics, including regular Mass attenders, considered the rape of an underage girl warranted the suspension of a general prohibition of abortion. For many, perhaps the majority of the ordinary Catholics we interviewed, it was commonsensical and rational–pragmatic to take due account of the situational context in moral decision-making.

Thirdly, this was related to the observable phenomenon of the 'loss of the fear of hell' among many of the younger Catholics we interviewed, one which was often recognised by their parents. Although we do not have any direct longitudinal evidence, our interview data provide good grounds for believing that there has indeed been a major reduction in the guilt-driven and hell-fearing forms of morality which persisted up to the 1950s. There seems little doubt that younger generations of Catholics are motivated to moral decisions by other means.

Finally, the result is that more and more Catholics are making up their own minds on more and more things and are getting on with the everyday tasks of living their lives, bringing up their families, and coping with the everyday problems of child-rearing, earning a living and making ends meet, unemployment or redundancy, being good citizens, and so on, as best they can, with whatever support they can get, from whatever source. It would seem that the days of substantial thought-control over all aspects of social life, powerful especially in the defensive ghettos of the fortress Church, are now well and truly over. With the removal of the threat of eternal damnation, going to church has to take its chance along with all the other claims on the discretionary time, energy and interest of Catholics.

10.4 The secularisation of English Catholicism?

The qualitative data we have reviewed in this book, and the quantitative data which were reviewed in the earlier study of structural aspects of Roman Catholicism in England (Hornsby-Smith, 1987) were all obtained in the decade between the mid-1970s and the mid-1980s. Directly comparable data from earlier periods, say the 1950s, are simply not available. Claims that there have been significant transformations in the nature of the beliefs and ways of legitimising religious authority in recent decades have therefore been made on the basis of reasonable inferences about what the situation was at some earlier point in time. Some independent validation of these inferences was provided by our interviewees (a) when they referred to changes which they had themselves experienced in the course of their lives, and (b) when they contrasted their own religious socialisation and beliefs with those of their own adult children.

Can the transformations which we have reasonably inferred have taken place be regarded as evidence for a process of secularisation? My own judgement is still heavily influenced by the arguments in David Martin's earlier writings (1965; 1969) and in particular by the twin problems of selecting an appropriate earlier time with which to compare the present situation, and selecting what is to count as really 'religious'. On the first point I have argued elsewhere that there never was a golden age (1987: 26–31). On the second I concluded that:

Theories of secularisation were ... difficult to substantiate because of the problematic nature of the relevant criteria for the measurement of the 'religious' and as a result of the changes in the meaning and significance of traditional practices which appeared to have taken place over the past two decades. (1987: 205)

I do not think that the detailed analysis of our focused interview data which we have reviewed in this book give us a warrant to change that judgement. My suspicion is that a more detailed comparison of our transcripts with the accounts of Catholic belief and practice in the early years of this century, such as are to be found in Hugh

McLeod's analyses of the Booth researches of religion in working class London (1974: 72–80), would indeed show substantial similarities in the categories of belief. When due allowance is taken of the special leadership role of the priest for Irish working-class immigrants in impoverished working-class ghettos, similar categories for the legitimation of religious authority are also likely. Certainly there is evidence of a less than total compliance to the priests and of some bitter struggles and contestation with the clerical leadership in this historical material.

In its simplest formulation secularisation has been defined as 'the process whereby religious thinking, practice and institutions lose social significance' (Wilson, 1966: xiv). Bryan Wilson has claimed that the well documented evidence of decline, in terms of many traditional indicators of involvement in institutional religion (for example, Mass attendance, priestly vocations, adult conversions, endogamous marriages, confessions, etc.), is a clear indication of a process of secularisation. Such an inference cannot be accepted without challenge, because it fails to allow adequately for the emergence of new manifestations of religious vitality (such as weekly communions, participation in new forms of communal prayer, emergent forms of social concern, etc.). Just as one would hardly say that soccer has less social significance in the 1990s than it had in the 1950s (although attendances were three times as great in the earlier period), so it cannot be inferred that the decline in the weekly Mass attendance figures by one-quarter since the 1950s (Hornsby-Smith, 1989: 2) demonstrates the declining social significance of Roman Catholicism in England.

This is not to deny that there have been significant changes as Catholics have moved, both socially and religiously out of the static, defensive, fortress Church, or, as Hammond has suggested (1988), as their identity has shifted from the involuntary 'collective–expressive' form to the voluntary 'individual–expressive' form. Rather it is to interpret these changes as major transformations of religious belonging, belief and authority, without the necessity of employing the ideological baggage associated with the concept of secularisation (Martin, 1965; 1969).

In a more recent work, Wilson has suggested that secularisation 'is the major contemporary transformation of religion' (1979: 112) which follows an inevitable 'gradual, uneven, at times an oscillating, trend, the general direction of which is none the less unmistakable, in the nature of human consciousness, towards what might be called a "matter-of-fact" orientation to the world' (1979: 11). It is certainly the case that our interview data have provided evidence for the growth of a rational–pragmatic world-view and its concomitant emphasis on 'making up your own mind'. But, in my view, Wilson's further claim that 'Christian faith is in serious decline' (1979: 6) is probably impossible to test empirically. Indeed the evident signs of new life and vitality in some parts of contemporary Catholicism seem clearly to point to the alternative conclusion, that there have been major transformations in the styles of 'belonging' to the Church (e.g. Nowell, 1982; Vardey, 1989), of 'being' a Roman Catholic, of religious meanings, understanding of the nature of the Church, and so on. Such transformations, innovations and vitality should not, in my view, be so lightly dismissed under the umbrella of a supposedly imperative evolutionary process of secularisation. In sum, in spite of Wilson's confident assertions, I believe there are good grounds for being wary of the concept of secularisation and for interpreting the changes of recent decades in terms of the less value-loaded notions of religious transformations.

It may be here that the distinctions suggested by Dobbelaere are most useful. Pointing out that secularisation is multidimensional, he distinguished *laicization*, or the process of structural differentiation whereby 'institutions are developed that perform different functions and are structurally different', from *religious involvement*, which 'refers to individual behaviour and measures the degree of normative integration in religious bodies', and *religious change*, which 'expresses change occurring in the posture of religious organisations ... in matters of beliefs, morals, and rituals, and implies also a study of the decline and emergence of religious groups' (1981: 11–12). In subsequent work he also distinguished societal, organisational and individual levels of analysis (1985).

In this book we have been mainly concerned with the individual level and only secondarily with the organisational level of analysis. We have noted evidence for an emergent pluralism, especially of religious beliefs and ways of legitimising religious authority. According to Dobbelaere, such 'religious pluralism stimulates the stripping of religious qualities from social problems in order to reduce tensions and conflict, and ... also promotes the development of a secular morality ... [and hence] laicizes society' (1981: 112). Furthermore 'religious and cultural pluralism ... stimulates the privatisation or individuation of religion' (1981: 116). Such processes seem to have been particularly evident in the contestation of clerical authority over contraception, in the criticisms we categorised as inadequate reasoning, and incoherent or resented authority, and confined, appropriated and redefined legitimacy (Table 8.1). Berger points out that a danger of 'subjectivisation', where 'subjective emotionality takes the place of objective dogma as a criterion of religious legitimacy', is that there is a relativisation of the religious content (Berger, 1973: 156–9; Dobbelaere, 1981: 117).

We would suggest, therefore, that rather than interpreting the empirical evidence as unambiguously indicative of secularising processes, it is helpful to make the distinctions suggested by Dobbelaere. The rich and varied interview data from English Catholics in the 1970s and 1980s, which we have reviewed in this book, provide evidence indicating a process of laicization at both the individual and organisational levels. This process manifests itself in the increasing differentiation of religious belief and moral decision-making where previously the priest was the sole focus of legitimate teaching and arbiter of morality. Secondly, the evidence indicates a decline of some traditional forms of religious involvement, but against this it is necessary to take due account of new, emergent forms of religious vitality, what Hervieu-Léger has called the 'paradox of modernity' (Hervieu-Léger, 1986: 224–7; quoted in Davie, 1989a). Thirdly, there is clear evidence of religious change from the pre-Vatican to post-Vatican models of the Church and theological legitimations (Hornsby-Smith, 1989). For the individual Catholic:

it is precisely at the crossroads between tradition and modernity, between old symbols of old authoritarian social structures and new social experience that the contemporary Roman Catholic is called to perform his bricolage. (Koopmanschap, 1973: 49)

It remains for the reader to evaluate the evidence which has been reviewed in this book and to 'make up his/her own mind' on its significance. Can it seriously be suggested that the rich plurality of religious thinking and practice reported by our respondents is indicative of a loss of social significance by Catholicism? The social significance of the contemporary parish has been considered elsewhere (Hornsby-Smith, 1989). The social and political significance of the Roman Catholic Church as an institution at the societal level remains to be investigated. In the absence of more convincing evidence, it is claimed here that the charge that the transformations in the beliefs and legitimations of religious authority among English Catholics are indicative of a process of secularisation remains unproven.

Appendix I

INTERVIEW GUIDE FOR COMMISSION
MEMBERS (1974/75)

There were four sections in the interview guide for the lay members of the bishop's commissions in 1974/5: the work of the commission, the religious socialisation of the member, interpretations of the present situation in the Church, and reactions to recent changes in the Church. For present purposes the guidelines for the last two sections only have been reproduced.

III Interpretation of present situation

A. Teaching of Church

1 Is there anything in the teaching of the Church you find difficult to accept?
2 Would you be prepared to accept changes in the teaching of the Church?
3 (If yes) What are the main points in the teaching of the Church which you would like to see changed?
4 What is the authority of the Church in the areas of your professional concern? Are there any conflicts?

B. Causes of tensions/conflicts in the present situation

IMAGES OF GOD:

5 It has been said that there are two contrasting images of God. The first image sees Him primarily as a transcendent being whose

action in the world proceeds from His will which guides humanity to its ultimate end. The second image conceives of God as one who is acting throughout history and as giving meaning to the individual and collective activities of humanity. Which of these images of God would you emphasise? How do you see it?

(First probe) Well, *either* God is the all-powerful creator whose will should be obeyed in all we do *or* God gives meaning to the changing activities and initiatives of man throughout history.

(Second probe) *Either* God tells us what we ought to do *or* it is up to man to look to God for the meaning of what we do in life.

CORRESPONDING VIEW OF AUTHORITY

6 How in general do you see the nature of authority in the Church? For example, do you see the Church primarily as an organisation which places decisions and power in the hands of a small group of persons whose authority is unquestioned? *Or* do you see the Church as an organisation, all of whose members play a more or less active role in decision-making, with the acceptance of authority depending on the general approval of everybody? Is authority regarded as a *value* or as a *means*?

7 (If authority sometimes questioned) Has it ever been *contested*? If so, how much? by whom? etc.
 (a) *What* is being contested?
 (b) *How* are people 'contesting'?
 (c) What *means* are being used?
 (d) What are the *reactions* of people in authority?
 (e) What are the *effects* of this contestation on the Church?
 (f) Has a further stage of *confrontation* been reached? If so, how much? By whom? etc.

8 What do you see as the authority of the Church in the areas of your professional concern?

AREAS OF TENSION/CONFLICT

9 Where do you *personally* find there are areas of tension/conflict?
10 Where do you think that in *the Church in general* there are areas of tension/conflict?

C. *General*

11 Should we encourage different types of liturgy or should there be a standard form for everybody? For example, some people like the

Latin Mass and are against using the vernacular. Others favour the use of mime, dance, etc. Do you feel there should be opportunities available for a wide diversity of liturgical worship? (Probe) Pluralism/diversity? Unity vs uniformity?

12 At the local level: some people have argued that there should be more concern for the development of small communities within the Church. What do you think of this idea?
(Probe) Breakdown of wider consensus? Strongholds of stagnation?

13 What do you think of notions of participatory democracy in the Church? To what extent do you think there should be unlimited scope for individual initiative? What advantages/disadvantages do you see?
(Probe) Dysfunctions?

IV The member as a Catholic

14 *Liturgy*: Reactions to new forms. If important/not, why? Personal preferences? Importance of the liturgy?

15 *Religious practice*: Personal practice? How important is going to Mass? Do you consider it a mortal sin to miss Mass? Attitude to practice? Prayer? Practice of children? etc.

16 *The clergy*: Their role; changes in it? Influence on parish? prime role there? In what ways has it changed? In what ways would you like it to change? Their relationship with laity? What should their priorities be? Comments on *Decree on Priestly Life*? Comments on celibacy? worker priests? married priests? women priests? For/against? Why?

17 *The laity*: Their role; changes in role? Relationship with clergy? Involvement and participation at parish, diocesan and national levels? Mission of laity?

18 *Authority*: Runs through all sections.

19 *Matters of faith*: Specific, e.g. papal infallibility? General faith in secular society?

20 *Moral issues*: Divorce? contraception? abortion? euthanasia? other?

21 *Controversial statements*: About belief in God, Jesus? etc.

22 *Personal concepts*: Of the Church? of religion? of Christianity? of faith?

23 *Needs for the future*: What are the needs in the Church? Are changes

necessary? for better? deepening spiritual life? more involvement in world? world of work? family life?

24 *The Catholic in Society*: His role? relationships with other Christians? with others? Do you feel different as a Catholic? fellow feeling? class barriers?

25 *The Church*: universally and in Britain? *Mission or Maintenance?*

APPENDIX II

INTERVIEW GUIDE FOR PARISHIONERS
(1974/77)

A. *Religious socialisation*

1 *Home*: Irish origins etc.; importance of religion in home; prayers.
2 *Community*: Catholics stick together? Importance of neighbours, friends, relatives?
3 *School*: Emphasis on R.E.; coercive? felt like rebelling?
4 *Work*: Entry into; what was most important?
5 *Marriage*: RC/convert? Pressure to change?

B. *Religious beliefs and values*

6 *Notion of God*: Transcendent cp. immanent. Importance to life? In what ways?
7 *Prayer*: How important in your life? Do you pray? How?
8 *Moral issues*: Teaching of Church e.g. on contraception, divorce and abortion? Authority of Church. Church and politics, e.g. race relations, social justice and Ireland cp. euthanasia, abortion?
9 *Catholicism*: How important to you is being a Catholic?

C. *Change in the Church*

10 *Liturgy*: Vernacular, priests facing people, communion in hand, lay readers, folk Masses, etc., Communion under both kinds (host and chalice), offertory processions? Decline of reverence, awe cp. joy, celebration? Views on Archbishop Lefebvre and Latin Mass. New Rite of Reconciliation. Benediction. Stations of Cross.

11 *Participation*: Relations between priests and laity; how have they/ should they change? Priest as remote 'man apart' cp. now? Role of women in Church? Own role in Church? Views on priests who marry?

12 *Ecumenism*: Mixed marriages? Intercommunion? Approval or disapproval?

13 *Mission or Maintenance*: Schools and buildings. How important are Catholic schools? Emphasis on dogma and rule-following cp. personal commitment? General attitudes to change? Role of Church in future?

D. The parish

14 *Community*: Would you say it is a 'community'? Are there house Masses? discussion/prayer groups? General comments. Importance of small groups? Religious education and self-help?

15 *Organisations*: Especially Social Centre/Club; its function and contribution to the parish; does the tail wag the dog? Parish Council? The choir and its relations with others in the parish.

16 *Change*: e.g. from all-embracing parish life, entertainment, processions, etc. to segregated part of life? Preston Catholicism and the Guilds.

17 *Priests*: Relations with laity; changes over time, etc.

18 *General*: Have I left out anything important? Any other comments?

THANK YOU VERY MUCH FOR GIVING ME SO MUCH OF YOUR TIME

APPENDIX III

INTERVIEW GUIDE FOR PEOPLE ATTENDING PAPAL EVENTS (1982)

Note for interviewers: We are envisaging an interview of only ten or fifteen minutes long. Please bear this in mind but feel free to improvise or rephrase questions as necessary without leading or prompting the interviewee in any way.

A. Introduction

Excuse me. Can I bother you for a few minutes?
I am from the University of Surrey and we are interested in people's reactions to the Pope's visit. Could I ask you a few questions about your own views?
(If agreed) Do you mind if I record you on tape?

B. The papal visit

1 How far have you come?
2 Why *did* you come here today?
3 What do *you* think is special about the visit of the Pope?
4 Are there any aspects of the visit and its preparations which have particularly pleased you?
5 And has anything troubled you about it?
6 What do *you* think the main job of a pope is?
7 What do you think about Pope John-Paul II?
8 Do you feel bound to obey all his teaching?
9 Are there any matters you feel entitled to make up your own mind about?

10 Do you think there will be any lasting effects of his visit?
11 (If yes) What sort of things? Why do you think this?

C. *Follow-up*

12 Are you yourself a Roman Catholic?
13 (If yes) We are hoping to recontact some of the people we have spoken to either personally or by letter in two or three months time. Would you be prepared to speak to us again if one of us visited you at your home, or could we send you a short questionnaire?
14 (If yes) Could you please tell me your name and address and telephone number?

THANK YOU VERY MUCH INDEED FOR BEING SO HELPFUL

BIBLIOGRAPHY

Abell, P. (1979) 'Hierarchy and Democratic Authority', in Burns, T. R., Karlsson, L. E., and Rus, V. (eds.) *Work and Power: the Liberation of Work and the Control of Political Power*, London: Sage, 141–71.

(1983) 'Accounts and Those Accounts Called Accounts of Actions', in Gilbert, G. N. and Abell, P. (1983), 173–82.

Abbott, W. M. (ed.) (1966) *The Documents of Vatican II*, London: Geoffrey Chapman.

Abercrombie, N., Baker, J., Brett, S., and Foster, J. (1970) 'Superstition and religion: the God of the Gaps', in Martin, D. and Hill, M. (eds.) *A Sociological Yearbook of Religion in Britain: 3*, London: SCM, 93–129.

Allport, G. W. (1950) *The Individual and His Religion*, New York: Macmillan.

(1966) 'The Religious Context of Prejudice', *Journal for the Scientific Study of Religion*, 5 Fall, 447–57.

Alton, D. (1987) 'The Life of a Member of Parliament', *Priests and People*, 1 (6) October, 222–8.

Anglican–Roman Catholic International Commission (1982) *The Final Report*, London: CTS/SPCK.

Anon. (1954) *A Catechism of Christian Doctrine* (Do.3), London: CTS.

(1981) *Liverpool 1980: Official Report of the National Pastoral Congress*, Slough: St Paul Publications.

Archer, A. (1986) *The Two Catholic Churches: A Study in Oppression*, London: SCM.

Bailey, E. (ed.) (1986) *A Workbook in Popular Religion*, Dorchester: Partners Publications.

Barta, R. (ed.) (1980) *Challenge to the Laity*, Huntington, Indiana: Our Sunday Visitor.

Beck, G. A. (ed.) (1950) *The English Catholics: 1850–1950*, London: Burns Oates.

Becker, H. S. (1960) 'Notes on the Concept of Commitment', *American Journal of Sociology*, 66, 32–40

Berger, P. L. (1971) *A Rumour of Angels: Modern Society and the Rediscovery of the Supernatural*, Harmondsworth: Pelican.

(1973) *The Social Reality of Religion*, Harmondsworth: Penguin. (Published in 1967 as *The Sacred Canopy*, New York: Anchor Doubleday).

Blaikie, N. W. H. (1988) 'The Use of Triangulation in Sociological Research: Ontological and Epistemological Considerations'. Paper Read at International Conference on Social Science Methodology, Dubrovnik, Yugoslavia, June.

Blumer, H. (1954) 'What is Wrong with Social Theory?', *American Sociological Review*, 19, 3–10.

Bossy, J. (1975) *The English Catholic Community: 1570–1850*, London: Darton, Longman and Todd.

Bowker, J. (1973) *The Sense of God*, Oxford: Oxford University Press.

Brown, J. M. (1982) 'A Facet Analysis of the Leadership Style of Pope John-Paul II'. Unpublished paper. Guildford: University of Surrey.

Brown, J. M. and O'Byrne, J. (1982) 'The Papal Visit to Britain: 28 May to 2 June, 1982: A Resource Paper'. Unpublished paper. Guildford: University of Surrey.

Burns, C. (1988) 'The Revolutionary Patience of a Housewife', *Priests and People*, 2 (3) April, 83–88

Burns, T. and Stalker, G. M. (1966) *The Management of Innovation*, London: Tavistock.

Butler, C. (1981) *The Theology of Vatican II*, London: Darton, Longman and Todd.

Canon Law Society of Great Britain and Ireland (1983) *The Code of Canon Law*, London: Collins.

Carroll, V. (1988) 'How Long Can We Sing the Lord's Song in a Strange Land?', *Priests and People*, 2 (8) October, 307–12.

Cartwright, A. (1976) *How Many Children?*, London: Routledge and Kegan Paul.

Catholic Information Services (1980) 'Synod '80: "The Family Today" No. 1', *Briefing*, 10 (32), 5–7.

Cheetham, J. (1976) 'Surveys Which Include Information About Roman Catholics' Attitudes Towards Legal Abortion', University of Oxford (mimeo).

Cipriani, R. (1984) 'Religion and Politics. The Italian Case: Diffused Religion', *Archives de Sciences Sociales des Religions*, 58 (1) July–September, 29–51.

Clark, B. R. (1960) 'The "Cooling-Out" Function of Higher Education', *American Journal of Sociology*, 65, 569–76.

Clark, D. (1977) *Basic Communities: Towards an Alternative Society*, London: SPCK.

Cologne Declaration (1989) 'Against Incapacitation – For an Open Catholicism', *The Tablet*, 243 (7751) 4 February, 140–2.

Coman, P. (1977) *Catholics and the Welfare State*, London: Longman.

Congar, Y. (1965) *Lay People in the Church: A Study for a Theology of Laity*, London and Dublin: Geoffrey Chapman.

Cornwall, M. (1987) 'The Social Bases of Religion: A Study of Factors Influencing Religious Belief and Commitment', *Review of Religious Research*, 29 (1) September, 44–56.

Coser, L. A. (1974) *Greedy Institutions: Patterns of Undivided Commitment*, New York: Free Press.

Cottrell, M. (1985) *Secular Beliefs in Contemporary Society*, Unpublished D.Phil Thesis, University of Oxford.

Davie, G. (1987) 'The Nature of Belief in the Inner City' in Aherne, G. and Davie, G. (1987) *Inner City God: The Nature of Belief in the Inner City*, London: Hodder and Stoughton, 19–74.

(1989a) '"An Ordinary God": The Paradox of Religion in Contemporary Britain' (Forthcoming in *British Journal of Sociology*).

(1989b) 'Believing without Belonging: Is this the Future of Religion in Britain?' Paper presented at CISR, Helsinki. (Forthcoming in *Social Compass*).

Denzin, N. K. (1970) *The Research Act in Sociology*, London: Butterworths.

Dobbelaere, K. (1981) 'Secularization: A Multi-Dimensional Concept', *Current Sociology*, 29 (2), Summer, 3–213.

(1985) 'Secularization Theories and Sociological Paradigms: A Reformulation of the Private–Public Dichotomy and the Problems of Societal Integration', *Sociological Analysis*, 46 (4) 377–87.

Dominion, J. (1975) *Cycles of Affirmation: Psychological Essays in Christian Living*, London: Darton, Longman and Todd.

(1977) *Proposals for a New Sexual Ethic*, London: Darton, Longman and Todd.

(1981) *Marriage, Faith and Love*, London: Darton, Longman and Todd.

(1989) *A Celebration of Marriage*. A Commentary for a Service at Westminster Cathedral, 29 April.

Douglas, M. (1973) *Natural Symbols: Explorations in Cosmology*, Harmondsworth: Penguin.

(1975) *Implicit Meanings: Essays in Anthropology*, London and Boston: Routledge and Kegan Paul.

(1978) *Cultural Bias*. Occasional Paper No. 35. London: Royal Anthropological Institute.

Doyle, E. (1979) Comments on 'Roman Catholic Opinion'. Video Interview. Hatch End: National Catholic Radio and Television Centre.

Droel, W. L. (1989a) *The Spirituality of Work: Nurses*, Chicago: National Center for the Laity.

(1989b) *The Spirituality of Work: Teachers*. Chicago: National Center for the Laity.

Dulles, A. (1976) *Models of the Church: A Critical Assessment of the Church in all its Aspects*, Dublin: Gill and Macmillan.

Durkheim, E. (1964) *The Rules of Sociological Method*, London: Collier-Macmillan.

Etzioni, A. (1961) *A Comparative Analysis of Complex Organisations*, New York: Free Press.

Fichter, J. H. (1954) *Social Relations in the Urban Parish*, Chicago: University of Chicago Press.

Fielding, N. G. and Fielding, J. L. (1986) *Linking Data*, Beverly Hills, London and New Delhi: Sage.

Foster, J. (1988) 'Facing Redundancy at Fifty', *Priests and People*, 2 (2) March, 52–6, 60.

Fox, A. (1985) *Man Mismanagement*, London: Hutchinson.

Fulton, J. (1987) 'Religion as Politics in Gramsci: An Introduction', *Sociological Analysis*, 48 (3) Fall, 197–216.

Gannon, T. M. (ed.) (1988) *World Catholicism in Transition*, New York: Macmillan, London: Collier Macmillan.

Gay, J. D. (1971) *The Geography of Religion in England*, London: Duckworth.

Gerard, D. (1985) 'Religious Attitudes and Values', in Abrams, M., Gerrard, D., and Timms, N. (eds.) (1985) *Values and Social Change in Britain*, Basingstoke and London: Macmillan, pp. 50–92.

Gerth, H. and Mills, C. W. (1954) *Character and Social Structure: The Psychology of Social Institutions*, London: Routledge and Kegan Paul.

Gilbert, G. N. and Abell, P. (eds.) (1983) *Accounts and Action: Surrey Conferences on Sociological Theory and Method 1*, Aldershot: Gower.

Goffman, E. (1952) 'Cooling the Mark Out; Some Aspects of Adaptation to Failure', *Psychiatry*, 15, 451–63.

Gorer, G. (1955) *Exploring English Character*, London: Cresset Press.

Gramsci, A. (1971) *Selections from the Prison Notebooks*, edited and translated by Hoare, Q. and Smith, G. N., London: Lawrence and Wishart.

Greeley, A. M. (1972) *The Denominational Society: A Sociological Approach to Religion in America*, Glenview, Illinois and London: Scott, Foresman and Co.

(1981) *The Religious Imagination*, Los Angeles, New York and Chicago: Sadlier.

(1985) *American Catholics Since the Council: An Unauthorized Report*, Chicago: Thomas More Press.

Greene, G. (1972) *Travels with my Aunt*, Harmondsworth: Penguin.

Hammond, P. E. (1988) 'Religion and the Persistence of Identity', *Journal for the Scientific Study of Religion*, 27 (1) March, 1–11.

Hammond, P. E., Salinas, L. and Sloan, D. (1978) 'Types of Clergy Authority: Their Measurement, Location, and Effects', *Journal for the Scientific Study of Religion*, 17 (3) September, 241–53.

Harding, S. and Phillips, D. (1986) *Contrasting Values in Western Europe: Unity, Diversity and Change*, Basingstoke: Macmillan/EVSSG.

Harris, C. C. (1969) 'Reform in a Normative Organisation', *Sociological Review*, 17 (2) July, 167–85.

(1980) *Fundamental Concepts and the Sociological Enterprise*, London: Croom Helm.

Harrison, P. M. (1960) 'Weber's Categories of Authority and Voluntary Associations', *American Sociological Review*, 25 (April), 232–7,

(1971) *Authority and Power in the Free Church Tradition: A Study of the American Baptist Convention*, London and Amsterdam: Feffer and Simons.

Hastings, A. (1978) *In Filial Disobedience*, Great Wakering: Mayhew-McCrimmon.

Hay, D. (1982) *Exploring Inner Space: Scientists and Religious Experience*, Harmondsworth: Penguin.

Hervieu-Léger, D. (1986) *Vers Un Nouveau Christianisme? Introduction à La Sociologie Du Christianisme Occidental*, Paris: Cerf.

Hickey, J. (1967) *Urban Catholics: Urban Catholicism in England and Wales from 1829 to the Present Day*, London: Geoffrey Chapman.

Himmelfarb, H. (1975) 'Measuring Religious Involvement', *Social Forces*, 53, 606–18.

Hoge, D. R. and de Zulueta, E. (1985) 'Salience as a Condition for Various Social Consequences of Religious Commitment', *Journal for the Scientific Study of Religion*, 24 (1) March, 21–38.

Hopper, E. (1971) 'A Typology for the Classification of Education Systems' in Hopper, E. (ed.), *Readings in the Theory of Educational Systems*, London: Hutchinson.

Hornsby-Smith, M. P. (1980) 'In Tears with His People: Reflections on the Role of the Roman Catholic Clergy in Four English Parishes', *New Blackfriars*, 61, December, 504–23.

(1986a) 'The Immigrant Background of Roman Catholics in England and Wales: A Research Note', *New Community*, 13 (1) Spring-Summer, 79–85.

(1986b) 'Some Aspects of Popular Catholicism', in Bailey, E. (ed.) (1986) *A Workbook in Popular Religion*, Dorchester: Partners Publications, pp. 10–11.

(1987) *Roman Catholics in England: Studies in Social Structure since the Second World War*, Cambridge: Cambridge University Press.

(1988) *The Everyday Lives of Lay Catholics: An Exploratory Study*, Occasional Papers in Sociology and Social Policy No. 15, Guildford: University of Surrey.

(1989) *The Changing Parish: A Study of Parishes, Priests and Parishioners after Vatican II*, London: Routledge.

Hornsby-Smith, M.P. and Mansfield, M. C. (1974) 'English Catholicism in Change', *The Newman* 7 (3) September, 62–70).

Hornsby-Smith, M. P., Lee, R. M., and Reilly, P. A. (1977) 'Lapsation and Ideology', *The Month*, 10 (12) 406–9.

Hornsby-Smith, M.P. and Lee, R. M. (1979) *Roman Catholic Opinion: A Study of Roman Catholics in England and Wales in the 1970s*, Guildford: University of Surrey.

Hornsby-Smith, M.P., Lee, R. M., and Turcan, K. A. (1982) 'A Typology of English Catholics', *Sociological Review*, 30 (3) August, 433–59.

Hornsby-Smith, M.P., and Cordingley, E. S. (1983) *Catholic Elites: A Study of the Delegates to the National Pastoral Congress*, Occasional Paper No. 3, Guildford: University of Surrey.

Hornsby-Smith, M.P., Brown, J. M. and O'Byrne, J. (1983) 'Second Thoughts on the Pope's Visit', *The Month*, 16 (4) April, 131–3.

Hornsby-Smith, M.P., Lee, R. M., and Reilly, P. A. (1984) 'Social and Religious Change in Four English Roman Catholic Parishes', *Sociology*, 18 (3) August, 353–65.

Hornsby-Smith, M.P., Lee, R. M., and Reilly, P. A. (1985) 'Common Religion and Customary Religion: A Critique and a Proposal', *Review of Religious Research*, 26 (3) March, 244–52.

Hornsby-Smith, M.P., Procter, M., Rajan, L., and Brown, J. (1987) 'A Typology of Progressive Catholics', *Journal for the Scientific Study of Religion*, 26 (2) June, 234–48.

Hornsby-Smith, M.P., Turcan, K. A., and Rajan, L. T. (1987) 'Patterns of Religious Commitment, Intermarriage and Marital Breakdown Among English Catholics', *Archives De Sciences Sociales Des Religions*, 64 (1) July–September, 137–55.

Hornsby-Smith, M.P., and Dale, A. (1988) 'The Assimilation of Irish Immigrants in England', *British Journal of Sociology*, 39 (4) December, 519–44.

Houtart, F. (1969) 'Conflicts of Authority in the Roman Catholic Church', *Social Compass*, 16/3, 309–25.

Inglis, K. S. (1963) *Churches and the Working Classes in Victorian England*, London: Routledge.

Ireson, D. (1988) 'The Ship of the Church: Standby to Put to Sea ... A Catholic Teacher's View of the Church', *Priests and People*, 2 (1) February, 23–7.

Jackson, J. A. (1963) *The Irish in Britain*, London: Routledge.

John-Paul II, Pope (1982) *The Pope in Britain*, London: CTS/Catholic Information Services.

(1989) *Christifideles Laici: Post-Synodal Apostolic Exhortation of His Holiness John Paul II on The Vocation and the Mission of the Lay Faithful in the Church and in the World* (Do.589), London: C.T.S.

Jowell, R. and Airey, C. (eds.) (1984) *British Social Attitudes: The 1984 Report*, Aldershot: Gower.

Kaiser, R. B. (1987) *The Encyclical that Never Was: The Story of the Pontifical Commission on Population, Family and Birth, 1964–66*, London: Sheed and Ward.

Kanter, R. M. (1972) *Commitment and Community: Communes and Utopias in Sociological Perspective*, Cambridge, MA.: Harvard University Press.

Kennedy, R. E. (1973) *The Irish: Emigration, Marriage and Fertility*, Berkeley, Los Angeles, London: University of California Press.

Kelly, M., Francis, M., and Johnston, J. (1988) 'Coping as a Single Parent', *Priests and People*, 2 (5) June, 163–8, 174.

Kerr, M. (1958) *The People of Ship Street*, London: Routledge.

Kokosalakis, N. (1971) 'Aspects of Conflict between the Structure of Authority and the beliefs of the Laity in the Roman Catholic Church', in M. Hill (ed.) *A Sociological Yearbook of Religion in Britain*, London: SCM Press, 4, 21–35.

Koopmanschap, T. (1978) *Transformations in Contemporary Roman Catholicism: A Case Study*, unpublished Ph.D. thesis, University of Liverpool.

Kuhn, T. S. (1970) *The Structure of Scientific Revolutions*, London and Chicago: University of Chicago Press.

Lees, L. H. (1979) *Exiles of Erin: Irish Migrants in Victorian London*, Manchester: Manchester University Press.

Lenski, G. (1963) *The Religious Factor: A Sociological Study of Religious Impact on Politics, Economics and Family Life*, Garden City, New York: Anchor.

Leo XIII, Pope (1949, fp. 1891) *The Condition of the Working Classes (Rerum Novarum)*, Oxford: Catholic Social Guild.

Lévy-Strauss, C. (1966) *The Savage Mind*, London: Weidenfeld and Nicolson.

Lodge, D. (1980) *How Far Can You Go?* London: Secker and Warburg.

Luckmann, T. (1970) *The Invisible Religion: The Problem of Religion in Modern Society*, London: Collier-Macmillan.

Lynch, L. (1988) 'The Changing Vocation of Social Work', *Priests and People*, 2 (7) September, 268–73.'

McEvoy, J. (1987) 'Rock Climbing: Reflections of a Life in Business', *Priests and People*, 1 (7) November, 259–61, 264.

McGaw. D. B. (1979) 'Commitment and Religious Community: A Comparison of a Charismatic and Mainline Congregation', *Journal for the Scientific Study of Religion* 18 (2) 146–63.

McKenzie, J. (1966) *Authority in the Church*, London: Sheed and Ward. (Quoted in Houtart, 1969).

McLeod, H. (1974) *Class and Religion in the Late Victorian City*, London: Croom Helm.

MacRéamoinn, S. (ed.) (1986) *Pobal: the Laity in Ireland*, Dublin: The Columba Press.

Mann, M. (1986) *The Sources of Social Power Vol. 1 A History of Power From the beginning to AD 1760*, Cambridge: Cambridge University Press.

Mansfield, M. C. and Hornsby-Smith, M. P. (1982) 'Authority in the Church: the Individual Catholic's Interpretation', *New Blackfriars*, 63, 450–60.

Martin, B. and Pluck, R. (1977) *Young People's Beliefs: An Exploratory Study*, London: Church of England General Synod Board of Education.

Martin, D. (1965) 'Towards Eliminating the Concept of Secularization', in Gould, J. (ed.) (1965) *Penguin Survey of the Social Sciences*, Harmondsworth: Penguin, 169–82.

(1969) *The Religious and the Secular: Studies in Secularization*, London: Routledge and Kegan Paul.

(1972) 'Church, Denomination and Society', in M. Hill (ed.) *A Sociological Yearbook of Religion in Britain*, London: SCM Press, 5, 184–91.

Mass Observation (1947) *Puzzled People: A Study of Popular Attitudes to Religion, Ethics, Progress and Politics in a London Borough*, London: Gollancz.

Matza, D. (1964) *Delinquency and Drift*, New York: Wiley.

Merton, R. K. (1957) *Social Theory and Social Structure*, London: Collier-Macmillan.

Merton, R. K. and Kendall, P. L. (1956) *The Focused Interview*, Glencoe: Free Press.

Merton, R. K. and Barber, E. (1963) 'Sociological Ambivalence', in Merton, R. K. (1976) *Sociological Ambivalence and Other Essays*, Glencoe: Free Press, 3–31.

Mol, H. (1978) *Identity and Religion*, Beverly Hills: Sage.

Moore, J. (1975) 'The Catholic Priesthood', in Hill. M. (ed.) *A Sociological Yearbook of Religion in Britain*, 8, London: SCM, 30–60.

Moore, S. (1989) 'Crisis over Contraception', *The Tablet*, 243 (7786) 7 October, 1146–8.

Mueller, G. H. (1980) 'The Dimensions of Religiosity', *Sociological Analysis*, 41 (1), 1–24.

Neal, M. A. (1982) 'Commitment to Altruism in Sociological Analysis', *Sociological Analysis* 43 (1) 1–22.

Nowell, R. (ed.) (1982) *Why I am Still a Catholic*, London: Collins.

O'Connor, K. (1972) *The Irish in Britain*, London: Sidgwick and Jackson.

O'Dea, T. F. (1970) *Sociology and the Study of Religion: Theory, Research, Interpretation*, New York, London: Basic Books.

Paul VI, Pope (1968) *The Regulation of Birth (Humanae Vitae)* (Do.411), London: CTS.

(1975) *Evangelization in the Modern World: Apostolic Exhortation Evangelii Nuntiandi* (S.312), London: C.T.S.

Pius XII, Pope (1957) *The Lay Apostolate: Address to the Second World Congress of the Lay Apostolate* (S.239), London: CTS.

Robertson, R. (1970) *The Sociological Interpretation of Religion*, Oxford: Blackwell.

Roof, W. C. (1978) *Commitment and Community*, New York: Elsevier.

(1979) 'Concepts and Indicators of Religious Commitment: A Critical Review', pp. 17–45 in Wuthnow, R. (ed.) *The Religious Dimension: New Directions in Quantitative Research*, New York: Academic Press.

Roof, W. C. and Perkins, R. B. (1975) 'On Conceptualising Salience in Religious Commitment', *Journal for the Scientific Study of Religion*, 14 (2) 111–28.

Rowntree, B. S. and Lavers, G. R. (1951) *English Life and Leisure: A Social Study*, London, New York, Toronto: Longmans Green and Co.

Rudge, P. F. (1968) *Ministry and Management: The Study of Ecclesiastical Administration*, London: Tavistock.

Ryan, W. (1973) *Assimilation of Irish Immigrants in Britain*, Unpublished Ph.D. Thesis, St Louis University.

Satow, R. L. (1975) 'Value-Rational Authority and Professional Organisations: Weber's Missing Type', *Administrative Science Quarterly*, 20, 526–31.

Schutz, A. (1972) *The Phenomenology of the Social World*, London: Heinemann.

Scott, M. B. and Lyman, S. M. (1968) 'Accounts', *American Sociological Review*, 33 (1) February, 46–62.

Scurfield, A. (1982) 'A Question of Orthodoxy', *The Tablet*, 236, 25 September, 954–6.

Shapira, Z. (1976) 'A Facet Analysis of Leadership Styles', *Journal of Applied Psychology*, 6 (1), 136–9.

Sieghart, P. (1989) 'Christianity and Human Rights', *The Month*, 22 (2) February, 46–53.

Spencer, A. E. C. W. (1966) 'The Structure and Organisation of the Catholic Church in England', in Halloran, J. D. and Brothers, J. (eds.) *Uses of Sociology*, London and Melbourne: Sheed and Ward, 91–125.

Stark, R. and Glock, C. Y. (1968) *American Piety: The Nature of Religious Commitment*, Berkeley, Los Angeles and London: University of California Press.

Thomas, K. (1973) *Religion and the Decline of Magic: Studies in Popular Beliefs in Sixteenth and Seventeenth Century England*, Harmondsworth: Penguin.

Thompson, E. P. (1968) *The Making of the English Working Class*, Harmondsworth: Penguin.

Towler, R. (1974) *Homo Religiosus*, London: Constable.

Towler, R. and Chamberlain, A. (1973) 'Common Religion' in Hill, M. (Ed.) *A Sociological Yearbook of Religion: 6*, London: SCM, 1–28.

Vaillancourt, J-G. (1980) *Papal Power: A Study of Vatican Control over Lay Catholic Elites*, Berkeley, Los Angeles, London: University of California Press.

Vardey, L. (1989) *Belonging: A Questioning Catholic Comes to Terms with the Church*, London: Macmillan.

Wallis, R. and Bruce, S. (1983) 'Accounting for Action: Defending the Common Sense Heresy', *Sociology*, 17 (1), February, 97–111.

Ward, C. K. (1965) *Priests and People: A Study in the Sociology of Religion*, Liverpool: Liverpool University Press.

Warren, N. (1988) 'The Life of a Welfare Law Solicitor', *Priests and People*, 2 (6) July/August, 205–7.

Webb, E. J., Campbell, D. T., Schwartz, R. D. and Sechrest, L. (1966) *Unobtrusive Measures: Non-Reactive Research in the Social Sciences*, Chicago: Rand McNally.

Weber, M. (1930) *The Protestant Ethic and the Spirit of Capitalism*, London: Allen and Unwin.

(1948) *From Max Weber: Essays in Sociology*, (translated, edited and with an introduction by Gerth, H. H. and Mills, C. W.), London: Routledge and Kegan Paul.

(1949) *The Methodology of the Social Sciences*, New York: Free Press

(1964) *The Theory of Social and Economic Organisation*, (edited with an introduction by Talcott Parsons) London: Collier-Macmillan.

(1966) *The Sociology of Religion*, London: Methuen.

(1968) *Economy and Society: An Outline of Interpretive Sociology*, Vol. 1, New York: Bedminster Press.

Willer, D. E. (1967) 'Max Weber's Missing Authority Type', *Sociological Inquiry*, 37 Spring, 231–39.

Willmott, P. (1986) *Social Networks, Informal Care and Public Policy* (Policy Studies Institute Research Report 655), London: PSI/Frances Pinter.

Wilson, B. (1966) *Religion in Secular Society: A Sociological Comment*, London: Watts.

(1979) *Contemporary Transformation of Religion*, Oxford: Clarendon.

Winter, M. M. (1973) *Mission or Maintenance; A Study in New Pastoral Structures*, London: Darton, Longman and Todd.

Wood, B. (1987/88) 'The Everyday Life of a Catholic Housewife', *Priests and People*, 1 (8) December/January, 297–302.

Worsley, P. (1970) *The Trumpet Shall Sound: A Study of 'Cargo' Cults in Melanesia*, London: Paladin.

Yeo, S. (1974) 'On the Uses of "Apathy"', *Archives Europeenes de Sociologie*, 15 (2) 279–311.

INDEX

Abbott, W. M., 6, 50, 166, 196, 198, 202, 218
Abell, P., 4–5, 48, 222
Abercrombie, N., 27, 31, 90, 111
abortion, 3, 13, 21, 38, 41, 54, 78–9, 84–6, 88, 133, 135–7, 160, 165, 168–9, 172–3, 178–83, 188–9, 223–6, 234, 236
Abrams, P., 66
abstinence, 7, 30, 112, 193, 215, 219
acceptance, 26, 56, 144, 146, 203, 217, 233
  of teachings, 70, 130–1, 133, 164, 194, 223
accommodation, 31, 207
accommodators, 149, 152–5, 157–8, 223
accounts, 4–5, 13, 18, 20, 22–7, 29–30, 32–5, 39, 44, 48–9, 51, 53–4, 62, 87, 89, 98, 110, 164–5, 214, 226–7
action, 13, 30, 39–41, 43, 55–6, 74–5, 79, 81, 85, 133, 154, 161, 177, 187, 196, 223, 233
  social, 24, 34, 36, 41, 221
  religious 27, 34, 41
activism, 42, 44
activists, 22, 26, 29–30, 35, 41, 92, 145, 198, 205
  justice and peace, 195, 209
  parish, 16, 25, 28, 34, 41, 224
activities, 59, 123, 129, 205, 233
activity, 42, 50, 209
  route-finding, 10
adaptation, 26, 154, 187

adherence, 146, 217
  to teachings, 72, 87, 139–40
adultery, 182
advice, 80, 83, 87, 174–5, 191
affiliation, 130, 159, 215
age, 142
  differences, 94, 118
  golden, 165, 227
aggiornamento, 7, 31, 201
Airey, C., 178
alienation, 59, 65, 110
allegiance, 72, 89
Allport, G. W., 40
Alton, D., 51, 57, 60, 64
ambiguity, 39, 40, 42, 221
ambivalence, 82, 221
annulments, 185–7
apathy, 21, 90, 92, 101, 111, 201, 203, 205, 219
Apostolicam Actuositatem, 50
appointment, 56
  of bishops, 144–5
Archer, A., 8–9, 120, 193, 203, 225
aspirations, 121, 207
assent, 54, 118, 188
associations, 57, 66, 207
assumptions, 189
  taken-for-granted, 47–8, 52, 65
attachment, 20, 24, 29, 43–4, 152, 221
  to beliefs, 34, 89, 98, 220–1
attendance
  Mass, 3, 28, 37, 76, 111, 118, 135,